D0498437

WITHDRAWN

WHAT IS JAPAN?

Contradictions and Transformations

Also by Taichi Sakaiya from Kodansha International
*The Knowledge-Value Revolution, or a History
of the Future*

WHAT IS JAPAN?

Contradictions and Transformations

Taichi Sakaiya

Translated by Steven Karpa

KODANSHA INTERNATIONAL
New York • Tokyo • London

Kodansha America, Inc.,
114 Fifth Avenue,
New York, NY 10011, U.S.A.

Kodansha International Ltd.,
17-14 Otowa 1-chome,
Bunkyo-ku, Tokyo 112, Japan

Published in 1993 by
Kodansha America, Inc.

Copyright © 1993 by Taichi Sakaiya.
All rights reserved.
Originally published in 1991 in Japanese by Kodansha Ltd.
as *Nihon to wa nani ka.*

Printed in the United States of America

93 94 95 96 97 6 5 4 3 2 1

Library of Congress Cataloging-in-Publication Data

Sakaiya, Taichi, 1935–
    [Nihon to wa nani ka. English]
    What is Japan? : contradictions and transformations / Taichi
Sakaiya ; translated by Steven Karpa.
        p.   cm.
    ISBN 1-56836-001-0
    1. Japan—Civilization. I. Title.
DS821.S24213 1993
952—dc20   93-16489
                                                                CIP

Book design by Cynthia Dunne

The text of this book was set in Caledonia.
Composed by Haddon Craftsmen, Scranton, Pennsylvania.

Printed and bound by Haddon Craftsmen,
Scranton, Pennsylvania.

Contents

2   PEACE, COOPERATION, AND THE ENVIRON-
MENT • 59

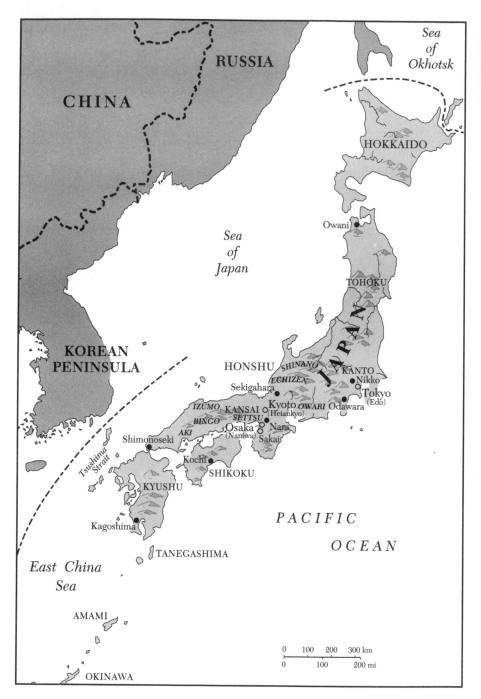

Preface to the English Language Edition

A few years ago a French journalist asked me if Japanese have some kind of national goal that motivates them to sacrifice their living standards for economic and corporate growth. Most Japanese would be surprised that such a question would even be asked. It would never occur to them that a country might have anything so lofty sounding as a "goal."

I responded to his question with a metaphor. A jet has a lot of different parts, like wings, a cockpit, a fuselage. These components all look different, they use different materials and require different levels of precision in their workmanship. Each performs a distinct function, but as a whole they have a single purpose: to fly. Now, countries like America and France are similar to jet aircraft. They have a sense of national purpose. America, for example, has the goal of promoting individual freedoms and democratic ideals. Japan on the other hand is more like a thousand clocks. All the clocks look the same, all mark time, but each is a separate machine that runs to its own rhythm. The Japanese government is quite assiduous in tinkering with them, but beyond ensuring that the clocks all keep the same time, the bureaucrats have no goal.

For more than twenty years I was a member of that bureaucracy. Even worse, I was one of those dreaded doyens of "industrial policy" so often accused of steering the course of "Japan, Inc.," at the Ministry of International Trade and Industry (MITI). During that period I can scarcely remember anyone discussing anything as grandiose as "Japan's national goals." All that the notorious MITI elite debated was how best to protect and support the industries in their purview. The effects that these efforts might have in achieving a broader national goal was not once mentioned. Japanese bureaucrats identify so strongly with their ministry that they work exclusively to achieve *its* objectives, not the country's.

Many non-Japanese feel a degree of uneasiness at this kind of intense Japanese identification with the group. But what they perceive as a lack of individuality in the Japanese is not a result of any powerful authority's fostering a common purpose; on the contrary, this single-mindedness occurs precisely because Japanese have no sense of a national mission, and thus no way to allocate different tasks to different people. Rather than a nation of jet engines, wings, and landing gear, Japan is a land of a thousand clock hands, ticking. No course is mapped to reach national economic goals, and yet when individuals make their own plans to increase their business and personal fortunes, those thousand hands tick and a single purpose is achieved: the Japanese economy grows.

How can Japan manage to make such a paradoxical system work? To state it in the most basic way, What is Japan? This question has recently evolved from an age-old concern of Japanese into an important consideration for the entire world. Modern Japan is now more than just an obscure Oriental island nation. It is an economic giant that accounts for one-seventh of the world's economy, an industrial giant that racks up mammoth trade surpluses. Japan's trade surplus, which topped $110 billion in 1992, has become a serious international structural imbalance. The trade surplus with the United States is particularly large.

This is not merely an American and world misfortune. It is also Japan's misfortune. An excessive trade surplus means that Japan does not use as much as it produces. It is not enjoying the fruits of its own labors.

Despite this surplus, Japan is not overall an efficient country. The productivity per hour of Japanese workers remains lower than in most industrialized nations. An extremely efficient manufacturing industry shields grossly inefficient distribution and agricultural sectors. In reality, modern Japan is an industrial power only in mass-produced products such as automobiles and electronics.

Why is this so? Japanologists have yet to come up with a convincing answer. Although a lot of research has been done recently on Japan and the Japanese, most of it looks only at contemporary Japan and barely touches on the physical characteristics of the land or the historical experiences that have shaped the country. Readers of this scholarship will find no connection between the "samurai country" of a scant century ago and the industrial country of today.

Opinions on Japan are thus radically divided. One school (primarily in Japan) determinedly praises the country for its high standards in technology and education and for its work ethic of diligence. The other school (primarily outside of Japan) criticizes the country's bureaucratically guided economy and corporation-centered social structures as economic imperialism.

People who praise Japan's industrial production figures and international competitiveness quite often attribute the country's success to the character of the Japanese people, as though industrial prowess were a natural consequence of being Japanese. They gloss over the fact that only a hundred years ago Japan was an agricultural country with virtually no modern industry.

And yet we cannot ignore that this rural country then proceeded to create the most advanced industrial society in the world outside the European and Christian cultural realm. After the Meiji Restoration of 1868 placed reformers in control of Japan's government, the country embarked on an effort to create a modern industrial society, one that succeeded in just 120 years. This was done by copying European and American technology and systems exactly.

This wasn't the first time Japan used the method of precise reproduction to master foreign models. Japan has in fact done exactly this repeatedly over the last 1,200 years. This aptitude for reproducing, absorbing, and then digesting foreign learning is in itself an important element that characterizes Japanese culture.

Critics of Japan's relentlessly expanding industrial production and trade surpluses often blame bureaucratic authoritarianism and nontariff barriers. They would do well to remember that none of the far more authoritarian and restrictive socialist countries and military dictatorships has succeeded economically. The postwar Japanese government has had no means or power to mobilize the population toward a single goal. In fact, few countries aside from Japan have governments so weak and reviled by their own people.

If Japanese work hard to foster economic growth and improve corporate fortunes, it is only to further their own happiness. Japan's climate and history have nurtured a deeply felt desire in individual Japanese to stay in favor with the groups of which they are members. After World War II, workplaces such as government and corporations became powerful focuses of that desire. The greatest happiness for postwar Japanese was to be on good terms with their co-workers.

Modern Japanese politicians, bureaucrats, and business leaders do not sit down together to craft national plans. They never have. Even at the height of World War II, the Japanese military command structure was not of one mind, and the army, navy, police, and economic bureaucrats constantly jockeyed for power. Japan raced into a war of great destruction not because it was an authoritarian country directed to a single national objective but because its governing organs were so divided they could not cooperate or compromise over anything. In Japan, everyone is loyal first and foremost to his organization. Japan is thus quite able to cope with minor developments; confronted by major changes, it falters.

This lack of directedness should be foremost in our minds as we consider Japanese trade surpluses and administrative guidance of industries by its government. While it is tempting to see Japan's mammoth trade surpluses, impenetrable administrative guidance, and competition-suppressing corporate groupings as the products of a vast conspiracy, a more realistic appraisal is that they are simply the cumulation of many diverse organizations and individuals protecting themselves and their interests. The policies of the last fifty years may have been crucial in shaping modern Japan's economy, but these policies arose from a national character forged through many centuries.

Modern Japan is the product of the interaction of an unusual geography and climate with distinctive events in Japanese history. For example, the spread of Buddhism did not erode the native religion, Shintoism. And the nominal government structure of the impotent imperial court endured eight hundred years after the military seized political power. These historic events still resonate today: the bureaucracy leads the country even though the Diet, Japan's Parliament, is freely elected. On this fertile soil of tradition and custom, deposited layer after layer by the flow of history, the system of administrative guidance and industrial cooperation was planted in 1941—and has thrived for more than fifty years.

In this book, I uncover modern Japan's relationship to the social and spiritual ground fashioned by the country's history and attempt to clarify how the system of administrative guidance and industrial cooperation that has grown up upon it really works.

Naturally, such a discussion requires a great deal of specific information about Japanese history as well as Japanese historical terminology that may not be familiar to Western readers. Although this will present some difficulties, I hope readers will take the time to acquaint themselves with some unaccustomed concepts. The reward is an otherwise unobtainable understanding of modern Japan.

In conclusion, I would like to thank all those who worked on bringing out this English language edition, especially the translator, Steven Karpa, and Minato Asakawa and Philip Turner of Kodansha America.

Taichi Sakaiya
December 1992

PREFACE TO THE JAPANESE LANGUAGE EDITION

What is Japan? This is a question Japanese ask themselves throughout their lives. As we enter the nineties, this question is more pressing than ever. Radical change surrounds Japan even as it grapples with a rapidly aging society and the greatest period of wealth in its history.

Perceptions of Japan and the Japanese have varied widely in the past. Since World War II, Japan in the Japanese popular mind has evolved from underdeveloped country to an admired "special case." The "special case theory" has today been further refined by foreign Japan scholars into veneration of Japanese-style management and Japanese-style government-business cooperation.

This perceptual evolution has paralleled Japan's economic development. A similar change occurred between the late nineteenth century and Japan's defeat in World War II. Up to the middle of the Meiji period (1868–1912), Japan predominantly perceived itself as lagging behind the European powers and the United States. Japanese denied their historic distinctiveness as they tried to trade in an "Asian" identity for a "European" one.

After Japan's victory against the Russian Empire in the 1905 Russo-Japanese War, a theory of Japaneseness emphasizing the peculiarity of Japanese culture gained currency, along with a growing longing and reverence among Japanese for the putative goodness of traditional Japan. This was succeeded by a growing tendency during the early twentieth century toward overconfidence in "Japan, the good country, the strong country." Criticism of the "modern" civilizations of Europe and America burgeoned. As a "good country," Japan was obliged to share its morally correct ways of thinking with the world; as a "strong country," Japan strove first and foremost for the superiority of its military power. The next logical stage was to perceive Japan as a divine country entitled to use all its military power to spread the Japanese way to the world. The prewar slogans "Building the Kingdom of Paradise" and "A New Order: the Greater East-Asia Co-Prosperity Sphere" epitomize the self-aggrandizement that enabled Japan to act aggressively and unilaterally. The slogans sprang directly from the country's self-image.

Always in the background of Japan's changing self-perception from the Meiji Restoration to World War II were Japan's military successes. After World War I, these had heartened the vast majority of Japanese. Despite the Japanese desire to be strong enough to stand up to foreigners, however, there was no ground swell for making Japan a great military power. The Japanese quest for strength and respect was the engine driving the Meiji period modernization. The result was a climate in which success was defined solely in terms of military power.

Although it seems strange in today's world, where economics reign supreme, in the 1930s many people said that countries far wealthier than Japan, such as the United States and Britain, should learn from the superiority of Japanese culture and the virtue of the Japanese social system. These voices were not limited to ultranationalists such as economist Shumei Okawa and General Sadao Araki—even such internationalists as Inazo Nitobe, the envoy to the League of Nations commemorated on the ¥5,000 note, struck the same chord. It is common for persons coming from underdeveloped nations to praise the qualities of their mother countries when they experience life abroad and learn foreign languages. The good fortune of succeeding victories in the Sino-Japanese War (1894–1895), the Russo-Japanese War, and World War I nurtured the self-laudatory belief that Japanese society combined the merits of modern Euro-American material culture and traditional Japanese spiritual culture.

Japanese look at cultures as systems and have a propensity for herd behavior that encourages easy surrender to the prevailing wind. So it should be no surprise that Japanese tend both toward uninformed conclusions and to completely succumb to the trend of the moment.

The "strong Japan" and especially the "divine Japan" schools of thought, with their overtones of infallibility, forced Japan into international isolation and before long led Japan to embroil itself in World War II. Likewise, the beginnings of a crisis are detectable in Japan's self-image today.

All countries and all peoples have unique cultures. In that sense, Japanese culture is certainly "special" as well. But if this specialness is used mindlessly to defend idiosyncratic government policies and management styles, only problems can result. It is a mistake to use "specialness" to defend the interests of particular groups or to protect the authority of individual government agencies. International society is a matter of the various distinctive cultures and peoples swallowing a bit of their mutual distaste so that they can work together to create common rules.

It is important for Japan to distinguish between the eccentricities that are merely changeable and those that can be easily changed. If a "special" behavior can be easily changed, then for the sake of international harmony it should be—even if a certain amount of domestic resistance must be overcome. Japan is fortunate in that its flexibility is one source of its distinctiveness.

For areas that are less tractable, Japan should carefully explain to the world why change is impossible, so that the international community will understand and recognize the Japanese position. Though this may bring upon Japan and Japanese some criticism, harsh words are certainly an improvement over more destructive actions.

This book is an attempt to give just such an explanation of Japan, by examining its origins and reality through history.

· · ·

A note on the order of Japanese names:
We have used 1868, the year of the Meiji Restoration, as the year to switch from Japanese name order (family name first, given name second) to Western name order (given name first, family name last).

1

JAPAN
IN THE
NINETIES

Almost Paradise

The Face of an Economic Giant

For more than a hundred years Japanese have worked to transform their country from an impoverished feudal nation into a modern industrial state. Today, Japan is extremely affluent. As they look at their country—peaceful, prosperous, and safe—Japanese ask themselves, Does Japan epitomize the ideals of modernity? The statistics say yes. And yet the Japanese are uneasy. Having tracked their progress by comparing themselves to others, they now look at the country around them and ask: Is this how it is supposed to be? Are we rich? Have we arrived?

The figures are plain: a per capita GNP like a small, rich European country, though in a nation of more than 120 million. Japan has the world's second-largest economy (after the United States), almost one-seventh of the total world economy, and great wealth as well. At the beginning of 1990, the average Japanese had assets worth triple the average American's and almost quadruple the average for British or German citizens.

In its international balance of payments, Japan is also a giant. Thanks to high-quality industrial exports, Japan's for-

eign trade surplus of $110 billion in 1992 was the highest in
world history. Clearly, Japanese industry is internationally
very competitive.

As an economic power, Japan has captured the triple
crown: world leader in per capita GNP and wealth, large
international balance-of-payments surpluses, and outstanding
industrial competitiveness. But these are international measures. To understand Japan today one must ask, How does
Japan fare domestically?

Very well. The unemployment rate has remained below 3
percent for long periods and was only 2.1 percent at the end
of 1990; this is well below the level modern economists consider full employment. And yet prices remain stable. The
annual rate of consumer price inflation between 1985 and
1990 was 1.8 percent, and wholesale prices actually dipped
1.2 percent.

Government finances are also on a sound footing. There has
been a complete turnaround from the debt crisis of the 1970s,
when 34.7 percent of government spending was financed by
borrowing. Today there is no longer any need to issue new
deficit-financing bonds. Although the reputation of Japan's
political life has lagged well behind its economic renown, any
government that can achieve such a massive reform of fiscal
policy without resorting to inflation must be deemed effective
indeed.

It sounds too good to be true. But peel back the curtain and
the supporting structures are just as healthy.

PROFITABLE BUSINESSES, SOLID FAMILY FINANCES

The size and strength of the Japanese economy can be seen as
easily in corporate ledgers and family budgets as it can in
weighty tomes of national statistics.

Corporate operating profits remain extremely good, even
after the early-nineties crash in stock and land prices brought

them down from their record 1989 high of roughly $31 billion. What is most remarkable is that companies have been able to increase the ratio of equity financing year by year, reaching 19 percent in 1989, even as they maintain private sector capital investment of 20 percent of GNP. And these figures do not include any unrealized capital gains from the land price boom. If these are included, equity-to-capital ratios are probably over 70 percent, even after the early-nineties collapse. Overall, Japanese corporations produce well, invest well, and have modern facilities and enormous bankrolls.

This financial comfort has not made them lazy: wage increases have maintained their relationship to productivity gains and stock dividend ratios have stayed down. A healthy climate for business prevails in Japan. Both employees and shareholders invest in corporate assets for the future without complaint.

Japanese family finances are also in good shape. The recent consumption boom and encouragement of imports has slightly lowered the Japanese family savings rate, but at about 14 percent in 1990 it was still among the very highest in the world. The liquid assets of individuals, including bank deposits, negotiable securities, and life insurance balances, were enough to maintain current life-styles for three and a half years from financial assets alone. When other assets such as real estate are included, Japanese have saved enough to take a nine-year vacation. The spirit of deferred gratification is alive and well in Japan.

Household debt levels are also low. At the end of 1989, households were carrying a total debt of ¥307 trillion, only one-third of their financial assets. Japanese families consume less today to prepare for tomorrow and have become very secure.

The Japanese male company worker's greatest protection is the system of lifetime employment. Employees very rarely leave companies except of their own volition, and they stand in little danger of losing their jobs. While this system has looked a little less desirable in recent years (because of increasing transfers for young workers and frequent business travel demanded of middle managers), it still receives strong support from Japanese society. A young person graduating from college and gaining a job can look forward to working in the same organization until retirement, unless he should resign. It is also assumed that the company will provide a loan for the purchase of a home.

In fact, companies do not dismiss significant numbers of personnel unless they have very specific, long-range plans of some kind. When they must lay people off, they consider it their minimum duty to try to arrange some other kind of employment for the dismissed workers. Most companies even help place retirement-age workers in other jobs, to ensure a certain level of income.

A Country Without Beggars, Where Thieves Take Only Cash

If we look only at the statistics presented thus far, Japan seems undeniably a rich country and the Japanese who live there seem very wealthy. But are the benefits spread fairly?

Virtually everyone in the entire country is covered by the national health insurance system. Clinics even find cash payments an unwelcome bother. And pensions for the elderly are high: a married couple, where the husband worked his entire career at a company that provides a state pension, would receive $1,500 per month, the highest in the world. Aid to single mothers with dependent children and to the poor is also generous. Monthly living assistance in Tokyo for a standard three-person household is about $1,000.

Beggars are not unusual in the wealthy societies of Europe and North America—many American cities, like New York, even run shelter systems—but in Japan there are no beggars. They do not exist.

Japan does have burglars. In fact, they are not uncommon. However, they will take only cash, negotiable securities, valuable jewelry, and the like; clothing, electronics, and other objects are safe, and cameras and bags can be left in hotel rooms without worry. Why are such goods perfectly secure? Because Japan has no place to sell secondhand clothing and electronics. If one cannot convert stolen goods into money, there is little reason to steal. The secondhand stores that used to exist in suburban commercial districts have now virtually disappeared, partly because no one is buying. The only items pawnshops carry are so nearly new they seem to have come from the warehouses of bankrupt companies.

If beggars have disappeared and buyers of used merchandise have vanished, clearly there are extremely few poor people in Japan. Not only is per capita income high in Japan, but income is also evenly distributed. There is a very small gap between the affluent and the less well-off. The measure usually used to compare the income distribution of nations is the multiple of the income of the top fifth of society to the bottom fifth. In the United States, this multiple is 9.1. In France and Britain, it exceeds 10. In Japan, it is only 2.9. In most developing countries the multiple is into the double digits, and it even appears generally to be higher in socialist countries than in Japan. While Japan has few extremely wealthy people, it also has few extremely poor ones. So Japan is not merely wealthy and secure, it also rates extremely well in measures of fairness.

The relative equality of income distribution is further compounded by a system of progressive taxation more aggressive than that seen in any other country. The minimum threshold for paying taxes is high. A household of a couple and two children pay taxes from a yearly income of $16,000 in the United States, $10,000 in Great Britain, but $25,600 in Japan. These tax laws and entitlements have overwhelming public support. The idea of giving priority to the wealthy and taxing the middle class does not even enter public debate. Modern

Japan is almost neurotic in pursuing economic equality and has achieved it to a degree not achieved anywhere else.

JAPANESE EDUCATION: APPROACHING EQUALITY IN OUTCOME

But income is not the only measure of class disparity. How about status? Surely this must vary greatly, especially in a meritocratic society like Japan. The truth is that there is little variation in one's income or place in society that correlates to one's school record.

This is true of not only starting salaries but also lifetime earnings. The lifetime income of graduates of top-flight universities is only twice that of noncollege graduates. There are innumerable ways of determining one's place in society, but effort, ability, and even luck play much larger parts in determining social standing than does school record. Two of Japan's last nine prime ministers have not even been college graduates (Kakuei Tanaka and Zenko Suzuki). And a survey of the heads of business organizations revealed that 30 percent did not finish college.

Nevertheless, the Japanese passion for education *is* as intense as its reputation. Japanese high school students study with maniacal passion to get into the best schools and get the best jobs, even though the pay is no higher and the advancement no faster. Virtually all Japanese children attend primary and junior high schools, 94 percent go on to high school, and almost 40 percent of high school graduates attend some type of institution of higher education. (If the 18 percent who enter vocational schools are counted, as they are in America, the total is well over 50 percent.)

An enormous amount of money is spent on education in Japan. In many cases students receive additional instruction in cram schools and prep schools and have home tutors. The effort that goes into education serves to further equalize Japanese society. Virtually all Japanese are literate and numerate.

Japanese society has in fact achieved real equality and fairness in almost every aspect. Because Japan is a mostly homogeneous society, the conflicts and discrimination caused by racial and ethnic diversity have not burdened the country. Since Japanese generally are not passionate about religions, religious discrimination does not exist either. And since the language is very uniform, there is no possibility of language discrimination. The minor variations of local dialect do not negatively affect one's social standing or income.

Of course, Japan does have some long-standing discriminatory customs and traditions, such as the different roles of men and women in society. But overall, the situation is better than that in other countries. Japan has not only achieved equality before the law and equality of opportunity; it has also come close to equality in outcome.

JAPAN IS VERY SAFE

Wealth, security and equality: Japan seems to be a paradise on earth. But is it safe? It certainly is.

First and foremost, Japan has been completely free of the horrors of war for almost half a century, since the end of World War II. Japanese troops have not once been dispatched to fight abroad. Japan has become so cautious with military force that even the dispatch of minesweepers to the Persian Gulf was a subject of much debate. Japan has no draft, nor is there a likelihood of one. Troops are volunteers and are in no danger of being sent to the battlefield.

During these forty-eight years, Japan has also been free of civil disorders. The most violent activities the country has experienced have been the 1960 riots over the Security Treaty, the Sanya and Kamagasaki incidents of 1961, and the student protests of the late sixties. These resulted in extremely few deaths. While small groups of extremists have perpetrated terrorist incidents, most of those injured have been the extremists themselves; the danger terrorism presents to ordinary citizens has been low.

Terrorism aside, the very low incidence of crime is a feature that characterizes Japan. In 1990, Japan had 1,238 murders, less than one for every 100,000 people. The rate for the United States is nine times higher, and those for France and Germany are four to five times higher. Japan's rates for other violent crimes—robbery, assault, and rape—are similarly low, one-tenth the rates of other countries.

It is generally believed that as nations become more industrialized and urbanized, crime increases. Japan is an exception. Despite its rapid industrialization and urbanization, crime has not grown.

Long life expectancies are another indicator of the safety of Japan. In 1990, the average life expectancies for Japanese were the highest in the world—81.77 for females and 75.91 years for males. Sanitation is superb. Cholera and smallpox have long since been eradicated and tuberculosis nearly so. There have been only a few thousand cases of AIDS, the scourge recently hitting America and Europe, and there are no signs of a rapid increase.

Safety is given plenty of consideration in more mundane affairs as well. There are few industrial accidents, and natural disasters claim few lives. Factories and construction sites have very thorough safety measures; roads and tourist spots are plastered with safety barriers. Seacoasts, dikes, and levees are sealed with concrete and hillsides tamed with retaining walls. Even famous ruins and natural wonders have been mercilessly "improved" or, where this is not possible, roped off.

Japan is also very clean. Roads and transportation facilities are kept almost spotless, and hygiene management for restaurants is quite strict. Most residences have baths and toilets, and young people today have increasingly developed the habit of washing their hair every morning. Many mothers today will stop their children from playing in sandboxes because it is "dirty." Urban children who go to rural farms to get a taste of nature by digging for potatoes wear gloves to keep their hands from getting soiled. Japanese are so used to this life-style they find living standards in the developing world intolerable and often refuse to ride the Paris or New York subways because they are "too dirty." Contemporary Japanese have pursued safety to such a degree that they have become obsessive-compulsives, afraid of natural dirt and bugs.

Pollution—in the sense of anything that damages the physical and spiritual health of human beings—is also a kind of danger. Since the seventies Japan has adopted the world's toughest standards in most spheres. These standards are strictly enforced. Laws on drugs and food additives are the most stringent in the world, and air and water pollution restrictions are tough. Auto exhaust restrictions are strictly adhered to, and Japan buys only the cleanest low-sulfur fuels. Noise abatement measures are far stricter than anything found abroad, so much so that European and American aircraft engine makers have to develop special low-noise engines for their planes to be flown in Japan.

Instances of pollution-related disorders have decreased rapidly throughout the country since the seventies, and the air and water quality in industrial areas is markedly improved. Japan today is an advanced nation in the realm of pollution control.

APPROACHING THE IDEAL MODERN STATE

If the ideal modern state is prosperous, peaceful, and safe, then of all modern states, Japan best approximates that ideal.

Since the overthrow of the feudal military government more than a century ago, Japan has striven to achieve the European and American model of the modern industrial society. Looking at Japan today, it is understandable that the bureaucrats, corporate managers, and engineers who put so much sweat and toil into realizing this "paradise" feel proud of the accomplishments of the "Japanese industrial model" and "Japanese-style management."

But is Japan really so ideal as a place for human beings to live? Not necessarily. The large majority of Japanese hesitate to express deep confidence and pride in their country. In fact, the overwhelming majority still instinctively feel that Japan is weak and vacillate over the country's future direction. They realize their affluence and security are dependent on the international climate and see a fundamental weakness in the structure of Japanese society itself, especially in its modes of capital accumulation and production.

While the ideals that Japan dreamed of in its many centuries of poverty have been achieved, doubts persist that what Japanese see before themselves today may not really be that wonderful. Japanese have believed that if they could sustain economic prosperity, equality of outcome, and personal security, they would certainly become happy. In a world where all this has been achieved, it has become quite obvious that happiness is not so simple.

What Japanese have discovered in the nineties is that "paradise" has its own peculiar set of problems.

THE RICH COUNTRY
THAT DOESN'T FEEL RICH

NO JOY IN HEAVEN

I remember thinking in high school, as I listened to the tales of the Catholic God, that heaven was the last place I'd want to go. After all, without struggle, deception, hate, and depravity, what fun is there? If the place called heaven were the abode of good, wise people chosen by God and if all actions there were virtuous and refined, it would undoubtedly be boring and tedious no matter how well appointed. And if the inhabitants of heaven thought of themselves as the selected "good people," they would certainly be roundly despised by all the others. For a person living in 1990s Japan, this scenario has an unpleasantly familiar ring.

Per capita income and wealth are tops in the world, income discrepancies are small, and there is little discrimination based on educational achievement. The reach of the education system is the best in the world, crime is low, pollution regulation excellent, and over two-thirds of the country is covered in green vegetation. Trains run on time, telephone connections are reliable, and families even own personal facsimile machines. Television broadcasts go late into the night, and people are free to criticize the government. Japan comes so close to the ideals of the modern state that its citizenry are unconcerned with politics. Its young people feel that nothing could be more natural or desirable than that their world continue as it is, unchanged.

But paradise has its own unique problems. Despite all Japan's efficiency, equality, and security, most Japanese say today that they do not feel wealthy. Just as Adam tired of life in Eden and tasted the forbidden fruit, Japanese are increasingly irritated by days that continue calmly, without incident.

Unfortunately for Japanese, this Eden cannot be changed simply by eating forbidden fruit, and in any case there are few bold and curious Japanese Adams to eat of it. The priests and bureaucrats have caged in all the mischievous snakes of temptation. While everybody feels growing irritability at a joyless present and the prospect of an uncertain future, Japanese continue to cling to the edge of the clouds so as not to fall from heaven. They even cry "ever upward." But where is "up" from heaven? A higher, more perfect heaven? Then this supposed heaven is only purgatory.

FINDING WHAT IS MISSING

Japan first became an economic power in the eighties. After the oil crises of the seventies—a period of marking time for the Japanese economy and a loss of faith in "big science"—the world economy leapt forward as oil prices fell and new technologies, chiefly electronics, broke exciting new ground. Japan made the most of these scientific advances, developing both its economy and a certain technological edge.

The fall of oil prices lowered the cost of Japan's imports and allowed it to accumulate capital. Advances in electronic technology increased Japanese industrial productivity. And Japan's international accounts swung into an ever-mounting surplus, leading to a rapid appreciation of the yen in the mideighties.

This revaluation pushed Japanese incomes dramatically up in international comparisons. The Japanese share of the world economy also surged upward, so that Japanese per capita incomes were soon the highest of the big industrial countries. The massive amounts of capital Japan was accumulating poured into a limited repository of land and stocks, the pressure of money driving real estate and share prices through the roof. Japanese corporations posted huge profits, and many Japanese became major moguls.

But while this transformation was happening, Japanese living standards hardly budged. More important, most Japanese perceived no change. Statistically, Japan became wealthy in international comparisons, but a large gap developed between what Japanese were experiencing in their daily lives and this distant concept of "wealth" they were hearing about.

In the eighties, Japanese vacillated between pride in this new economic power and a dissatisfaction with living standards. Japanese asked themselves where all this reputed wealth was. The country launched a search to find out what the "real" rich countries had that the Japanese did not. Surely, if the Japanese did not feel wealthy despite their statistical achievements, something must be lacking.

The first answer was housing. Compared to the cities of Europe and America, with their neat rows of stone buildings, Japan's unplanned mazes of low-rise wooden buildings seemed indigent. They gave the impression that Japanese housing was cramped. An unflattering comparison made in a European Community cross-country study of middle-class living standards—that Japanese homes were like rabbit hutches—stuck sharply in the Japanese consciousness. Cramped housing was the answer; cramped housing was why Japanese did not feel rich.

Unfortunately, this answer did not hold up to closer scrutiny. It turned out that the number of housing units exceeds the number of households by 10 percent, and the average unit area is eighty-five square meters. While this is a smaller

amount of space than in the average residence in the United
States or the former West Germany, it compares favorably to
French, British, and Italian dwellings. In particular, Tokyo
and Osaka boast substantially bigger units than London and
Paris. On top of that, Japan has a higher rate of home ownership (61.4 percent) than any other industrialized nation, when
the same measurement standards are applied. The fact that
Japanese continue to leave more spacious dwellings in outlying regions for cramped houses in Tokyo also demonstrates
that the connection of living space to a feeling of prosperity is
not a strong one.

At the same time, bureaucrats hungry for budgetary increases began to claim that Japan's roads and parks were too
small and its waterworks backward. But the populace did not
agree. Movements sprang up opposing parks, objecting to
messy trees and increased cicada noise. Usage rates of new
sewers were low. Rural regions often found that only 10 to 20
percent of local residents were using sewers even ten years
after completion. Even in Tokyo it is not unusual for such
usage to reach only 30 percent, because buildings had septic
tanks in place before public sewer construction.

It seems obvious that an increase in the number of urban
parks and sewer lines would not lead to a sudden upswing in
the feeling of prosperity. Japan's "poor infrastructure," so
widely touted by the government and media in the eighties,
was not the source of the Japanese feeling of discontent.

PEOPLE UNABLE TO UNDERSTAND WEALTH

What is wealth, anyway? This is currently a topic of much
debate in Japan. The debate has yet to produce any concrete
answer that has found widespread acceptance or provided a
direction in which to move.

Government bureaucrats and some academicians tallied
Japanese income and material consumption totals and told the

Japanese people that if they wanted to know what wealth was, they should take a look at themselves. This attitude found few subscribers. Others said true prosperity was a matter of the soul, but this was too abstract and left people pondering how to go about making their souls rich. To some it sounded like a moral lesson: be thankful for what you have.

A more successful explanation was that the answer was to provide ample welfare so the entire population felt secure. But medical insurance and old-age pensions were already generous, and many Japanese doubted that augmenting them would make people feel richer. The largest expense of those elderly currently receiving pensions is said to be gifts to their grandchildren (if grandchildren do not receive money they won't come to visit). This suggests that giving the elderly pensions that are 10 or 20 percent larger will not significantly increase their happiness. In fact, financing such generous raises for the retired would result in an increase in taxes and social insurance charges on workers, which might increase the feeling of deprivation, especially as Japan is now heading into a crisis of aging.

Some people have found great satisfaction in volunteer work or community service. But Japan has little history of allowing a place for volunteer efforts, and there are few community organizations to help. Unskilled volunteers are considered a nuisance by city officials, and in towns inhabited largely by company employees and school-age children, holding neighborhood meetings or helping with children's sporting activities is considered meddlesome.

Still others say that increasing the natural richness of the environment is the way to make prosperity tangible. But in a society in which mothers scold their children for playing in "dirty" sandboxes and teenagers run at the sight of a bug or a snake, there are really very few who sincerely believe this. Many housewives state a preference for organic vegetables, but when shopping time comes around, they don't buy misshapen cucumbers or blemished fruit. The young people

raised in this safety-first environment are extreme in their
cleanliness and utterly domesticated. When they say they
love "nature" they are referring to lush, spotlessly kept-up
parks and ornamental and flowering plants raised in green-
houses.

The more Japanese debate the meaning of wealth, the less
they understand it.

Slaves to Magazine Trends

While pundits and opinion makers debate, ordinary Japanese,
in their role of consumers, have found a way to experience
wealth in quite a different form. In the eighties, Japanese
rushed to buy more things than ever before and stampeded to
purchase famous foreign brand names.

Since the Meiji days, the foremost goal of the Japanese
nation has been the creation of a modern industrial state. To
that end the government promoted standardization in every
field to make mass production easier. It is fair to say that all
postwar government policy has been directed at this aim in
order to help a peaceful Japan develop economically. And the
Japanese people were squarely behind this effort.

In the forties, the Japanese dream was to be able to eat a
full belly of white rice. In the fifties, everyone wanted the
"three magic machines": a black-and-white television, a re-
frigerator, and a washing machine. In the sixties, these became the "three Cs": color television, cooler (air conditioner),
and car. The items had changed, but the idea of lining up
material possessions was the same. And providing these items
at the lowest price and greatest quantity was the goal of the
state and the hope of the people.

By the seventies, most people had their three Cs. By the
time differentials of income were low and everyone had these
standard products, people no longer wanted them. The Japanese began piling up money because there were no more
standard items left to want.

In the eighties, people stopped accumulating standard products and began to want anything that seemed a little different, a little trendy, a little conspicuous. But postwar Japanese had all been through an educational system that extinguished their individuality and turned them into clones suited to the mass-production workplace. They did not really know what "a little different" or "a little trendy" was. Nevertheless, full of consumer energy, they could still turn to famous foreign brand names: Louis Vuitton handbags, Hermès ties, Wedgwood china. The eighties were boom years for companies like these. Louis Vuitton exported more than a third of its products to Japan. Add in the merchandise purchased by Japanese abroad, and Japan was probably taking over half their wares. Prices of hundreds or even thousands of dollars for consumer goods are nothing unusual for ordinary Japanese.

The purchase of high-profile items that the elite of Europe and America had long enjoyed did help give Japanese a feeling that they had made it. But it was not enough. Those Japanese born after the war had been educated to be patient and cooperative, and to have standard levels of skills so that they would be good workers on the factory floors. They found that the task of selecting individualized items and dreaming up creative combinations was more than difficult, it was burdensome. As consumer options became diversified and brands became trendy, most Japanese, especially young people, came to want someone to inform them what products were in, what brands they could feel good about owning. A stream of new magazines flooded Japan to inform the trend-buying public what brands were famous, which products were must-haves.

By the end of the eighties, there were more than a hundred of these trend magazines catering to both men and women. To fill up each one, the articles became ever more detailed, describing the elements of ideal dates or the most comfortable position of chairs at gourmet restaurants. And young people took up these hints by the thousands.

What greater contradiction is there than having a magazine inform you of what is unusual and undiscovered, and reflects your own unique taste? A write-up in a magazine sells products, and yesterday's unusual item is suddenly seen everywhere; your unique taste is suddenly everyone else's. Most Japanese responded by relying even more on trend magazines to tell them even sooner what brands were hot. This insatiable flurry of restless, endless pursuit of fashion regardless of cost left no room for leisure.

Since everyone had bought the same products to show their individuality, a "common individuality" developed. Japanese had believed that economic prosperity would provide a feeling of abundance, but when everyone becomes rich, no one feels rich. Likewise, once everyone had bought the brand names that people were using to distinguish themselves, people had even less individuality than before. By the early nineties, a feeling was rising throughout the country that something was wrong with Japan.

FRUSTRATION AT FOREIGN PRESSURE

Pressure from abroad only makes Japanese dissatisfaction and uneasiness worse.

When Japan began really to prosper in the eighties and its industrial competitiveness dramatically improved, the United States and other countries began bombarding Japan with new requests and demands, which ranged from voluntary export restraints to import expansion, from allowing foreign companies to bid on public-works projects to financial liberalization and increasing aid to developing countries. In 1985, the Plaza Accord induced a rapid appreciation of the yen. To the Japanese people, this was perhaps the most surprising effect any international agreement has ever had. To understand how the Japanese were caught unawares by this accord, a brief look at postwar international monetary policy is in order.

For close to thirty years after World War II, the Bretton Woods agreement called for currencies to be fixed in value (they were generally tied to the American dollar). But in the early 1970s, a new system of freely convertible currencies was instituted. The idea behind this move was that floating exchange rates would adjust naturally to keep international payment balances in equilibrium. Japan, which had concentrated solely on its own trade and keeping its economy moving, had no understanding of this concept. In the early eighties, President Ronald Reagan began simultaneously running huge fiscal deficits and tightening monetary policy. As a result, the United States racked up huge trade deficits even as dollar interest rates rose. In building his "strong America," Reagan ignored the international adjustment function of the floating exchange-rate system and instead worked only to promote domestic economic growth and build up national defense.

While this had very positive effects in speeding up the victory over the Soviet system in the Cold War, disequilibrium in the world economy increased. Thanks to the cheap yen, Japan's exports increased massively and its industry thrived. The Plaza Accord of 1985 was an attempt to correct the distortion that had developed and restore the adjustment function of the floating exchange-rate system. Japanese, who were relatively unfamiliar with the system, were stunned by the rapid appreciation of the yen. They were gripped by uncertainty and anger because they feared that exports would contract and corporate profits would decline.

Since a rise in a country's currency exchange rate means that its income and assets increase in international value, it seems like something that *should* be welcomed. In fact, most citizens of West Germany were quite happy when the mark also appreciated after the Plaza Accord.

The Japanese reaction to foreign pressure is always the same, especially to demands from the advanced nations of Europe and America. First surprise, then a feeling of threat, then anger. Japanese always feel that foreign demands are

intended to harm Japan. Japanese never stop to investigate
the actual demand or forecast the actual effects. The media
are loath to report voices that argue for compliance. The
Japanese media have always found their best market in the
nervousness and dissatisfaction of their readership.

But no matter how the facts are reported, no matter how
people feel, the economy always responds in real ways. The
result of the yen appreciation was that the Japanese economy
boomed and its economic position within the world improved.
Corporate profits grew and individuals became rich. Japanese
bought more world-famous brands and took more vacations
abroad. And many Japanese felt that all this was due to the
abilities and diligence of the Japanese people themselves. The
consensus was that the foreign plot had fallen through because Japanese knuckled down to foil it and achieve greater
prosperity than ever.

The reaction of the Japanese people to foreign pressure is
typically to act like "capable weaklings" and to cast themselves as the underdog nation. Japanese fear outsiders, im-
pugn foreign motives, and attribute Japanese success to their
own efforts and abilities.

JAPANESE BEWILDERMENT AS THE WORLD CHANGES

Japan has a new emperor for the nineties and a new era
name, the Heisei. And this new era brings with it an entirely
new kind of foreign pressure. What has been demanded of
Japan in the Japan–U.S. Structural Impediments Initiative,
the Uruguay Round of the GATT negotiations, and most recently in the Gulf War is greater participation. The world has
also demanded a faster response. For Japan, accustomed to
security and equality, this provokes great pain and anxiety.
Since the end of World War II Japan has concentrated on
security above all. Courage and decisiveness have not been
thought of as virtues. In a society that enshrines equality,

avoidance of strong leadership has weakened the country's ability to coordinate planning for the benefit of all.

Japan had been through other types of pressure, such as export restrictions and import liberalizations, but each of these dealt with single products or with problems confined to single industries. For that reason they were easy for Japanese to understand and easy to respond to. Japan's government usually has enough protective structures in place to sacrifice a few of its "administrative guidances" and still have enough left to amply protect individual industries.

The first foreign challenge came from the American negotiators of the Structural Impediments Initiative. What the United States asked for in this new negotiation was the reduction or abolition of the very structures that protect and coddle Japanese industries. The Americans asserted that Japan was not a true free market but a managed economy guided by the hand of government. If Japan wished to continue free trade with the United States, the Americans said, it had to change to a free economic system.

So what is this free economic system that the European and American countries, led by the United States, envision? It is a system in which sales patterns of products and services and the fortunes of corporations are determined by consumer choice. It is a system that enshrines "freedom of choice."

In specific terms, there are many examples that can be given of the changes requested. Among them were the abolition of the Large-Scale Retail Store Restriction Law, which restricts the retail market, strengthening the antimonopoly laws, and the vigorous pursuit of actions against cartels that inhibit consumer choice, so that consumers can shop at the stores they desire. These are all examples of the single overarching reform that is being proposed. At its core, the Americans wanted nothing less than the abolition of the system of close bureaucratic involvement in the industrial world through administrative guidance, and its replacement with a regime that relies on consumer choice and free competition.

. . .

The agricultural issues raised at the Uruguay Round of the GATT talks in the late eighties and early nineties are based on the same principles. The American position is that the fortunes of agriculture and the specialization of each country's agricultural industry should be guided by consumer choice. Subsidies and protection given to agriculture should be reduced throughout the world and agricultural goods should have access to consumer markets with no discrimination between foreign and domestic products.

Agriculture is an ancient industry and is dependent on natural conditions and social structures in many ways. For that reason alone, it is harder for Japan and European countries to be as ruthlessly competitive as America. While the conflict between Europe and America has been quite intense, Japan has been cornered into a position of even greater difficulty. Japan's extremely protective agricultural policies for rice cultivation are rooted in the system of administrative guidance, and Japanese conceptually see absolutely nothing wrong with them.

Japanese became quite terrified when they encountered these two types of foreign pressure on their industrial and economic system. The pursuit of efficiency, security, and equality made Japan a utopia: it made it an economic dynamo that was highly competitive in industrial exports. It made Japan clean, lowered its rate of accidents, and increased the life expectancies of its people. It made Japan the world's most peaceful country, gave Japanese high incomes, and eliminated much educational discrimination. It made Japan a society of equality in outcome. But this Japanese utopia lacked one critical element: freedom. When America demanded that freedom be introduced into Japan, the limits of this utopia were exposed.

THE ANXIETY OF JAPANESE ASKED TO JOIN
THE WORLD ORDER

The third element of this frightening new foreign pressure hit Japan in 1990 and 1991. Japan was asked to participate in the Gulf War against Iraq.

In the past two thousand years, Japan has very rarely played a significant role in the affairs of the world or the international order. For great lengths of time, Japanese have lived exclusively within the bounds of their island nation. Rarely has Japan thought to occupy territory outside its home archipelago, and Japan has never been even close to being made part of another country. Although Japan has often studied foreign thought and culture, rarely has it made any attempt to proselytize the world with its ways. There have been few instances of foreigners settling in Japan in any significant numbers or organized fashion, and there has never been a large-scale, planned transfer of Japanese abroad.

Of course there have been military adventures abroad, such as the Japanese Mimana domain on the Korean peninsula in the fifth and sixth centuries and the dispatch of troops to the Pak River in the Korean state of Paekche in 663, but these were minor incidents of well over a thousand years ago. Toyotomi Hideyoshi's invasion of Korea in 1592 was a more recent and larger scale event, but the goal of the invasion was never clear. It did not have the passionate support of Japanese society and did not have a lasting impact on the Japanese sense of nationhood. It was followed by 250 years of isolation and peace. Naturally, Japanese gave no thought to concepts like "world structure" and "international order."

The only time Japan has interacted with international society in a significant way was during the thirty years in the first half of the twentieth century, from World War I to World War II. And this too ended in disaster. The defeat in World War II was a crushing tragedy. Ultimately Japan's actions and ideals were totally repudiated not only by other countries but also by the Japanese themselves.

The experience that had the strongest impact on the Japanese consciousness has been the postwar years. A defeated Japan had absolutely no role in the crafting of new world structures and the international order. It promoted no specific measures, and it had no opportunity to offer its opinions. Though fortunate to be occupied by America alone, Japan had no maneuvering room to select its international position. As when the country opened to the world in the Meiji days, it was only after some time that Japan was allowed to enter, head bowed, a world that had already been completely shaped by others.

As it happened, the Japanese economy was able to develop tremendously within this postwar world. The contrast with the prewar world it had tried to shape was clearly burned into Japan's consciousness. Japanese learned the importance of using the world structure and international order and the danger of trying to change it. To contemporary Japanese, the world order seems to be a natural phenomenon, such as gravity, not something that can be controlled by mere human beings.

So being asked to participate in maintaining the international order is as perplexing to Japan as being asked to lend a hand in maintaining gravity. Japan does not have in its repertoire any tools or skills to help maintain the international order.

The call to help and the subsequent confusion are having a continuing impact on Japanese thinking. Japanese have learned that their utopia does not float apart from other countries but is located on the ground, connected to a world of war and poverty and violence and plotting. And Japanese have become a little more appreciative of their wealth, security, and equality. The series of events that occurred at the start of the decade have provoked Japanese to re-examine Japan.

More and more Japanese are thinking, Is the utopia that Japanese believe in real? Is it possible to raise that utopia higher, to separate it from the "ground" of the world even more? And would that even be the road to true happiness for Japanese? When one looks at Japan again through these eyes, utopia assumes a new, different shape.

THE REALITY OF
PARADISE JAPAN:
THE INDUSTRIAL
MONOCULTURE

THE INEFFICIENT ECONOMIC POWER

It is easy for a people whose socio-economic position ascends rapidly to drift into one of two extreme ways of thinking about themselves. They may gain an exaggerated opinion of their own capabilities, attributing their climb solely to their own efforts. Or they may develop a kind of self-hate that arises from the cold way that everyone else looks at them.

This psychology can lead them on the one hand to engage in ostentatious displays of wealth and misuse of power, and on the other to nurse an excessive feeling of being wronged. The internal desire to be liked by others can become quite strong. This is the psychology of the nouveau riche, which is clearly Japan's position within international society at the moment.

Japan's exaggerated opinion of itself informs Japanese administrative, industrial, and cultural organizations. It is widely prevalent in Japanese individuals, who cherish an image of the country as an immense economic power. It is the self-image of the Japanese: hardworking, talented, upstanding. The bureaucracy publishes the statistical information to support these verdicts, which are picked up by the media for further amplification by the opinion makers.

The various statistics used to illustrate the economic power described earlier are accurate and contain in themselves no hidden agenda. But the way the figures are selected and reported clearly encourages an image of Japan as a country of economic efficiency, a society that has created an economic system so good it should be adopted by the entire world.

It is true that Japan is extremely competitive internationally in fields that employ mass production, such as automobiles and electronics. These products are not only cheap, their quality is also superior and deliveries are prompt. The rate of defective products is low and breakdowns are few. Twenty-five years ago Japanese products were seen as cheap and shoddy and Japanese were hotly criticized for dumping goods and paying low wages; such complaints are rarely heard today. The extensive steps taken to make Japanese factories more efficient and to incorporate high technology have shifted Japanese products toward higher added value. Even the ball bearings used in residential door hinges are crafted to the same ultrafine precisions used for aerospace rockets. Factories equipped with automated machine tools with submicron tolerances produce such products cheaply and in high volume.

This approach is seen in all fields of industry, fostering an impulse to boast that Japanese economic power and technological prowess is the best in the world. This in turn leads to the belief that Japanese society itself is very efficient. These areas of efficiency, however, are but one part of the total picture. When we step back from this image to look at the totality of Japanese society, a different reality comes into focus.

When the per capita gross national product is converted to other currencies at current exchange rates, Japan's ranking is the highest in the world. However, when we look at real gross national product, which takes the cost of living in various countries into account, Japan, the former West Germany, and the United States come out roughly the same. In fact, according to Bank of Japan international comparisons, the former West Germany and the United States rank slightly higher. Britain and France are only marginally lower than Japan. The differences are far smaller than when viewed in currency exchange terms.

A survey of worker productivity performed in September 1991 by the Japan Productivity Headquarters placed Japan at the bottom of the major industrial nations, above only Sweden. Japan's percentage of employment, at 49 percent, remains the highest of any industrialized nation.

Japanese also work longer than inhabitants of the other industrial nations. The 2,044 hours the average Japanese worker puts in each year is 10 percent longer than the hours worked by Americans, 20 percent more than British and French works, and an incredible 30 percent longer than the Germans' work year.

When the time consumed in commuting is added to the total work-related time, this discrepancy increases further— to 20 percent between Japan and the United States and 40 percent for Japan/Germany. To state this most broadly, the American worker needs only ten months to produce what the average Japanese worker produces in a year, and the German needs only eight months.

As a result of their greater productivity, Germans have three times as much discretionary time as Japanese. Whenever commuting times in the Tokyo area grow, the average worker's discretionary time shrinks even further. Between the seventies and eighties, the average Japanese worker's sleeping time actually decreased eighteen minutes.

The high figures for per capita gross national product for Japan are due not to high social and industrial efficiency, but merely to long working hours. To use a little hyperbole, only by working all night has Japan managed to equal the level of Europe and America.

THE IMMENSE WASTE OF THE JAPANESE SYSTEM

Japan is reputed to be an advanced, technological nation. Its factory automation is the best in the world, and its office automation first class. These days, even ordinary families have facsimile machines at home, junior high school students carry the popular Famicon portable computers, and housewives write letters on word processors. The extent of the spread of these electronic technologies not just to factories but to ordinary life is quite amazing.

Japan is a country that does not spend money or manpower on anything other than the economy. Defense counts for a mere one percent of GNP. America spends six times as much. Even Western Europe spends almost four times what Japan does. Japan's military forces account for only 0.39 percent of the workforce, which is one-half to one-fifth the level in Europe and America. Religions account for a similarly small share of Japanese personal and pocketbook activities. The majority of priests and religious officials work only part-time, and only very rarely is religion allowed to impede economic activity. Volunteerism is a fringe activity in Japan, and it never slows down the corporate march. Japan concentrates its financial and human resources earnestly on economic matters without regard to defense or religion.

Japan is proud of the high quality of its labor force. Education is widespread and evenly provided, as I described earlier, and students are indeed earnest. The skills and knowledge of Japan's average worker are said to be substantially higher than those of counterparts in Europe and North America. The vast majority of Japanese are overwhelmingly, almost poignantly, responsible and loyal to their organizations. They are rarely absent from work, and strikes are remarkably rare.

Japan also has what has been called the most ideal population structure in the history of the planet: people of working age account for an incredible 70 percent of the population (the rise of the elderly to 13 percent of the population has been counterbalanced by an even faster decrease of the young). This makes Japan more productive per capita than Europe, with its high proportion of elderly, and the United States, with its high proportion of young.

In contemporary Japan, technology is advanced, the quality

of the labor force high, the population well educated, and modern machinery found in every facet of life. The country spends little of its money or personnel on anything other than the economy, and the bulk of the population is in the prime of its working life. Yet despite these optimum conditions, the real product per worker hour is far lower than in America and western Germany. It is lower even than in France, Britain, and Spain. How can this be? Why, despite the abundance of loyal, diligent workers laboring in highly automated factories to produce cheap, high-quality products, is the country as a whole so inefficient? Somewhere, outside the efficient factories, there must be enormous waste.

Behind the face of the astonishing international competitiveness of its industrial products lie all the other fields, in which Japan's cost of production is remarkably high. The small scale and low productivity of Japanese agriculture is already infamous. In fact, price supports and government assistance account for 75 percent of farm incomes.

The distribution industry is also amazingly wasteful and inept. One widely heard aphorism is that while America needs two people to build a car and one to sell it, Japan requires one person to build the car and two to sell it. The average retail price in America is 1.7 times the factory invoice price; in Europe, it is also less than 2 times factory price. Only in Japan does it hit an incredible 3 times the factory price. It costs Japan 2 to 3 times as much to sell a car as it does for Europe and America.

Of course, we cannot ignore the high quality of service in the Japanese distribution industry, or at least in its retail end. Japanese retailers are open late and they hardly ever run out of stock. Delivery is free and after-sales service is thorough. And best of all is the packaging. The paper used for wrapping, the boxes, and bags are of excellent quality, and wrapping an item in three layers is standard practice. Surely this must be an object of national pride! And that is the level of service the Japanese consumer wants.

Even allowing for this, it is hard to deny that the Japanese distribution industry is inefficient and replete with redundancies.

Service in hotels and restaurants is also fairly good. A top-quality dinner out will never exceed three hundred dollars in New York or Paris, but it is not unusual to be presented a thousand-dollar tab at a traditional Japanese restaurant in the Akasaka or Shimbashi areas of Tokyo. At a Ginza or Kita-Shinchi club, a few whiskey-and-waters might cost three hundred dollars. Nonetheless, these clubs are quite well attended by regular salaried employees. Within that very specialized world called business entertaining, the service demanded is far more luxurious than for private entertainment.

Financial and information costs are also higher than in other countries. As the scandal of stock brokerage houses covering losses for their largest corporate clients so vividly illustrated, Japanese securities commissions are roughly double what they are in Europe and America. The high cost in the television industry of surveys, planning, design, production, and editing is another example. The Japanese system requires that large numbers of people gather in offices built on ridiculously expensive Tokyo land to talk and get friendly, which sends these costs way up.

So even though Japan is a great economic power, the truth is that the only industries competitive and productive enough to be able to boast about quality and quantity are the manufacturing industries, especially those that exploit mass production, such as automobiles and electronics. The reality is that Japan is not superior across the entire range of economic activity, but is rather a mass-production power, one whose development of mass-producing industries has vastly outstripped its waste and inefficiencies in other areas.

THE WARPED PROSPERITY OF
THE INDUSTRIALLY OPTIMIZED SOCIETY

The severity of this imbalance—mass-production industries
that overwhelm the rest of the world with their volume and
efficiency alongside distribution, information, and knowledge-
value creation industries mired in inefficiency and waste—is
the key to understanding modern Japan. Emphasis on the first
quality has crowned Japan as the world's most dynamic economy and the world's closest approximation of industrial utopia; emphasis on the second causes Japanese to view the
country as an inefficient and unenjoyable society in which
they cannot feel wealthy.

How did this imbalance arise? It is clear that manufacturing
did not become dominant because it attracted the best people
or benefited from economies of scale. The inefficiency of agriculture is in part due to natural conditions, but there are no
such conditions in modern Japan that place distribution and
information at an intrinsic disadvantage. The government did
have a role in directing capital toward manufacturing industries from the midtwenties to the midsixties, but that hasn't
been true for twenty years now. Manufacturing is not considered a particularly desirable form of employment for young
people today, and it has not necessarily attracted a more
skilled or capable part of the workforce. On the contrary, the
fact that young people are increasingly attracted to finance
and to the information industry is creating concern that manufacturing will decline.

It is also difficult to explain the imbalance in productivity by
the scale of the corporations. It does make some sense for
distribution, which has the Large-Scale Retail Store Restriction Law to protect the many medium-size, small, and minia-
ture offices and outlets that characterize that industry. Yet
even that cannot be considered the entire cause, since inefficiency is not limited to small retail outlets. Even in the whole-

sale market, which is not so restricted, roundabout distribution and high costs seem to be an ineradicable part of the system. Financial and information companies are as large or larger than counterparts abroad. Even the knowledge-value creation industry has quite a few large corporations. That does not prevent them from being inefficient and expensive; in fact, it seems to further the trend.

In short, despite the fact that all these companies have the same high quality of people, are organized along the same lines, and obtain the same level of passion and diligence from their workers, the mass-production manufacturing companies achieve world-class levels of productivity and competitiveness while the distribution and information industries produce incredible inefficiencies. Why the difference? At its simplest level, it is because the attitudes and culture that permeate the entire fabric of Japanese society are conducive to standardized mass-production manufacturing but inappropriate for any other kind of industry or social activity.

The fact is that the Japanese government has expended prodigious energy to boost mass production and standardization. One example of such policy over industrial products is the use of the JIS (Japan Industrial Standards) mark, which encourages conformity for all kinds of products from screws and bolts to steel to electronics. Building codes and fire codes are also exceedingly strict, placing astonishing limits on building design and interior space, so much so that the building codes determine the building design more than the architects do. Road, park, and electrical facility regulations are also exceptionally strict. Operation of these facilities is then further restricted by the Road Transport Act, park management regulations, and the like, so that free use is virtually prohibited. Japanese cities are notoriously short on parks, and the few they have are becoming more and more difficult to use. Medical care is standardized into accepted "standard treatments," and hospital charges over the insurance coverage (for private rooms and the like) are viewed in the strongest negative terms.

Standardization of the gamut of commercial products, facilities, and services decreases the number of commercial services, narrows the scope of consumer choice, and thereby creates an environment more advantageous to mass production of standardized products. When companies tried to diversify their products and services in the eighties, their changes were limited largely to the color and shape of the containers and other cosmetic matters.

STANDARDIZATION OF EDUCATION AND INFORMATION

Bureaucratic control of education is complete. In the half century since the National Schools Ordinance was promulgated in 1941, Japan has pursued a policy of public primary education that prohibits the construction of new private schools in the primary grades. A compulsory system of drawing students strictly from a single catchment district, one per school, has been strictly enforced. This allows no room for any sort of choice on the part of students and parents, who are ultimately the root source of educational demand. The individual likes and characteristics of children are ignored; students are forced into schools designated by bureaucrats.

Within schools that they are forced to attend, students are mechanically fed a bureaucratically designated curriculum, advancing through the system month by month, year by year. Bureaucrats also stipulate instructional outlines that dedicate the educational system to eliminating defects, providing instruction in inverse proportion to ability—the less accomplished one is in a subject, the more one studies it. Even more frightening, recent years have shown a strengthening of school rules to enforce norms of clothing, haircuts, and even student posture and manner of walking, all because some "bad students" still exhibit signs of personal likes and dislikes, or individuality. School rules are the final method of control used to outlaw any expression of those last vestiges of student individuality.

This homogenizing educational system eliminates all pleasure from school life and destroys student creativity and individuality. On the other hand, it is effective in instilling a common level of knowledge and skills and in getting students used to enduring long hours filled with discomfort. In sum, it is effective in training a labor force suitable for employment in the workplaces of standardized mass production.

Japan's industrial and professional organizations were also created under the guidance of the bureaucrats. They have their headquarters in Tokyo, and civil servants from the "old boy" network customarily head their secretariats and serve as managing directors. These industrial and professional organizations fulfill the directives of the bureaucratic structure, both directly and through the networks of ex-officials in the secretariats. This practice suppresses competition between corporations and between professionals, which has the result of raising consumer prices and enforcing standardization of industrial products. But it is useful for preventing excessive competition within industries.

The system of centralizing all distribution of broadcasting and print media in Tokyo also has a half century of history. This system ensures that all of Japan has a single informational environment. This not only minimizes the variety and distinctiveness of regions but has also been undeniably important in transforming the country into a single, unified market to facilitate the sale of standardized products and services.

Under the rubric of "administrative guidance," Japan also permits its bureaucrats unlimited power to intervene administratively outside the system of law. The bureaucrats show no compunction about using legal rights in a manner completely at odds with their original purpose and intent if doing so is useful in forcing compliance from corporations and regional governmental entities.

For example, the Supreme Court ruled that prohibitions against pharmacies opening branch stores were unconstitutional, since they contravene the constitution's "freedom to select employment." The bureaucracy then sidestepped this judicial ruling by directing pharmaceutical companies not to sell to such pharmacies. Should a pharmaceutical company go against the bureaucracy's wishes, it has to live with the prospect of its drug approvals dragging on for decades. In this way the branch pharmacies that bureaucrats frown on remain unopened.

The same environment makes possible schemes like the securities scandal exposed in the summer of 1991, which has been mentioned earlier. The Japanese financial community is governed by the Ministry of Finance, which limits competition so that commissions can be collected at high ministry-stipulated rates. Guaranteed enormous profits, the securities companies were able to guarantee certain customers that they would cover any losses in order to land fat accounts. The interests of ordinary investors were sacrificed for the profit of large corporations.

In many other cases, administrative guidances like these suppress competition, raise consumer prices, and provide effective protection for producers. This allows corporations to accumulate capital useful for forward-looking investment and introducing new technologies.

Contemporary Japan thus acquiesces to restricted competition under the aegis of administrative guidance to create a social system advantageous to the expansion and development of mass production. As a result of fifty years of this system of administratively guided industrial cooperation, consumer choice in Japan has been narrowed and consumer prices have increased. Student individuality and creativity have been stunted and regional distinctiveness has lessened. Access to information and management operation are also less than free. In return for these restrictions, Japanese society is optimized for industries of standardized mass production.

Today's Japan is both an industrially optimized society and an industrial monoculture. Because of this industrial monoculture, Japanese quality and quantity in mass-production industries like automobiles and electronics are the wonder of the world; because of it, fields that do not use mass production, such as publishing, financial services, and advertising, are inefficient and wasteful.

THE ADVANTAGES AND DISADVANTAGES OF JAPANESE-STYLE MANAGEMENT

Most of the characteristics of which Japanese are so proud today spring from the industrially optimized society. To say Japanese are proud of these things, then, is no more than saying that they are proud of being optimally suited to standardized mass-production industries. Most Japanese, for example, would pick the concept of "Japanese-style management" as the element of Japanese culture that the world would most benefit from adopting.

Broadly speaking, there are three foci to characteristic Japanese-style management. The first is a closed labor system that is characterized by lifetime employment, a seniority wage system, and company unions. The second is the group orientation symbolized by the dispersion of decision making throughout lower echelons and the use of consensus. The third is extremely low dividends and extremely high business-entertainment spending that unifies the community of employees. These three characteristics are interrelated. Because the system of lifetime employment is used, corporate employees think of themselves as a community; because they are a community, they can be group oriented with dispersed authority; because they are group oriented, it is difficult to leave the community, and lifetime employment is strengthened.

Japanese-style management strengthens the loyalty of the employees, increases the undistributed profit, and pushes the corporation toward aggressive, forward-looking investment. Since decision-making powers are dispersed down to the furthest echelons, more time is required to come to a corporate decision. But in-house agreement is produced, and once made, the decision can be carried out with the cooperation of the entire workforce. Japanese corporations have grown strongly, with little labor unrest, and have often been able to institute technological changes and management restructurings with companywide involvement. The aggregate of many such companies has provided the growth and productive force that has made the Japanese economy as a whole so internationally competitive.

These achievements have induced Japanese managers, bureaucrats, and opinion makers to point triumphantly to Japanese-style management as the single thing the world should learn from Japan. And there is some truth to this. But when one turns to look at fields such as distribution, information, and knowledge creation, one sees that this same Japanese-style management can also lead to a structure where costs are far higher than they are abroad.

The lifetime employment system is prone to overemployment (this phenomenon is known as in-house unemployment). The group orientation that disperses decision making through the company makes definitive decisions slow. Communal corporations that pay low dividends tend to shelter one another, and their expenses are high. In manufacturing, which has relatively steady operating rates, lifetime employment has its advantages, but in the information and knowledge-creation industries, prone as they are to feast or famine, such a system is dangerous. Similarly, while group orientation has many advantages for mass production, in the distribution and information industries, where there are many opportunities for spontaneous creativity and decision making, it is a drawback.

The major advantages of Japanese-style management can be exploited only in constantly growing mass-production manufacturing industries that require little decision making and are focused inward. When applied to low-growth (or shrinking) industries, this system of management quickly leads to overemployment, as was clearly the case in the old Japanese

National Railways and is currently true of agricultural and forestry organizations. When Japanese-style management is instituted in manufacturing industries that rely on small production runs and high variety, they too suffer in costs and time because they must make many decisions. Japanese-style management is what makes Japanese information industry and knowledge-value creation costs so high. When foreign companies encounter it, friction causes a barrage of criticism.

CORE TENDENCY TO HOMOGENIZE EVERYTHING

At the start of the eighties, Japanese-style management was the rage in Europe, Asia, and America. The Japanese economy had shown admirable stability and recovered quickly after the Iran-Iraq war caused a worldwide fear of a new oil shortage, plunging many economies into chaos. The successful injection of electronics technology into its industries attracted worldwide attention and envy. Foreign scholars identified Japanese-style management as the key, some even calling it capitalism with a human face.

One foreign scholar wrote, "Japanese-style management is a wonderful method that develops the national economy, spreads technological innovations to all of society, nurtures corporations and provides employees with security. People are seen as part of the company's assets and the training of personnel and learning of new technology is part of the long-term corporate plan." Malaysia promoted its "Look East" approach and exhorted its population to study the excellence of corporate management and diligence of the workforces in Japan and Korea.

As the eighties ended, however, the sheen of Japanese-style management had dimmed considerably and had come to be more criticized than praised. In the nineties, criticism by Europeans, Asians, and Americans on the closed nature of "Japanese-style management" is far more likely to be heard.

There is no single simple reason for this—neither Japanese

corporations acquiring movie studios and large amounts of real estate nor their developing too large a presence in Asia accounts for it. Rather, the true essence of Japanese-style management has been discovered, its inefficiency in anything other than mass production recognized, and the underlying assumption of a continually expanding company made clear.

One very important part of Japanese-style management, with its three pillars of lifetime employment, group orientation, and communization-company identification, is that all employees are forced to share the same set of attitudes and values. Everyone has to believe that the development of the corporation is a social good and that the accomplishment of the work of the company is a goal of society. The explanation that something is "for the corporation" then permits one to ignore the expectations of others outside the company and even to break laws. One must believe that work is a sufficient excuse to skip family functions and break family promises. Part of Japanese-style management is that an employee is a "good employee" only if he or she subscribes to these beliefs.

This keeps Japanese eyes perpetually on the workplace community and causes everything to be evaluated in terms of whether it is good or bad for the company community. This not only asphyxiates any individuality or creativity, it also pushes out of the company anyone who does not buy into the value system of the workplace community. In other words, to be a "good employee" under Japanese-style management one must give up one's own thoughts and one's sense of belonging to family and regional society and be loyal only to the workplace community; one must belong only to the workplace.

For the corporation, such a strong sense of employee loyalty and belonging is a management advantage. But when the employee believes that the only good is the profit of the corporation to which he or she belongs, society pays the price and international friction increases. The "kanban" system or "just in time" method of inventory control, one product of the system of Japanese-style management, places a heavy burden on Japanese roads, as inventory is shipped constantly. It is symptomatic that even the Ministry of International Trade and Industry is unable to restrict this practice.

BUREAUCRATIC ORGANIZATIONS WORK FOR THE MINISTRY, NOT THE COUNTRY

These tendencies are not so bad that they cannot be tolerated by the private sector in some form, but the same problems are very serious when they apply to government bureaucracies. Japan's bureaucrats are loyal not to Japan or the Japanese government but to their ministries and agencies, within which they have lifetime employment.

Japan's bureaucrats work passionately for the interests of the ministry to which they belong, in order to expand its authority and protect its traditions. Authority and traditions are the source of bureaucratic power and the basic elements used to expand the ministry organization and increase its budget. Loyalty of a bureaucrat to his or her ministry means a passion for extending the authority and guarding the traditions of one's particular ministry.

The result is that the ministerial eye focuses of necessity on the activity under its jurisdiction, and its ideas concern the protection and nurturing of that activity. When that activity does grow, then the ministry's existence is strengthened. The authority of the ministerial bureaucrats themselves is increased and their traditions protected.

Japan is periodically lauded for the quality of its bureaucrats. In their passion for their work and their depth of knowledge in their field, they are perhaps unequaled in the world. But their gaze never strays from the boundaries of their ministry and its specialty. In their value system, there is no room for any consideration other than the interests of the ministry and of its bureaucrats. For that reason, they do not have— indeed, they must not have—any room to consider whether the policies and programs of the ministry are good or bad for Japan or Japanese society.

It is only natural that they strive solely for the interests of their area of jurisdiction. Unfortunately, this makes it impossible to draft basic policies for the nation, because no ministry can submit to overall coordination of government policy.

The setting of basic national policies and the overall coordination of those policies are at root the primary work of government. If politicians try to enforce coordination, bureaucrats react strongly to what they perceive as an attempt by an outsider to destroy their authority and traditions. In Japan, the mass media is fused to the bureaucrats and supports them. A politician who is "cooperative" can be promised the ardent support of the bureaucrats and can count on help from the industry under the ministry's purview.

For this reason, despite the fact that individual bureaucrats are extremely passionate and long on specialized knowledge, the Japanese administration as a whole is extremely inefficient and uncoordinated. When one ministry hammers out a policy in one direction, another will issue an opposing counterproposal, afraid of following the first ministry's course. Since the spheres of authority of the ministries overlap in complex ways, any new policy expands the authority of the ministry that proposes it, so the others inevitably resist. In addition, slow Japanese responses to international problems have repeatedly caused friction with other countries; these delays are caused by poor coordination among ministries.

If the quality of a bureaucracy is determined by how objectively it makes its decisions and how quickly it implements them for the overall benefit of the nation or the people, then the Japanese bureaucracy cannot be judged superior.

EDUCATIONAL SYSTEM WORKS FOR
THE ADMINISTRATORS AND TEACHERS

The fields in which Japan finds cause to sing its own praises are those, such as Japanese-style management and Japanese bureaucracy, that can be evaluated by the ultimate measure: they are good for mass-production industries. Japanese education is another example.

Japanese education is currently the object of a great deal of criticism—student violence and teacher misconduct are the most disturbing trends—but overall, Japanese primary education is still quite highly regarded. The consensus seems to be that the higher the level, the worse the education. A typical view is that primary and junior high schools are orderly and students achieve well, but that college students do not study and have no personalities. There is little creative or original study and research being done in Japanese universities.

It seems very strange that Japanese universities should suffer from a poverty of creative force when compared to European and American institutions of higher learning at the same time that primary and junior high schools perform so much better. Educators cite three measures as evidence of this achievement: high attendance rates, order in classrooms, and high scores in international comparisons of knowledge in science and geography. However, are these enough to say that Japanese primary education is excellent?

The high attendance rates, for example, do not show any excellence of school curriculums or systems but rather reflect Japanese traditions. In the year of the Meiji Restoration, 1868, Japan already had 40 percent of its male population and 25 percent of its female population attending educational institutions such as temple schools, where they were taught to read, write, and use an abacus. In Great Britain (then the world's most developed industrial nation) that very same year, only 25 percent of the male population had been through any kind of schooling. Not a single university in Europe then accepted women. So we see that extremely high school-attendance rates in Japan today are a continuation of long-standing practices.

Similarly, it is difficult to consider the order found in the Japanese classroom a good measure of educational quality, since it is primarily enforced by the strict supervision of teachers, not imposed by the students on themselves. After all, armies and prisons are quite orderly throughout the world, but this does not make them optimal forums for education. Japanese schools are so tightly constrained by instructional supervision and school rules that they bear some resemblance to armies and prisons. It is also undeniable that this quality has serious negative effects in dampening student initiative and creativity.

In common international tests given in the subjects of science and geography, Japanese junior high school and high school students rank near the top with students of Korea and Israel, but this achievement cannot be definitively linked to a high quality of education either. It seems more likely that it is a result of the incorporation into the Japanese educational system of the test-taking skills that students need to pass entrance exams. In a recent experiment, Japanese-style test-taking instruction was provided in a three-hour lecture at a school in Germany. The students quickly exceeded the Japanese test-taking performance. If good test results are the measure of educational excellence, it is Japan's cram schools that deserve the praise, not the public schools.

To praise the quality of education because the entire nation undergoes primary education, submits politely to teacher control, and acquires basic knowledge and basic skills is to assume that the purpose of education is to produce human capital easily employable in mass-production industry.

A broader view of quality might suppose that the first goal of education is to equip human beings to live happy lives, the second is to enable them to contribute to the prosperity and progress of the human race, and the third is to achieve this efficiently with the least pain to the student and least burden on parents and other relatives.

Modern Japanese education is not highly regarded in other countries for its achievements in these areas. It is not enjoyable, it does not foster the individual creativity needed to contribute to the advancement of the human race, and it imposes a high cost in student suffering and parental expense.

It is very important to remember when considering Japanese society that Japanese educators virtually never seek to evaluate or criticize school education from a whole-life or whole-society perspective. There is a tendency to leave evaluation of education to the teachers and educational bureaucracy.

JAPANESE ORGANIZATIONS CANNOT SEE THE BURDENS THEY IMPOSE ON OTHERS

There is another area of Japanese pride that bears close resemblance to the educational situation, and that is public security. Japan has a low crime rate and an extremely high conviction rate. But it is hard to be comfortable with the supposition that this shows the superiority of the Japanese police system. Japan has had good public security since the Tokugawa days, and the incidence of crime was very low even in rural mountain areas and cities like Osaka that had only minimal police systems. Japan has been a very governable society for a very long time. Today's good public security is largely attributable to this tradition.

The other side of the picture is that modern Japanese police are so concerned for safety that they do not hesitate to impede the free movement of people. Whenever an important international visitor arrives, or there is a significant national function, all of Tokyo is thrown into gridlock and people's lives and jobs are seriously disrupted. The police have absolutely no awareness of the burden they impose on the city's population.

In their attempt to provide perfect protection they are completely blind to the social inconvenience and the havoc they wreak in quality of life.

The same can be said about the safety codes for buildings and park management. Japanese building costs are far higher than costs abroad. One reason for this is the very strict building codes and fire laws. The Ministry of Construction and the Fire Defense Agency, which are responsible for building safety, give no thought when fulfilling these duties to the inconvenience and expense placed on the construction and use of buildings. Yet the number of deaths per building fire in Japan is twelve times that in Europe and America.

I have already mentioned how the hard-and-fast formality of park management makes parks difficult to use. Standards and regulations are designed for the convenience of the people who manage these facilities. Urban parks are classified into city parks and children's parks based on their size, and each must have a certain complement of trees and facilities per square meter. These stipulations cover everything down to the level of how many large trees, medium-size trees, and small trees a park must have for each hundred square meters. For the smaller children's parks, "directives" guide even the construction of swings and of any play equipment using old tires.

These strict regulations virtually eliminate the need for thought when building a park and greatly simplify management. Local officials, who are the "suppliers" of parks, are presumably grateful for these rules, since they simplify their work. But for the park users, the rules make parks uninteresting and remove any distinctiveness from the neighborhood. Parks are supposed to be for the city's residents, but it is no exaggeration to say that their construction and design are guided primarily by the convenience of the builders and managers. Given the Japanese bureaucratic structure, criticism of these standards and regulations is basically unheard of. Since the bureaucrats focus their attentions inward, all that matters is avoiding responsibility within the bureaucratic structure and making their own jobs easier. As a result, they have no idea of what kind of inconveniences or burdens their actions impose on the outside world.

CONCENTRIC GROUP MEMBERSHIPS

The object of this internal focus can be sometimes narrowed, sometimes enlarged, depending on the degree of identification of the individual. Even within a single corporation, Japanese clearly favor their own department, section, or branch over all others. Different branches of the same corporation can even become bitter enemies in the fight to attract customers. But once a common enemy appears, they seek their common interests and join together. Entire industries coalesce over issues of taxation and government policy. Industries join with one another to ward off incursions from abroad. Corporate managers are bound by a strong sense of connection to their industrial community. Different corporations in the same industry that compete fiercely under normal circumstances will join forces for the benefit of the industry to respond to the government or to compete overseas. The seamlessness of the cooperation can be quite eerie.

Japanese, by and large, feel senses of belonging to a ranked series of concentric groups that are strongly distinguished from other groups of the same rank. Belonging in the world as a whole is naturally placed on the furthest rim of this system. In the minds of Japanese, a huge chasm yawns between Japan, of which they are strongly aware, and foreign countries, which are lightly regarded. If there is a plane crash anywhere in the world, the first question is always, Were there any Japanese on board? If there were not, it is of no concern; if there were, the news is an account of those Japanese. Any non-Japanese are either ignored or treated with utter disregard.

If this is the attitude for something like a plane crash, which involves the loss of human life, it is even more pronounced in intellectual spheres of endeavor, such as economics or social customs, in which awareness of non-Japanese can disappear entirely. Japanese are keenly alert to trade friction when imports from other countries cause damage to some domestic industry but completely insensitive to any harm that Japanese exports may cause to foreign industries or workers. Japanese by and large lack the capacity even to imagine how conditions are in other countries. Japanese don't feel this is coldhearted or unusual. They believe everyone else in the world feels the same way.

As Japan entered the nineties, the idea that the country could exist alone in peace finally began to be criticized. No one honestly believed it would continue into the future. Postwar Japanese have been afraid of Japan's getting embroiled in war but have not given a thought to maintaining world peace. Japanese have wanted to believe that the world was filled with countries like the island nation of Japan, separated from others by protecting seas, just wide enough. Japanese even developed amnesia about the tone of Japanese society only a half century earlier, when Japan itself aggressively waged war. Most Japanese came to believe that peace would automatically prevail if they simply stated their opposition to war and asked everyone to be nice. They did not extend their imaginations to the efforts that must be made to preserve world peace. Inward-looking Japanese are not in the habit of exercising their powers of imagination on the rest of the world.

The Faceless Economic Power

When the question is asked outside of Japan, What do you know about Japan? the answers are generally product names—Toyota, Nissan, Honda, Sony, Panasonic, Canon.

Many non-Japanese can quickly reel off ten or twenty Japanese brand names, but they know very little of Japan's culture, systems, and customs. The names of some food—sushi or yakitori—and martial arts—judo and karate—are about the extent of their knowledge. It is a rare individual who knows the names of some Japanese. Even in America, which has a close relationship with Japan, fewer than one in five can name a Japanese person, other than a personal acquaintance. According to a survey done by a Japanese television station in 1987, the most widely known Japanese in America was Emperor Hirohito, and he was only named by 7 percent of respondents.

The survey also asked, What comes to mind when you hear the name of this country? When asked about countries other than Japan, the results were quite different, even in Japan. When asked about America, for example, the first things to come up were people's names—Washington, Lincoln, Chaplin, Kennedy, Marilyn Monroe—followed by cultural things, like baseball, jazz, hamburgers. For Britain, Shakespeare, Churchill, and Queen Elizabeth were followed by horse racing, double-decker buses, and whiskey. Germany brought to mind Beethoven, Goethe, Hitler, music, and beer; China conjured up Confucius, Yang Yu-huan, Sun Yat-sen, Mao Zedong, Chinese food, poetry, and calligraphy.

Of course there are many countries, both in Japan and elsewhere, about which little is known. Anyone who had much to say about the Seychelles or Belize would be either a specialist or quite well informed, indeed. But then again, neither are their product names known.

In fact, there may be no other country whose brand names are widely known and yet whose people and culture so obscure. Sri Lanka with its tea and Saudi Arabia with its oil are the only comparable cases. Probably only in Japan's case could people around the world come up with ten brand names and not a single person. Japan is a faceless economic power, a black box that belches forth industrial products.

One reason for this comparative anonymity is that authority in Japan is typically dispersed to lower levels of organizations in Japan, making it difficult to assign credit for product design and corporate management to specific individuals. If there were such a person, that individual would be subjected to heavy criticism from jealous colleagues, which is something that inward-directed Japanese fear most.

Except for politicians and artists (for whom name recognition is an important part of their profession), the overwhelmingly vast majority of Japanese tell pollsters that they value the approval of their peers over fame in their fields or internationally. Even scholars and artists pay more attention to their personal reputation in scholarly, literary, or artistic circles than to public acclaim for their work and fame for themselves. That is the "smart" way to pursue a career.

It is difficult for the type of creative and distinctive individuals who achieve individual fame abroad to make their way into the coterie of specialists in Japan. One is going to have a far easier time and enjoy life far more if one suppresses one's individuality and opinions in favor of inoffensive people-pleasing in the corporate, government, scholarly, literary, or artistic community to which one belongs. Many people become seriously regarded in academia and the arts simply by keeping this up for decades. It is not unthinkable for scholars and artists to reach the pinnacle of their worlds without ever producing a significant work of scholarship or artistic achievement.

The reputations of these caretaker people, who are known only within their own cliques of specialists, are completely untranslatable. The extreme acclaim that Japanese bestow on them is void of international credibility. This shows no sign of changing, even now that so many Japanese travel or live abroad. In fact, younger people tend to value such cliques the most.

It is true that Japanese culture has more peculiar traditions and subtleties than cultures of other countries and that the

Japanese language contains nuances that are difficult to translate. But the idiosyncrasy of Japanese culture does not arise solely from such historical qualities. The contemporary introspection of the Japanese and their strong desire for peer approval are major factors—perhaps the most important ones—in explaining why Japan is an economic power without a face.

THE GREATEST INDUSTRIAL MONOCULTURE

The inward focus and approval-seeking that permeate Japanese society in the nineties are linked to the spiritual underpinnings of Japanese-style management. Looking inward helps make people dependent solely on the workplace for identity and makes a closed labor system easier to maintain. The desire for the approval of one's peers encourages a group orientation and thus the downward dispersion of authority. When these two characteristics persist for a long time, the entire corporation naturally becomes an employee community. The same pattern has spread to government and bureaucratic organizations, politics, academia, and the literary and artistic worlds. In the nineties, the principles and values of Japanese-style management run through the entire fabric of Japanese society.

If Japanese-style management is the organizational principle best suited to a manufacturing industry of standardized mass production, then its spread to society as a whole implies that the society has become optimized for standardized mass production.

This optimization has enabled Japan to achieve the world's highest levels of manufacturing prowess and competitiveness in its mass-production industries. Japan has managed to become the largest and most competitive producer of a given product—transistors, automobiles, calculators, semiconductors—only when the product entered the stage of mass production. Even in computers Japan lagged behind the United

States when the market was characterized by small lots of a wide variety of large products. Japan achieved its lead only when the market turned to smaller, mass-produced machines—that is, when it became a commodity market. The end of this trend is the personal computer and Famicon-type simple portables. There will be no change in this situation so long as Japanese values and organizations remain optimized for mass production of standardized goods.

In technology fields like aerospace, which produce complex products in small volumes, and in the information and distribution industries, the labor rigidity and group orientation of Japanese-style management are at the very least a disadvantage. All these fields require rapid decisions and diverse creativity.

When Japanese-style management is incorporated into governmental structures, it metastasizes into supplier-biased policies that defy overall coordination. In politics, as in academia and the arts, the only result is a stagnant, sealed room. Japan today has become an industrially optimized society, geared to mass-produce, and the nation has become an industrial monoculture state in which these industrial values and organizing principles have taken root throughout society.

Model monocultures of the past were often agriculturally based. For example, in Sri Lanka and Cuba land use was optimized for production of a single product (tea and sugar cane, respectively). The "best" workers were those who could work in the tea plantations or cane fields. Government bureaucracy was organized in terms of knowledge and skills relating to tea or sugar, and informational structures were organized to optimize reporting about these subjects. In these extreme monoculture societies, production in the specialty industry was very efficient and production in other industries was inefficient, disordered, and disorganized. Once a society has become a monoculture, it is not easy to change.

This is the situation Japan finds itself in today. In its attempt to modernize industry, Japan recrafted its systems, organizations, education, market structures, regional structures, and even its values and motivations for the benefit of mass-production manufacturing. Other fields become inefficient, disordered, and disorganized. But very few people have noticed that this is the result of a social system and value system that was created to conform to the needs of mass production. For that reason, most Japanese do not view the unease and dissatisfaction that swirl through the country as a problem of the basic nature of the society. Instead, they see a series of isolated problems that can be corrected through specific measures—by changing the person in charge, by retraining, or the like. The search in the eighties for that missing "something," which I described earlier, is an example of this approach.

"WEALTH" IS SATISFYING DESIRES

Industry (which is Japan's monoculture specialization) is certainly not a single product like tea or sugar. It uses a wide variety of skills and technologies. By developing new products, demand can be increased seemingly without limit. For this reason, specialization in standardized mass production has industrialized not only the Japanese economy, but all of society as well. There is far less danger of Japan's being influenced by the fluctuations of the international economy than there is for monocultures that rely on a single agricultural commodity. If this pattern is viewed purely in economic terms, Japan picked a very good field in which to specialize. But specialization in a specific industry inevitably means that diversity and choice within society as a whole is impoverished, even though industrial products have a high rate of growth in demand and employ a wide base of technological skills. That is why Japan is a faceless economic power. It is also why Japanese do not feel rich, even though all the statistics say they are.

What makes people feel rich is their ability to fulfill their desires. At extremely low levels of living standards, one's daily bread is of overriding importance, and a decent meal is enough to satisfy that desire. Surveys have shown that a mere $600 per month would be needed for the average family of four to survive in Tokyo today at the living standards of 1949 (assuming the family owns a home). In 1949, people were no longer starving and the birth rate was at its highest; therefore, with this amount of money, it is possible to meet the physiological needs of a human organism to survive and raise children. People seek higher incomes and consume more than that level because they have psychological or social desires they want to fulfill.

But money alone is not sufficient to fulfill those desires. Having money (or a high salary) is a necessary condition, in that one has the economic possibility of fulfilling the desire, but it is not in itself sufficient. What good is money, after all, when all the stores stock the same items and everyone is too busy to shop?

Because Japan has tailored its entire society toward mass production, its goods have a certain sameness and there is not enough freedom of choice. Primary education is designed to extinguish individuality through homogenizing instruction, and medical treatment is restricted by a system of standard protocols. The same applies to shop and park construction. And if one has the misfortune to choose one of the professions involving tertiary functions that have been concentrated by government policy in Tokyo, crowded living conditions and long commutes are unavoidable. If one seeks to live outside of Tokyo, employment is limited to working in a factory or in a local service industry. These provide precious few outlets for creativity. It is virtually impossible in Japan to fulfill one's life-style and work desires simultaneously.

For Japan to become a country in which people can feel rich, a greater diversity of supply must be permitted and freedom of choice opened up. This means that some of the advantages of an industrial monoculture society—an industrially optimized society—must be relinquished. Late-twentieth-century Japan has been shaped into such a society by the islands' climate and terrain, Japan's history, and the long traditions of Japanese culture that the environment has fostered. Japan has succeeded economically by developing and expanding its mass-production industries. The greatest issue for the nineties in Japan will be whether it can depart from that path.

When we think of the future, we must start with an understanding of the present. To know the present, we must search the past. To consider Japan's future we must uncover its origins. The coming years will be an extremely important period for determining Japan's position in the world and reforming the domestic system. It is now time for Japanese to re-examine themselves and find out just what is Japan.

2

PEACE, COOPERATION, AND THE ENVIRONMENT

JAPANESE CULTURE BEGAN
IN THE RICE FIELD

WHY JAPAN ABSORBED WESTERN TECHNOLOGY SO EASILY

In Part I, I called Japan an economic power and explained that since this economic power applies exclusively to industries that can exploit mass production, Japan is an industrial monoculture. I also described how this monoculture was a logical consequence of Japan's creation of the ultimate industrial society. But this ultimate society is a relatively recent phenomenon. The broad spectrum of Japanese industry truly gained international competitiveness only in the seventies, when trade surpluses became a structural characteristic of the economy. That strength became definitive in the eighties.

This prosperous decade is but a flash in the long history of Japan. Understandably, many people have raised their voices to rebut the notion that the 1980s are evidence that Japan and the Japanese are somehow different in character than other countries. But even if this is only a brief moment, it is still very much a real one; Japan somehow arrived at this remarkable, bright place.

Why has this island nation suddenly become the world's purest industrial society? The answer to this question is both the story of Japan and the primary topic of this book.

Discussions of Japan's modernization and industrialization usually focus on the period starting at the Meiji Restoration in 1868 and continue through the high-growth days after the end of World War II. However, this approach promotes some misconceptions, because Japan's transformation into a modern, industrial nation was not a departure from its historical and traditional path.

Since the Meiji period, Japan has acquired many technologies from Europe, the United States, and Canada. It has learned the West's methods of organization and studied its systems and institutions. Without this knowledge, Japan's industrial development would not have proceeded so rapidly or so far.

But Japan was not the only country to come in contact with the modern technology of Europe and North America in the middle of the nineteenth century. The Islamic world and India encountered this technology and knowledge far earlier than Japan; China too had substantial contact with Western countries. And the countries of Central and South America, the destination of many emigrants from Europe, naturally were far better acquainted than Japan with European and American culture and technology.

Why, then, did not these countries develop a flourishing modern industry? Why was Japan the only country outside of Europe and North America to develop a fully industrial society? This same process is currently occurring with great speed in South Korea, Taiwan, Singapore, and other newly industrializing countries, but it does not detract from the significance of Japan's early development into a state more industrial than any in Europe and North America.

If contact with knowledge, technology, and systems was sufficient, every country would today be a modern industrial state. This is clearly not the case. To digest and internalize these inputs and spread them throughout society takes a certain set of values, attitudes, and social systems. This is a very important consideration for industrializing countries now on the path of economic development.

THE WEST'S THREE HUNDRED YEARS OF
IDEOLOGICAL CONFRONTATION

To really find the answer to this question we must dig even deeper and ask why Europe and North America were alone until the late twentieth century in creating a modern industrial civilization. One certain fact is that the industrial revolution of the eighteenth century simultaneously saw rapid technological advances and growing availability of the resources required to exploit them. But technological discoveries are as old as mankind and sudden bursts of new knowledge are not the exclusive preserve of modern Europe. Ancient Greece and Rome had their flurries of material advances, and during the Song dynasty China produced such technologies as well. Western Europe itself was the scene of remarkable progress in the twelfth century. The fifteenth and sixteenth centuries likewise saw many important new discoveries and inventions.

But none of these advances and technologies in the end became linked with industrial production, and none created an industrial revolution. For technological advances to trigger modern industry, they must be utilized on a large scale, and certain societal conditions have to exist so new knowledge can spread throughout society. Ideas that would permit technological advances to be accepted and used on a wide scale are needed; the values and attitudes of modern civilization must be firmly established throughout society.

Europe underwent years of conflict between competing ethical and aesthetic systems from the sixteenth-century Renaissance to the eighteenth century before an ideology receptive to modern industrial civilization could take root. Religious reformations and wars occurred repeatedly through this period. Developers of new technologies were sometimes burned as witches and discoverers of previously unknown natural laws were tried in religious courts. Religious wars and pursuit of witches were far more severe in the seventeenth century, as the modern age was being born, than during the Middle Ages, when the Catholic church dominated Europe.

By the eighteenth century, after Europeans had passed through this very painful ideological conflict, society was finally ready for the spread of technology.

This technology did not become widely used or cause upheavals in the Islamic world, India, and China primarily because the ethical and aesthetic foundations had not been laid. The spread of Western-style modern industry in these areas is even today encountering strong resistance, as was clearly dramatized in Iran's Islamic revolution of 1979.

Japan, by comparison, accepted modern civilization in an extremely short period: from the end of the military-feudal *bakufu* government to the early years of the Meiji Restoration in the 1860s. Its rapid spread through society amounted to a social revolution. The technology and systems entering the country were then digested and adapted to the Japanese context in about forty years. There has been no other case of a people introducing and spreading modern civilization with so little resistance, with such order. This process was virtually painless compared to the centuries of ideological conflict that Europe had to undergo.

The implication is clearly that the social and spiritual groundwork that permitted Japan to accept and exploit these advances had already been laid well before.

This does not mean that Japan had already been through the same painful conflict of values and ideologies that Europeans had. Rather, the "premodern ideology" that opposed modern industry had never become established in Japan in the first place. Japanese had never become accustomed to the religious mode of thinking, which says that cultures are self-contained systems that must be accepted or refused in their totality. Instead they looked at all events as discrete and unconnected, making piecemeal adoption of new ideas natural. This pragmatism is another defining characteristic that has been constant throughout Japanese history.

How did this trait of pragmatism get established in Japan?

It was caused by neither a single incident nor any concordance of events. It involved everything that went into producing Japan and the Japanese. And the most important of these things is the physical environment, the climate, which not only shapes the psychological experience, personal character, and behavioral standards by which Japanese live, but is also the major influence in shaping the entire society, down to its modes of production and organizational principles.

THE ENVIRONMENT MANDATED DILIGENT, COOPERATIVE WORK

There are many elements that govern the shape of civilizations and cultures. The three most important are population, resources, and technology. In my book *The Knowledge-Value Revolution,* I termed these formative factors "the disrupters of civilization" and described how they act as the basic elements that mold each civilization.

Since before the dawn of history, the climate of the Japanese archipelago has been marked in unusual ways that are not found many places worldwide. (When I refer to "climate," I mean resources and the natural environment.)

In his book *Environment,* the philosopher Tetsuro Watsuji emphasized the influence of the natural environment on human culture. This type of theorizing had always been very popular with Japanese. Japanese novels usually begin with descriptive passages of scenery. Yasunari Kawabata's novel *Snow Country* starts out, "When we left the tunnel we were in snow country." Most non-Japanese novels begin with descriptions of characters.

In Japan, people now tend to attribute everything to this concept of environment. It is common for people even to cite the physical environment in which a person grew up as a formative factor in that person's character. Since Christ grew up in the warm environment of the Middle East, to give a popular if simplistic example, some observers have ascribed

Christ's message of love to that warmth. Of course, Shichi-hei Yamamoto has pointed out extremist ideologues were far more common in Christ's time and place. Another more commonly heard claim is that the aggressive, active nature of Oda Nobunaga was due to his upbringing on the wide, wild plains of Owari, but when Oda was alive, his home county of Kudashi in the Owari region was not the rolling plains we see today but a quite different landscape of flooded rice fields and swamps.

Explanations of the sources of the character of specific individuals in terms of the physical environment they grew up in are too specious to be credible. The fact that persons of radically different characters grew up in the same environment is so basic it hardly needs stating. The fact that so many Japanese believe this kind of explanation is, in another light, evidence of the strong influence of the physical environment on Japanese culture.

The Japanese climate is warm and humid, and Japanese geography is characterized by steep mountain ridges enclosing narrow plains. Such terrain is suited not to herding but to paddy-based rice cultivation. Japanese history lacks any period when cattle raising was prevalent, and animals were rarely used to assist in agriculture. Japanese began rice cultivation before ever experiencing a period where the primary economic activity was hunting or animal husbandry. Japanese history and civilization essentially started with the cultivation of rice.

Flooded-field cultivation of rice exploits the nutrients carried by water, so fields can be cultivated year after year and harvest yields per unit of area are high. Corn and wheat quickly exhaust the potential of the land unless chemical fertilizers are applied, and yields are low, so fields must be rotated and allowed to lie fallow periodically.

Although rice cultivation has advantages, it is very labor intensive. First, the field must be leveled so it can be flooded. Slopes must be terraced, and even on level ground, levees must be built so that water does not drain away, and narrow channels must be built to distribute the water. These structures require constant maintenance.

This amount of labor means that communities must work together in units larger than individuals or even families. Japanese early on accepted that it was their lot in life to form village communities and work together diligently.

A PEOPLE WITH LITTLE CONTACT WITH ANIMALS

A history that begins with community-oriented rice cultivation is quite different from one that springs from hunting and herding, and Japanese society shows the effects of its origins in many ways. The first of these is the lack of contact with animals.

Some archaeologists have claimed that horse-riding nomads from the Asian continent arrived in Japan, settling there in ancient times and at one time establishing a nomadic state, but there is little evidence for this assertion.

The Japanese language is clearly related to the languages of the Mongols and the Tungus. The nomad theorists thus postulate that the Japanese are linguistically and ethnically related through the Korean peninsula to these two nomadic peoples. While the ethnic origins of the Japanese people are varied, linguistically the Mongol and Tungus lines predominate, according to this academically influential theory.

Research recently done on the blood types of Japanese dogs indicates that they are closest to the blood types of Mongolian dogs. Since dogs migrate with people, they are usually found where people are. The methodology of searching for the roots of the Japanese through their dogs seems quite sound. But even the conclusion that Japanese are descended primarily from the Mongols and Tungus is not evidence that the Japanese were once horse-riding nomads. Native Americans are also thought to be related to the Mongols and Tungus, but they were not horse-riding nomads. The horse was unknown on the American continents in pre-Columbian days. So the fact that peoples ethnically related to Japanese formed nomadic nations does not imply that the Japanese themselves did.

In fact, it seems unlikely there was ever a nomadic state in Japan. Cut up as Japan is by coastlines and mountains, horseback mobility is rather limited. In the past, the country was far swampier than it is today, so horses were of limited utility and expensive to keep. Only a single mention is made of horses in the entire *Kojiki,* Japan's oldest text, and that is of a "no-good horse." The "Men of Wo" section of the *Wei Zhi,* an early (third-century) Chinese work of history that mentions the Japanese, states that Japan was without horses and sheep, and horses play no important role in any of the old fables and tales. There isn't even any report of emperors riding horses prior to the Meiji period.

A large number of the myths and stories of Mongols and the peoples of North China and Central Asia concern horses, but Japan's fables and folktales feature other animals, such as dogs, raccoon dogs *(tanuki),* monkeys, rabbits, turtles, crabs, pheasants, and kites. None of these animals are generally thought of as useful for nomadic migration.

Japanese also has only one word that means horse *(uma).* All other words for horses are compound words such as malehorse and female-horse. This stands in contrast to Mongolian, which has individual words such as stallion, mare, clippedtail-horse, gelding, and even horse-that-runs-by-putting-bothfront-or-both-rear-feet-forward-together. The prevalence of such words is a clear indicator of the role of horses in Mongolian culture. Japanese has fewer ways of naming animals in general than do the languages of other peoples.

But Japanese does have a lot of words for natural phenomena, especially rain. *Tsuyu* (spring monsoon rain season), *yudachi* (sudden or evening shower), *shigure* (late autumn or early winter rain) and *samidare* (early summer rain) are but some of the native (non-Chinese-derived) words in the language. Japanese also has many words for fish, including the unique Japanese word *shusseou*, for fishes that have different names at different stages of growth.

For the Japanese of old, the rain that nourished the rice fields and the fish that supplied their protein were topics of vital concern. They do not seem to have had as much interest in animals.

JAPANESE HISTORY HAS NO SLAVERY AND NO CITY STATES

Japan had no period of a herding-based culture. It also had no experience of animal-assisted agriculture. Compared to the other peoples of the world, Japanese have, in fact, had extremely little contact with animals throughout their history. While some implications of this are relatively minor—such as the low percentage of animal protein in the Japanese diet and the fact that Japanese have longer intestines than most other peoples—the impact on the Japanese psyche and the structure of Japanese society are profound.

To raise and exploit animals, one must control and suppress a willful opponent. Sheep, cattle, and horses have surprisingly strong wills. When they stampede, no human being can control them. To control and use animals, a relationship of dominance and submission must be established. When one has experience establishing such relationships, one acquires not only the knowledge of how to do so, but also the feeling that such practices are morally correct. These skills can then be applied to animals with higher intelligence and stronger wills—namely, other human beings. A life of herding, animal husbandry, and animal-based agriculture makes the formation of a slavery system much easier.

Perhaps because of this lack of experience in dominating willful opponents, Japan never became conducive to a large-scale system of slavery. No proof has yet been discovered that a large-scale institution of slavery ever existed in Japan. Although some theorists have postulated that slaves were common in the period when the tomb of the Nintoku Emperor (313–399) was constructed and the ancient Asuka and Nara periods (seventh and eighth centuries), these theories are the result of Meiji period and modern scholars applying the lessons of Western history to Japan.

It also seems that a system of slavery cannot be established until human beings have the technological know-how to produce far in excess of subsistence. Slavery thus had to await the development of irrigation technology and the rise of classical cultures that adopted a materialistic outlook. It then follows that Japan probably did not have a large-scale system of slavery in the days when the ancient tombs were constructed because such agricultural technologies had yet to be introduced. Slavery is not found thereafter either. There are no descriptions in Japan's legends and fables that would lead us to posit a large-scale system of slavery, nor are there any records of slave revolts. No implements of captivity that would indicate a culture of slavery have yet been unearthed. Japanese does have the words _yakko_ (valet) and _nuhi_ (servant), but except for a few household servants, so-called _yakko_ and _nuhi_ were in actuality more like serfs _(noudo)_.

Another historical landmark that by its absence helps define the Japanese physical environment is the city state or an age of city states.

The Japanese archipelago is broken up by a patchwork of mountain ridges and a tortuous coastline. Flat lands suitable for rice cultivation are found in small alluvial plains and tiny valleys. The valleys and plains are very small, as are the mountain ridges and the ocean distances. This made it difficult for small regions to establish any lasting autonomous political authority. Since rice cultivation requires prodigious labor input, a conqueror must rule not only the land, but the inhabitants as well. A "king" who ruled over a neighboring land would then make the land's inhabitants work rather than killing them. Yearly tribute and labor taxes could be levied, but the people could not be slaughtered.

Japanese thus did not feel the need to construct solid walls to resist conquerors. No city states surrounded by stone walls were constructed.

The ruins at Yoshinogari indicate that ancient villages had wooden walls and lookout towers that surveyed the surrounding areas. These extended only around the village itself, however, and the walls themselves were insubstantial, a far cry from the stone walls that European, Middle Eastern, and Chinese cities encircled themselves with. Autonomous regional authority in Japan never lasted long enough to earn the name "city state."

This had a decisive influence on the pattern of political authority and urban culture in Japan, a point I will return to later.

The peculiar nature of the Japanese climate and terrain thus meant that ancient Japanese never experienced animal husbandry, a socially significant slavery system, or city states. Their absence had a greater direct effect on Japanese culture than did the climate and terrain itself. It made Japanese very jealous and egalitarian, with a dislike for relationships involving extremes of dominance and submission.

BUFFERED BY A PROTECTING OCEAN, JUST WIDE ENOUGH

A Unique Geographical Position

The warm climate of the Japanese archipelago and the steepness of its mountain terrain had profound effects on the Japanese people. But there is more to the natural environment than just these two factors. Other important environmental conditions were the separation from the Asian mainland by an ocean that was "just wide enough" and Japan's comprising four large and close islands, which formed a geographically cohesive entity.

If the straits between Japan and the Korean peninsula and the Chinese mainland were as narrow as the Strait of Dover or as wide as the Taiwan Strait, Japanese history and culture would have been drastically different, even if everything else about the climate remained the same.

There is no other country on the globe that was situated close to an area of ancient civilization (in Japan's case, China) and yet was separated from that civilization by several hundred miles of water. The only similar case is Taiwan, but the area across from Taiwan on the Chinese coast, Fujian Province, was one of the last areas of China to develop. Chinese civilization developed first on the Yellow River, gradually spreading south, and the relatively unyielding soil of Fujian Province developed only in the Song dynasty (960–1279), long after fertile Guangdong Province farther to the south. Taiwan is also far smaller than Japan, and was less populated, so it did not have the necessary conditions to develop a historically independent culture and economy. The island was only fully developed in the time of the Qing dynasty (1644–1912).

Another region roughly the same size as Japan and located an equivalent distance off its respective mainland is Madagascar. The Mozambique Channel is far more difficult to cross than the Tsushima and Korea straits. The flora and fauna of Madagascar are for that reason quite distinct from the opposite African mainland. The opposing coast was also exceedingly slow to develop, so the island was eventually settled not by Africans from the close-by mainland but by Malays riding currents from far away. Culturally, Madagascar was completely isolated.

Japan is thus unique in its proximity to an advanced region of civilization and its sharp geographic integrity. The effects on Japanese history were crucial.

CULTURAL INTERCHANGE WITHOUT POLITICAL PENETRATION

The bodies of water that separated Japan from China and Korea were not so wide that they could not be crossed using ancient technologies. Japanese were thus able to establish an interchange with the mainland early on.

The first mention of the Japanese people in written history came in the *Later Han History* chronicle of the year A.D. 57. Emissaries of a Japanese king came to the court of Chinese Emperor Guang Wu in Lo-yang, who gave them a seal for the king of the "country of Wo" (Japanese, Wa). This record predates by a full 180 years the more famous record of the woman called Himiko of the country of Yamatai who appears in the *Wei Zhi* account "People of Wo."

Recently written histories of this early period have placed more emphasis on the account of Himiko because, although the events described in the *Later Han History* occurred earlier, the account itself was written later. Therefore, the *Wei Zhi* is considered more authoritative.

In China, histories of dynasties are commonly written after the end of the dynasty. The *Later Han History* was written during the Jin dynasty, which succeeded the rather short-lived Wei dynasty. The events at the court of Guang Wu were thus described 250 years after they occurred. The record may thus include errors and speculations, although recent excavations have tended to corroborate the *Later Han History* records. The most striking substantiation was a gold seal unearthed in Fukuoka Prefecture in 1748, which matches the description of that given to the emissary of the "kingdom of Wo" by the Han emperor Guang Wu down to the exact characters it bears.

By the middle of the first century A.D., Japanese emissaries were apparently being dispatched to Lo-yang. Although the reports of these emissaries to the Chinese emperor undoubtedly contained many exaggerations, the Later Han dynasty nonetheless recognized Japan as a "kingdom." The proof of that status was carried back to Japan in the form of a seal. China of that period was very thorough in its conduct of foreign relations and bestowed status based on the integrity of the country and the state of development of its culture. The status of "king" was not lightly granted. The emissaries of Japan seem to have been able to present objects and verbal accounts that were sufficient to convince the rigorous Chinese officials that Japan merited such status. Since this occurred 180 years prior to the accounts of Himiko of the country of Yamatai, this Japanese state was probably a kingdom of villages that was still small in area. But clearly the sea between Japan and the mainland was narrow enough to be crossed with the navigational technology of the day.

Nevertheless, it was also wide enough to prevent the organized movement of large numbers of immigrants or armies. The seafaring technology of these ancient days did not permit a fleet to cross the East China Sea or the straits of Tsushima and Korea and arrive on the far shore in one coherent unit. This made effective military movement into Japan impossible. Japan was able to interact with the mainland and receive an inflow of knowledge and culture, but major movements of people and organized military incursions were prevented.

The only such expeditions sent against Japan during the premodern period were the two Mongol invasions of 1274 and 1281; both failed in their attempts to cross the seas, because of storms. The second time a landing was made in the autumn at Hirado (in Nagasaki Prefecture), and the armies advanced as far as Fukuoka Prefecture before a fierce typhoon destroyed nearly all of the invading fleet. (These storms were called the *kamikaze* [divine winds] by the Japanese, although they had no special religious significance.)

The Mongol troops of 1281 brought many horses with them; their strategy was to wage war from horseback in the autumn. Being horse-riding nomads, they were unable to fight well without their horses. When the Mongols arrived in Japan, however, they found little room to land their animals. The infantry had to land first and search for good landing sites for the horses while the navy sailed up the coast. Autumn is typhoon season in Japan, so the Mongols were sitting ducks as they sailed along the coast searching for landing sites.

No other organized attempt was made to invade Japan until World War II. No large-scale battles were waged on Japanese soil with alien peoples. There were few significant influxes of immigrants from abroad, either, and few serious conflicts between established residents and newer arrivals. It is thought today that there were large numbers of immigrants at the end of the Asuka-Nara periods and Warring Countries period (1477–1573), but because of the weather conditions of the East China Sea and Korea and Tsushima straits, these immigrants were not able to consolidate geographically to form a major presence. The mainland culture arrived in Japan, but its military and political domination did not.

VILLAGE COMMUNITIES BONDED BY THE TASK OF GROWING RICE

There are few barriers to movement between the four major islands that compose the Japanese archipelago. This impeded the rise of long-lived geographically distinct kingdoms. As far as we know, the archipelago has always been a single country.

The *Kojiki* contains stories of the subjugation of the Ebisu people by Yamato Takeru no Mikoto, but does not indicate whether they had established an independent country. Further back in the "age of the gods," conflicts between the god Izumo and the god Yamato are reported, but these belong to the realm of myth.

What is known is that no independent kingdom has been proclaimed within the Japanese archipelago since the establishment of the Yamato Court in the seventh century. Taira Masakado took on the name of "new emperor" and tried to establish a regime independent from the imperial court of Kyoto, but it is unclear whether even Taira Masakado himself considered this a country. There is also evidence that in 1869 Takeaki Enomoto tried to carry on independent foreign relations with France from his headquarters in Hakodate, but this lasted only for a period of months.

The country was partitioned during the Warring Countries period, but no daimyo lord ever proclaimed that his own authority was that of a different country, unrelated to Japan. All were powers fighting for authority within the country of Japan. And the "country of Japan" of that period was almost identical to the principal territory and population of modern Japan. Before Japanese came to develop the concept of a state, they already thought quite naturally of Japan as a single, whole entity.

This is another feature of Japanese history not seen elsewhere. It helped Japan develop into a highly homogeneous nation with a concept of itself as a "natural state" independent from international relations, virtually a world of its own. Because Japanese civilization developed from the patterns of rice agriculture, it contains a tendency to homogenize everything. Rice cultivation required collective labor; water maintenance and management required communal work and communal allocation. In a rice-cultivating agricultural society, individuals and families could not survive independently of the group. To deny a family water was to sentence them to death.

Since all the canals were connected, everyone had to work together to repair roads and levees. Communal living and work were constantly required and instilled in Japanese a spirit of cooperation. In this the Japanese differed from peoples who herded animals over the plains or hunted in the woods, since in these instances a family could conceivably survive alone by herding its own animals.

According to the *Secret History of the Mongols* (1240), which records the story of Genghis Khan (Temüjin), Temüjin's father, a clan leader, was poisoned and died. His longtime rivals usurped power. Temüjin's mother, Höelün, did not accept the rival family and separated her family from the clan. The family lived alone for ten years. Animal-herding nomads could have these strong passions; but in Japanese society, water-based agriculture meant that to be excluded from the community was to starve. For instance, when Oda Nobunaga exiled Sakuma Nobumori, Sakuma fled from Koyasan to the mountain reaches of Kumano, but before long he starved to death. The mountains were not available as a refuge to flee to if one was excluded from the rice fields.

The phrase "blood is thicker than water" is stood on its head in Japan, where water matters most of all. Water is a connection to the land, a relationship in which everyone shares the same life-giving flow of water between the fields; blood is a tie to relatives, shared only with one's parents and ancestors.

In ancient Japan, one's sense of belonging was to the water and to the communal village group that cultivated the rice. The method of food production and the social structure made this a necessity. Adoption of children not related to one by blood was very common, and the preservation of the means of production—land, house, reputation—mattered most of all.

A Society That Eschewed Strong Leaders

The rice agriculture that Japan embraced early in its history required diligent, communal work. The same tasks had to be repeated year after year, and there was no need to decide how to respond to sudden changes. China and India practiced the same kind of rice culture, but they drew water from major, continental river systems that would periodically flood; the same rivers drew them into conflict with the other peoples who shared the watershed. Japanese had their narrow valleys and small rivers safely to themselves, so experience and memory of that which had worked traditionally were more important than decisiveness and foresight, which might have been required if wars, raids, and floods were common.

Having never engaged in animal husbandry, Japanese lacked experience with relationships of dominance and submission. It is thus not surprising that Japanese developed a culture of working together and a strong focus on the importance of the group. Separated from the continent by its "sufficiently wide ocean," Japan did not fear invasion from abroad and had few conflicts to draw ordinary people into war. The strong leadership so indispensable in wartime was thus not highly valued in Japan.

What Japan looked for in its leaders was neither decisiveness nor foresight, but a gentleness that helped rice cultivation proceed smoothly and a spirit of self-sacrifice to take the lead in getting to work. It is not surprising that Japanese did not come to believe that greater capabilities entitled one to greater income or consumption. Today, Japanese very jealously seek to maintain equality.

The most important thing in a Japanese-style communal group is that the leader be selected by objective criteria that everyone recognizes. Straying from this rule rattles the peace of the group. The most objective criterion and the least subject to debate is age. Age is easy to correlate with experience, and everyone can expect to become leader in turn. There is no safer way to govern a community peacefully than the seniority system. If a leader is chosen on the basis of ability instead, the group will be divided by the debate over who is the most capable. And when a capable person is made leader, that person draws authority to him or her, concentrating power. This not only raises the jealousy of the other members of the group, who lose some rights, it also sets people against one another as they compete to be designated the next leader. To avoid this, Japanese always preferred guarding against leaders who were too strong over selecting leaders who were exceptionally capable.

Methods of suppressing leadership and eliminating conflicts caused by leader selection were devised even for smaller scale situations. The most extreme solution was to have no leader at all. *Kasa-renban* (umbrella joint signature) is just such a method. In the latter half of the Muromachi period (the fifteenth and sixteenth centuries), documents committing an entire group to a common fate were executed, and the signatories would write their names in a circle, in the shape of an umbrella. If the names were written horizontally, one name would have to come at the front and an order would naturally follow. The *kasa-renban* sought to avoid that ordering.

Much earlier in Western Europe, England had also seen the Knights of the Round Table. In this case, the knights who surrounded the table were there in the context of a clear leader, King Arthur, and the table symbolized that they would not be divided. On the surface, the shape is similar, but in the Japanese case, this pattern negated the idea of leadership, while in the English one it aimed at fortifying the closeness, loyalty, and relationship to the leader.

The *kasa-renban* custom gradually spread and by the sixteenth century had permeated the country. The custom died out during the Warring Countries period, when leadership became important to large-scale conflicts.

In groups without clear leaders, authority is diffused and everyone cooperates to achieve goals. If the foundation of the Japanese spirit and temperament is to be named, its second quality, after pragmatism, is this group orientation.

JAPANESE HAD NO CONCEPTION OF STATE

Japan's communal villages did not require strong leaders. Since Japan as a whole was an aggregation of such communities, it had little need for a state as a structure for authority.

In the formative stages of the classical age, when interchange with the peoples of the Korean peninsula and the Chinese mainland was common (and many Koreans assimilated into Japanese culture), there was little reference to states in records, songs, and poetry. When this interchange slowed in the Heian and later periods (794–1185), consciousness of nation *(kuni)* and state *(kokka)* disappeared almost entirely. The consciousness of the state sharpened dramatically when the Mongols attempted their invasions, but otherwise the vast majority of Japanese remained unaware of any structure of authority embodied in a state from the latter half of the Heian period through the middle of the sixteenth century. The idea of national defense appears many times in the *Manyoshu* (eighth century) but disappears almost entirely in the *Kokinshu* (905) and later works.

The arrival of the southern barbarians (Europeans) and the dispatch of troops to Korea in the late sixteenth century did little to change this. Toyotomi Hideyoshi felt some alarm at the increase in the number of Christians and outlawed the religion, but this was the maximum extent of the concern. The invasion of Korea is best characterized as the reckless action of an intemperate dictator and a few runaway daimyo lords filled with a wild desire to conquer territory. They had no conception of themselves as agents for a "state" called "Japan" that was invading a foreign country. The Japanese daimyos of the time thought that wherever their military power went was their territory and made little distinction between the Tohoku region, the island of Kyushu, and the Korean Peninsula. Granted, the resistance of the Korean people soon disabused them of this notion.

There are contemporary scholars who profess that Japan does have nationalist traditions, but these traditions were created from the model of Western imperialism that was adopted in the process of Meiji period modernization. They do not spring from Japan's older, indigenous traditions. Japan was transformed for a few decades into an ultranationalist authoritarian state not because that was in its traditions, but because, lacking a tradition of nationalism, it had little experience with brutality and aggressiveness of state power and, unable to detect the warning signs, had no way to guard against it.

It was also caused in part by the lack of definition of the relationship between the people and the state. People who excuse the aggressive war waged by Japan in the 1930s and 1940s as the crime of a state distanced from its people base their arguments on this lack of definition.

A Peaceful Society
That Trusts Its
Superiors

Europe and America Have No System of Residence or Census Registers

About ten years ago, I attended the Japan–United States Symposium in Aspen, Colorado, which the United States attorney general was also attending. The attorney general's role is to represent the United States federal government when it is in court. I asked him what U.S. government case was currently the most difficult.

He responded that it was the suit brought by the cities of Los Angeles and Detroit that the 1980 federal census was incorrect.

The United States of America conducts a population census once every ten years. The results affect many things, including the districts of the House of Representatives. The two cities in question had alleged that their population figures were incorrect. Since the amount of aid they receive from the government is based on population figures, a smaller population means less money. And so they had gone to court. The problem was that there was no way to determine accurately the population missed by the census.

Japanese find it hard to believe that a country as advanced

as the United States would have difficulty compiling accurate statistics of its population. Yet the attorney general said the census could have missed as many as 5.8 million people. That is more than 2 percent of the American population.

The primary reason cited for the lack of accuracy is the existence of illegal aliens. They enter the country illegally, or as students or tourists who then go underground. There are many such, who may or may not have left the country. There are also criminals or homeless who disappear from records.

In Japan, such a large discrepancy could not occur because Japan has census registers and residence registers.

When I told the attorney general that Japan had this system, he asked me what kind of incentive was used to get Japanese to register. I explained that children cannot enter school if they are not registered in both registers. He then asked what the penalties were if a private school accepted a child who was not registered.

I was stumped. Japan has no such punishment and does not even try to find unregistered people. I realized that if I said the school would worry that it would later be difficult for an unregistered student to get a job without a census register or residence register, the next question would be what method is used to find out if companies are hiring unregistered people and what punishments there are for them.

As Americans see it, a carrot or a stick is required to get the population to do something. European countries and most other Asian countries share this outlook. The bottom line is that people in these countries would rather not be known to the government. In Japan it is the reverse: even without carrot or stick, the population would rather be known to the government.

Only three countries in the world have a strict census register system: Japan, South Korea, and Taiwan. The institution of such a system in Europe and America would be opposed as an untoward violation of privacy. People do not want the government to know about them or their lives.

Japanese feel that they would be inconvenienced if they did not report themselves to the government because they could not receive government assistance when they needed it. The Japanese people have great trust in the Japanese state and government. The fact that the Japanese, who had no conception of "state" for so long, have such trust in the nation and government is again closely related to the environment of the island nation in which they live.

THE STATE WAS BORN OF DEFENSE

Japan's separation from the continent by a buffering sea made Japan into a tranquil world never at war with alien peoples. This is turn shaped modern Japan.

In most areas of the world, the state was born of a need for national defense. When humanity first began agriculture, it lived in the very limited arable land on continental riverbanks and in oases. In the surrounding wide expanses of grasslands and forests, many hunting and nomadic people wandered freely. The first agricultural peoples had to organize in groups under strong leaders to protect life and property from these roving groups, and they built structures to fend off attacks from others. If a state is defined as an organization with authority to govern a defined population and territory according to set rules, then the first states, no matter where in the world, were city states that started life as these kinds of groupings. They were walled areas of agricultural settlement. As soon as human beings settled, they began to live in military fortifications.

Military defense not only requires great expense and consumes valuable labor, it also places limits on the conduct and movement of people. Simply constructing the city walls that defined the city states required great labor and expense. To govern the way they lived within those walls, strict rules were needed. To maintain a force ready to repel aggressors at any time, citizens had to be accustomed to obeying orders, doing military training, and staying alert to danger. This placed a large physical, psychological, and economic burden on the populace.

Defense is the typical public good. Regardless of who pays for it, everyone benefits. If someone were to pay for the construction of city walls, everyone inhabiting the city would be protected from outside enemies. There is no way for an enemy to attack only those who have not shouldered part of the cost and there is no way to protect only those who have served as soldiers (and their close kin). Everyone suffers from a defeat in war; everyone benefits from peace.

It is human nature that people try to avoid shouldering the burden for public good as much as possible. Everybody wants to avoid serving as a soldier and paying for defense, benefiting only from the security that is created by defense. But this would render national defense impossible. So states implementing defense try to compel payment of taxes and military service, to thereby share the burden equitably. To do this, the state must determine citizens' income and wealth and expend its energies in collecting taxes. It thus must also be able to keep the public peace. These three functions— defense, tax collection, and keeping the peace—are the basis of state authority.

Although modern governments have many other responsibilities and mandates, the roots of authority are the same. For defense, military power has been supplemented by foreign diplomacy; the public peace is secured by police forces and the administration of justice. Even in peaceful postwar Japan, the prime minister's secretariat comprises the Foreign Ministry, the Ministry of Finance, and the Police Agency. Before the war, the inner cabinet was composed of representatives from five ministries—Army, Navy, Finance (tax collection), Internal Affairs (police), and Foreign Affairs.

Many countries still use this format. It is difficult to call any entity that lacks the three powers of defense, tax collection,

and keeping public order a "state." Were there any other
organization that had these three powers in a stable, continuing manner, it would in effect become the state, as happened
to the Nazi party under Hitler and Communist parties in
socialist countries.

It is also difficult to term other responsibilities state powers.
Modern governments have many agencies with specific mis-
sions and consultative functions. The Ministry of Construction
and Ministry of Transport oversee public works, the Ministry
of Posts and Telecommunications performs mail service, and
the Ministry of Education performs education work. Consultative agencies include the Economic Planning Agency and
the Science and Technology Agency. Many of these functions
have historically been solely performed by the private sector;
in many countries, they still are today.

Non-Japanese Don't Want to Be Known to the State

When the state is born of a need to provide defense as a public
good, the citizenry naturally wants to hide its affairs from the
government. When the government knows, it taxes and con-
scripts. Best of all for the citizens is to have the state completely unaware of their very existence. The more the burden
of defense grows, the more citizens want to hide from the
state. China's population records showed dramatic plunges
during the Warring States period, becoming suddenly several
times greater in times of peace.

With its narrow valleys and small plains, Japan never had
nomadic peoples, so there was no threat of marauders when
rice cultivation first began. Its island status spared it from
devastating wars with other peoples. The burden of defense
was consequently light even in ancient times, and there was
rarely a need to raise troops. And so the Japanese became the
only people on the globe to develop without city states.

All the cities that predate the Middle Ages—Athens, Rome,
London, Paris, Frankfurt, Baghdad, Delhi, Beijing, Nanjing—

had thick city walls. Only Japan had cities without city walls. There were towns alongside castles, but no towns within castles. (I will return to this topic in part 4.)

Even though there were wars in Japan, these were almost all civil wars, fights of Japanese against Japanese. Almost all of these Japanese were agricultural folk. The battles were largely for the right of the ruling class to rule over land and people, and the conflicts ended when the leaders of the losing clan committed suicide. There is only one example of a war in which the ordinary population was massacred, the Ise-Nagashima campaign of Oda Nobunaga. Were local residents to be massacred, there would be no one left to grow the next year's rice crop, so there would be no tribute coming into the treasury. It was far more common that to win the favor of the local residents a victorious daimyo lord would lower the amount of tribute required.

The citizenry had no inclination to work with the ruling daimyos for a common defense, because there was no need. There was likewise no need for walls to protect cities from enemy attack. Ordinary citizens could temporarily flee to another location during war, returning as soon as it was over.

The people adopted quite a relaxed attitude toward war. There are reports that large numbers of rural residents would come to sixteenth-century battlefields to watch the fighting. Large crowds gathered on the hills on either side to watch the great battle for control of the mountain pass road at Shizugatake. The victorious Hashiba Hideyoshi (later Toyotomi Hideyoshi) bought umbrellas from the spectators and gave them to the injured to protect them from the sun.

If people were this relaxed about war even during the violent Warring Countries period, other periods must have been more so. The military expenses of the Japanese were rather low. Taxes must also have been correspondingly low and conscription rare. The relationship between the state (government) and the people (citizens) was formed within this context.

THE JAPANESE STATE CONCENTRATES ON WELFARE

It is my view that defense was not the sole source of state authority. It seems clear that the preservation and management of seed was another source.

When human beings first began agriculture, the amount of grain harvested was only three times the amount sown. One-third of the harvest thus needed to be reserved for the next year's crop. In bad years, or when enemies had stolen grain, even more would be needed. It seems hard to believe that individuals and families would be able to exercise the discipline needed to accomplish this.

A story has been widely told of the "dutiful farmer" Sakubei of Iyo, who died of starvation with a little straw bag of seed rice under his pillow during the great famine of the Kyoho Era in the early eighteenth century. It is easy to see how the ancients needed the compulsion of a "royal authority" to ensure that they preserved the seed they needed.

One of the reasons that a centralized state developed in the absence of a state authority based on defense was that rice cultivation required both seed storage and pooling of water channel management skills. The large number of seed storage granaries found in old ruins are evidence for this theory.

If so, the tax burden on the Japanese people must have been light and the Japanese state's primary orientation was toward the welfare of its people. The Japanese people would then have every interest in notifying the governing body of their existence and situation. This would be the only way to receive their allocation of good seed grain and get help in maintaining riparian works. Tamuramaro Sakanoue, who "subjugated" the Tohoku region of northern Japan, used farmer-soldiers to distribute farm tools to surrounding residents and encouraged use of cold-resistant seed strains. The Yamato Court could rapidly extend its authority into the eastern provinces with little resistance because the court brought with it new rice cultivation technology.

From the fifteenth century on, local rulers spent great energies on the use and management of water; they also tried to develop mines and public works. Though this was done to increase the daimyos' income and extend their power, the ultimate effect was to improve the lives of the local residents.

In the age of the Tokugawas, from about 1600 to 1868, when the Tokugawa family ruled all of Japan, the main duties of the daimyos and chief magistrates were land development and encouraging production. They worked feverishly on the sale of local products. The daimyo of Toyama, Maeda Masatoshi, always brought local medicines whenever he went to Edo Castle, the seat of Tokugawa government, giving them to any daimyos he saw looking pale or peaked. Since these daimyos, though sick, had after all managed to come to Edo Castle, their symptoms were generally light and they recovered readily, thus earning Toyama medicines good repute. When the daimyos returned to their native provinces, the sales of Toyama medicines increased.

Many of Japan's famous regional products—Yamagata safflower, Awa indigo, Yamato-Kooriyama goldfish, Ako salt, willow-bark luggage of Toyooka—were developed in the Tokugawa period under the patronage and direction of the daimyos and chief magistrates.

"SIX PARTS FOR THE STATE, FOUR PARTS FOR THE PEOPLE" WAS ACTUALLY THREE FOR THE STATE AND SEVEN FOR THE PEOPLE

Taxes, which were low to begin with, were further lowered in the Tokugawa period. The only official tax was an in-kind harvest tax on land, and the farmers who worked the land were the main taxpayers. In addition, merchants and processing industries often had a "self-rule charge" assessed on buildings. The taxation system was rounded out with compulsory contributions called *myogakin*, which were levied from time to time.

Textbooks today still write of the "Six Parts for the State, Four Parts for the People" rule, but the 60 percent tax was merely a formal rule. It was not followed in practice. At the beginning of the Tokugawa period, the actual levy on farmers was only 30 to 40 percent of their harvest; by the later years of the period, the average levy had dropped to under 20 percent nationwide.

The great majority of the Japanese population in Tokugawa times were farmers (though many also had other occupations), and rice was the principal crop. It was plainly impossible for the ruling classes to eat 60 percent of the harvest. Since there were no exports during this period of national seclusion, there was obviously no way such a situation could endure, so the nominal levy was lowered from 60 to 50 percent. And while the officials had stipulated what appear to be quite strict procedures for this purpose, the collecting officials consciously worked out systems to lower this amount further.

First, when the crops were measured, they winked at misreporting. Harvests were measured based on a "test harvest" of a standard field surface area (usually 30 *tsubo*, about 120 square yards) to determine the amount of yearly harvest per unit area. But low-producing areas were chosen for those test harvests, and the outer crop rows on the perimeter, both horizontal and vertical, were excluded when the area was measured. This alone reduced the area by almost 10 percent.

Next, the farmers always did the work of actual harvesting themselves, and they were sure to leave plenty of seed rice in the straw. It was part of the chief magistrate's duty to provide plenty of opportunity to hide seed rice that was later retrieved from the matting. In some regions, it was the practice to hide seed rice under layers of mats that were laid while the official stepped outside to sample a cup of tea. Through such sympathetic treatment, it was common for the reported harvest totals to shrink an additional 30 percent.

Areas and harvests were also lowered for newly developed fields. Sometimes there were even hidden fields not subject to any taxes at all. In most such cases, these "hidden fields" were shielded by the collusion of the officials. The phrase "bad magistrate" persists in the rural regions, meaning a bureaucrat who lacks such sympathies and applies the rules by the letter.

As a result of these many dodges worked out by the officials and the citizens, the nominal harvest was reduced to only half the real harvest. So although on paper the government was receiving 60 percent of the harvest, it was in fact receiving only 30 percent. This was further reduced through various means, so only 23 percent of the harvest was ultimately delivered to the government. The tax rate on nonfarm income, for crafts and the like, was even lower—about 20 percent in most areas. The tax on a chicken, for example, might be ten eggs per year. Averaging roosters and chicks in, the yearly yield was figured to be seventeen eggs.

The public tax burden in Japan in fiscal 1990 (the ratio of taxes, social insurance charges and the like to GNP) was about 40 percent, which is higher than the tax rate in the later Tokugawa period.

JAPANESE METHODS LEAVE AMPLE ROOM FOR DISCRETION

If the harvest estimates were so drastically minimized, why not simply change the rule to "Three Parts for the State, Seven Parts for the People"? Well, this is simply not the Japanese way. The difference between the form and the substance is the source of the official's power. Were the farmers to grumble about the amount of the tax, the official always retained the power to make an accurate count. Since the farmers knew that this would increase the amount of the tax, they had to keep quiet. This gave officials the power to issue arbitrary decisions in other administrative areas and to conscript labor.

By collecting less than the legally stipulated taxes, they ingratiated themselves with the farmers and simultaneously gained the power to give orders in other areas beyond their legally stipulated powers. This tradition is alive and well in Japan today.

The tax rate on real estate, for example, is 1.6 percent, and reaches 2.4 percent when the urban planning tax for large cities is included. The appraised value of the land on which these taxes are levied, however, is kept down to 30 percent of the current market value. If the property tax were actually levied at current values, landowners would probably quickly go bankrupt.

The value of the land when appraised for inheritance tax is more than double the appraisal for the property tax. The appraised value for determining real estate income tax or real estate acquisition tax is roughly triple the property tax appraisal. Even allowing for differences between local taxes and national taxes, it is remarkable that appraisals should vary by a factor of three. But Japan would never consider upping the property tax appraisals and lowering the rates to one-third of current levels. The difference between the apparent and the real is an important source of official discretion. The citizenry feels comfortable with this arrangement because of the sense of collusion and common interest between citizens and government.

The applications of this system do not stop with taxes, however. In modern Japan, the arbitrary powers of the bureaucracy have been institutionalized in the form of "administrative guidance." Generally, governments enact laws to prohibit things; things not prohibited by law are permitted. In a democracy, the enacting of laws is the charge of the assembly elected by the vote of the people. This is to prohibit arbitrary actions by the bureaucracy. However, in Japan, administrative guidance is used by bureaucrats to prohibit activities that are not covered by law. They use it freely, and they do not see anything wrong with this practice. The bureaucrats' feeling of moral rightness springs from the traditions of official discretion.

GOVERNMENT-CITIZEN COOPERATION THE RESULT OF A COMMONALITY OF VALUES

Japan's separation from other cultures by its buffering waters brought the state and citizenry closer together. The low military burden and low taxes helped create a sprawling network of collusionary façades and the arbitrary powers of administrative guidance. But there was another important factor that engendered this system: except for the few years directly after World War II, Japanese were never ruled by an alien people. Throughout history, both rulers and ruled have been Japanese.

It is easy for people raised in the same specific environment, with the same traditions and work patterns, to develop common ethical and aesthetic views. In Japan, this is strongly the case. When a citizen petitions the government, the decision will generally be what the petitioner expects. And so Japanese have developed the habit of appealing to those above them for solutions to their problems. In Japan, the ethical outlook of populace and officialdom are the same, and both see the same things as virtues. Differences arising between the two are largely those of viewpoint, not of differing ethics.

This situation does not pertain when the ruled and ruling are of two different peoples. In the Yuan dynasty, when Mongols ruled China, and during the Qing dynasty, when the Manchus ruled, these nomad peoples had different successional principles from the Chinese, favoring the last-born over the first-born. When Mongol courts decided questions of inheritance among Chinese farmers, the results were not as the Chinese expected. Chinese farming people could not expect what they considered a just decision from those above them.

The custom of "the people deciding the matters of the people" became established.

In Nara period and Heian period Japan, Japan was affected in many ways by the adoption of the Tang dynasty system of *lü-ling* government (in Japanese, *ritsu-ryo*, a system of separate criminal and civil laws). The *lü-ling* system had detailed provisions for criminal law; its civil law was less precise, since it was founded on the premise that the government did not interfere much in the affairs of the people. The system Japan assembled on this model also lacked such provisions, but because the officials held the same ethical beliefs prevailing in the culture, they were able to fill in the gaps with their "good sense." The *ritsu-ryo* system was thus not implemented strictly in keeping with the letter of the law.

Roman law, which like the *lü-ling* system is considered one of the finest examples of classical law, has numerous civil provisions. The Mediterranean was rife with intercultural exchange, so laws had to be written out very explicitly. Officials were given little discretion in applying them subjectively so that plaintiffs were able to obtain a predictable outcome. Since Japanese officials and citizenry shared the same outlook and the populace trusted those above them, they did not see such a need. People felt at ease going beyond the written law in difficult situations to appeal to common sense, about which there was ready agreement.

Japanese today still place little faith in written agreements and laws. It is a characteristic of Japanese to differentiate between appearances committed to paper and underlying reality, which is possible because they believe that everyone is playing by the same rules. This is also the root of the system of administrative guidance in place today.

Europeans and Americans seem to believe that the Japanese population and corporations go along with the directives of government administrative guidance because they are forced to or are given profit incentives. Even today they have many questions: Why do Japanese register, without exception, in the census registers and residence registers? Why do Japanese corporations follow government administrative guidance? What incentives and punishments does the Japanese government use?

These are "Japanese secrets" that foreigners will never decode no matter how they investigate. This causes some to feel that Japanese as a whole have some kind of common plot to reach specific goals. Some recent revisionist theories contain these kinds of latent assumptions.

But the Japanese government does not have any special methods of punishment or reward, and the Japanese people are not joined in any kind of national goal. Government direction simply is seen, through long habit, as arising from the views of the majority, and the Japanese people have no difficulty complying with it. This attitude is firmly established among Japanese. The practice of administrative guidance, which has such a bad reputation around the world, is not thought of as the government and bureaucrats pushing their ways upon Japanese society, but as a process that thoroughly reflects majority opinion.

JAPANESE SOCIETY LACKS A MILITARY IDEOLOGY

A final feature of Japanese society that springs from its environment is the complete lack of a military ideology. This has not arisen from the defeat in World War II but predates it. Military ideology has never, in the history of the country, become the criterion for decisions or actions either socially or personally.

In 1942, I entered primary school, then called a national people's school. It was a school in Osaka associated with the Kaigyosha, a club of commissioned army officers, and the principal was a retired major general. Every morning he addressed the school. "The Japanese are a militaristic people of the Far East," he would say. "Our officers are peerless in courage, so our imperial army and navy are invincible. One of our army divisions can hold off three American and British divisions!"

I didn't know where he got this ratio of three to one, but, being a small child, I believed what the great soldier told us.

Many Japanese people of the time believed that with the same equipment and troop strength Japanese troops were stronger than American or British troops. Even now, many Japanese believe that the Japanese are bellicose and skilled at war. Such fancies are likely somewhere in the mind of "civilized" opposition party politicians who feel that any Japanese military expansion will lead to war but are not worried at all about the military preparations of the Russians, Chinese, and North Koreans.

Once World War II started, however, Japanese troops proved to be rather weak. For six months after Pearl Harbor, the Japanese military posted a string of victories. But once the Americans and British got on war footing (around the time of the Battle of Midway), the Japanese encountered defeat after defeat. Japanese troops sought to react and stubbornly defend. All offense came from the enemy side. And during this time, well-equipped Japanese troops were defeated time and again because of strategic errors, insufficient mobilization, and lapses in military thinking. Despite what it called a wartime system, "militarist" Japan was unable to come up with any decent warlike ideas.

The way food was provided in the battles of the South Pacific is a good example. To the very end, Japan supplied its troops with rice, despite the fact that rice requires prodigious amounts of cooking water, is heavy, spoils easily, and is difficult to package. Worst of all, it must be cooked just before it is eaten, so smoke from cooking fires gives positions away. Japan alone among twentieth-century nations fed its frontline troops such a militarily unsuitable food.

Once war came, the societies of Europe and America placed themselves on wartime footing, doing without peacetime luxuries. Despite being amply provided with food, the

American army's first priority for the food supplies of front-line troops was that they be militarily functional. Japanese looked first to the quality of life for frontline soldiers, figuring that they deserved rice, since they were risking their lives; the needs of warfare came second.

This type of thinking is seen in ancient Japanese artifacts of war as well. Japanese armor is beautiful, but not very effective for defense and hard to move in. Japanese swords are good for skilled individuals, but in a battle they are not very useful. European and Chinese weapons may not be graceful, but they get the job done in battle. Japanese always select their weapons using peacetime criteria.

If military thinking is absent in war, it is hardly likely to be more present elsewhere in Japanese social organization. The need to respond rapidly to an emergency of war is nowhere reflected in the design of cities, the layout of fields, regional communities, family structures, the educational system, or religious observances.

The absence of military thinking is related to the rejection of strong leadership. When strong leaders were rejected, all ability to rapidly respond to emergencies was lost. Another Japanese defect that showed up in World War II was the inability of Japanese cities and factories to repair themselves quickly. Japan lacks a system for responding to wars and disasters and cannot mobilize for emergencies.

Even today, after forty-eight years of peace, Japan lacks a clear procedure for succession should the prime minister, the highest leader of government, meet with an accident. Nobody would even think to ask what would happen if the entire cabinet resigned during a big Tokyo earthquake.

In the recent events in the Persian Gulf, Japan's lack of ability in crisis management was clearly evident. Japanese news organizations are set up only to handle peacetime business information; they crumble in the face of war. During the Gulf War Japan's only source of real information was foreign television news.

Because of its poor leadership, the Japanese government

cannot make quick decisions and is reduced to going to amateur analysts for information. At a crossroads, certain voices call for Japan to have its own foreign policy and not follow the lead of the United States; however, Japan lacks the ability to gather its own information and make its own decisions, and it has neither the habit nor the inclination to respond to crises. Those who call for Japan to formulate its own policies never happen to clarify just what those might be.

The narrow fields and valleys of these islands, buffered from the world by sheltering seas, encouraged the labor-intensive cultivation of rice. This safe environment has not been as conducive to either effective crisis management or the development of a system in which strong leaders can make decisions.

3

RAISED
TO BE
GOOD
LEARNERS

Shinto and Buddhism: Two Religions at Once

In May 1986, the Japan Traditional Crafts Fair was held in Paris. An exhibition was staged in the foyer of the Palais de Congrès (an international conference center), and events and performances were held in the hall. I was producer for this exhibition and spoke on the topic of "The Traditional Japanese Aesthetic and the Modern Consumer Marketplace."

It was not a major event, but it drew forty-eight thousand attendees and was the subject of lengthy television programs on two channels and more than twenty articles and columns in newspapers. One prominent newspaper ran its article under the incredible headline "First Encounter with Japan."

Now these days, there are many ways to get to know Japanese culture, even in Europe. Exhibitions of Japanese painting, kabuki performance, and even sumo tournaments are held, especially in Paris. Japanese painting has had a major influence on the Parisian impressionists ever since they discovered ukiyo-e painting, and the French are quite interested in Japanese art. More than twenty thousand Japanese presently live in Paris, and artists, particularly visual artists and fashion designers, are especially numerous. Tens of thousands of Japanese visit Paris as tourists each year. With all this interchange with Japan, how could such a small exhibition be called a "First Encounter with Japan"?

This extraordinary billing was given the exhibition because it was perceived as shedding light not only on Japan's traditional crafts and performances but also on their connection to contemporary Japan. It emphasized the effect of traditional ways on the modern industrially optimized society, which chalks up huge trade surpluses with its highly competitive mass-produced industrial products; in the process, it shed some light on why Europeans have such a difficult time selling their wares in the Japanese marketplace.

For Europeans, it is almost impossible to connect the nation ruled by samurai with the incredible industrial might of today's Japan. For them Japan is a "black box" belching boatloads of high-quality industrial goods, a nation whose cultural forms are obscure and whose inhabitants have names they do not know.

What has in the past been emphasized in Europe is the role of European and American systems and technology in Japan's rapid advance as a modern nation, starting from the great revolution of the Meiji Restoration. Westerners naturally know very little about how the culture and traditions of the Tokugawa period and earlier Japanese history are connected to modern Japan. I should add that Japanese themselves do not think about this very much either.

Japanese have often explained to industrializing countries trying to modernize that they need to import modern systems and technology as Japan once did. The reality is not so simple. In the half-century since World War II, there have been only a handful of countries that have managed to integrate modern industry into their societies—namely, the so-called Newly Industrializing Economies (NIEs) of South Korea, Taiwan, Hong Kong, and Singapore.

Japan is not the only country to have encountered Western

social systems and industrial technology in the nineteenth century. Turkey, Iran, India, and China all came into contact with the Western world earlier, and in larger scale. But Japan, last of all to encounter the West, was fastest to form successfully a modern industrial state.

Why were the other countries of Asia and Africa unable to incorporate successfully these European and American innovations into their societies while Japan was? The answer is intricately bound up in Japan's traditional, pre-Meiji cultural and societal climate. This has been little explored to date.

Some of those who have researched this topic find that at the end of the Tokugawa period, Japan had rather advanced craft and financial industries, and that the elements needed to incorporate modern industry were already in place. While this may be true, it does not explain why Japan leapfrogged over so many other already industrialized countries to become the world's most industrial nation. The answer is that Japan has traditions that facilitate the embrace of foreign technology and systems and their digestion.

120 MILLION SHINTOISTS, 120 MILLION BUDDHISTS

As part of the theme of the Paris exhibition, a Shinto shrine was placed on one side of the entrance and a Buddhist shrine on the other. The caption for these shrines read: "These are symbols of Japan's two religions. The Shinto shrine is a part of Japan's ancient 'Way of the Gods' while the Buddhist shrine is the symbol of Buddhism, which was brought to Japan 1,400 years ago."

The following series of questions and answers was repeated by French and Japanese many, many times as the French inspected this display.

"How many Buddhists are there in Japan?"

"A hundred and twenty million."

"How many Shintoists are there?"

"A hundred and twenty million."

"What is the population of Japan?"

"A hundred and twenty million."

There were a lot of wide-eyed French during those several days. With the strictness of the French approach to religion, they could not understand this, but it in fact is an accurate description of today's Japan.

Virtually all Japanese have a Shinto marriage and a Buddhist funeral. They visit Shinto shrines for New Year's prayers and Buddhist temples for the *Bon* Festival of the Dead, and some may even celebrate Christmas. Masayoshi Ohira, Japan's only Christian prime minister, prayed at the famous Shrine at Ise, joined in *Bon* dancing, and meditated in Zen temples. Japanese feel no pangs of conscience for such behavior.

This has been explained by simply labeling Japanese behavior pantheism, but such a conclusion not only fails to understand Japan, it also compounds the misunderstandings. Buddhism is a monotheistic religion as strict as Christianity. Shintoism is even more pantheistic than Hinduism. And yet Japanese can believe in both of these fundamentally disparate religions at once. This phenomenon is a rare one indeed.

In the Greco-Roman world, Jupiter was worshiped as the main god flanked by the other gods of Olympus. Ruins of temples dedicated to Jupiter, Neptune, Apollo, and Venus can still be found dotting the Mediterranean. None are in active use today. Christianity swept over the region in the latter days of the Roman Empire, and when the Emperor Constantine declared Christianity the official religion of the empire, the gods of Olympus lost their believers. Although they endure in works of art and literature, no one believes in them literally anymore and no ceremonies for them are ever held.

At the same time, the Germanic peoples north of the Alps had their own distinctive gods of Valhalla. These objects of reverence were also displaced by Christianity, not even leaving ruins to mark their forgotten presence.

Even in the Middle East, the birthplace of Christianity,

when Islam swept over the land, Moslems and Christians remained quite distinct. The Moslems became numerically overwhelming, but tens of millions of Christians still live there. Conflicts between Christian and Moslem militias occur regularly in Lebanon.

The Indian subcontinent was the birthplace of Hinduism, but the Moslems spread their religion into the region in the tenth century and Islamic kings founded a dynasty. Moslems and Hindus both live in the subcontinent today but still remain quite distinct.

In Korea, Confucians, Buddhists, and Christians intermingle, but their believers are also distinct, and the total of adherents of the three matches the total population of the country, give or take a little error for evangelical exaggeration. In most countries in the world, one person believes in one religion at one time. After all, religions are by their nature exclusivist.

At first glance, China appears to follow the same pattern as Japan. Individuals adhere to the rites of Taoism, Buddhism, Confucianism, and ancestor worship all at once. But these have blended together over so many years that they now constitute, in the words of Yu Ying-shi, a "comprehensive Chinese religion." Individuals are not really worshiping a large variety of distinct religions.

In Japan, Shintoism did not lose its believers when Buddhism entered the country, and yet Buddhism was accepted as a religion by the entire population. People continued to follow the same Shinto rituals and came to believe in Buddhism at the same time. So Japan, with a population of 120 million, has 120 million Shintoists and 120 million Buddhists. On a given day it may even have 120 million Christians. No other country in the world is like this.

This phenomenon, which is so hard for non-Japanese to comprehend, sprang from the same basic attitude that allowed Japan to accept Western civilization so easily.

SHINTO: A CREED WITHOUT TEXTS OR DOCTRINES

Why do Japanese manage to believe in multiple religions at once, and how and when did this characteristic emerge? If this Japanese social climate is in part connected to Japan's modernization, the answers to these questions are extremely important for understanding Japan. Any explanation should start with the nature and origins of Japan's native religion, Shinto.

There are few religions in the world as misunderstood as Shinto. Shinto is a very sparse belief system that seems to have spontaneously generated. Foreigners interested in Shinto often start by asking what Shinto's holy books are. There are none, which clearly separates Shinto from other religions. Christianity has its Bible and Islam its Koran. Even Buddhism has its basic texts, since the word of the Buddha was spread in organized fashion, although there is not one single text but many, such as the Prajna Paramita Sutra and the Sukhavati Sutra. Since different sects focus on different texts, it is difficult to say which is the primary text, but it is possible to pick out a range of most important texts for Buddhists.

Shinto, however, has no bibles, korans, or sutras.

Astute foreigners then ask about the texts priests appear to be reading at weddings and ground-breaking ceremonies. These are a few words that the priests write for the occasion, words that seem to fit the day. They are not drawn from any specific books. People of other religions find this surprising. In Shinto, anybody, at any time, can become a prophet, receiving the word of the gods.

Nor does Shinto have any precepts or commandments. Although one should not do bad things, there are no enumerations either written or oral of such bad things. The *Kojiki,* an ancient text that records the doings of the Shinto gods, does not contain so much as a hint of such precepts.

The Shinto concept of innumerable gods is an overlapping of a reverence for natural manifestations like thunder, typhoons, mountains, waterfalls, and large rocks with worship of ancestors. This is a common basis for early religions and can be found throughout the world. What is rare is for such early religions to endure to modern times without developing holy books and precepts. Shinto, as a religion, has no system of absolute values and no divine words and teachings. That fact gave Shinto eternal life. Since it has no absolute values, it can coexist alongside other value systems.

In time, Japanese encountered a religion that had more strictly articulated values. Buddhism entered the country, first from Korea, then from China. By then, a thousand years had passed since Buddhism's birth in India, and the religion had become highly refined as it passed through Central Asia, China, and Korea.

The *Kojiki* indicates that Buddhism may first have entered Japan during the age of Emperor Kimmei (539–571). The Emperor Kimmei received a statue of the Buddha from Paekche (Japanese, Kudara), an ancient Korean kingdom. He presented it to Soga no Iname and commanded the Soga family to worship it.

Buddhism may have entered Japan even earlier than this. There were many Koreans who settled in Japan in these early days, becoming Japanese, and it is reasonable to suppose they brought Buddhism with them. This account in the *Kojiki* of the emperor and the Buddha is best taken as indicating government approval of freedom to worship the Buddha, thereby giving the people permission to follow these beliefs. Since Shinto had no clear regulations, principles, and commandments, this approval of Buddhism was in all likelihood easily accomplished.

How Buddhism Became a Political Issue

Once freedom of worship was recognized for Buddhists, the new religion spread rapidly as the numbers of immigrants increased and interest in the new culture grew. This spread was accelerated by the new learning and technology that accompanied Buddhism. New techniques in medicine, building, water use, agriculture, and metallurgy followed the immigrants, most of whom were Buddhists. People's productive abilities and lives were improved. The new religion seemed extremely vigorous because of the advanced technology, and people were drawn to it by motivations of profit and by cultural interest.

The Yamato kingdom flourished, industry thrived, and land was developed. The political power of the Buddhists also increased, and they began to demand not just freedom to worship but also that the government and the emperor himself convert to Buddhism. This demand was in part motivated by the expectation that this conversion would accelerate economic development and technological advances. Proselytization of new religions is always linked to expectation of a better life in the here and now, as seen in the evangelism of Christians in Japan since the sixteenth century and the spread of the so-called new religions there today.

The growing tensions were diffused somehow during the reign of Emperor Bidatsu (572–585), who followed Emperor Kimmei. But the *Kojiki* records that when Emperor Yomei took the throne (585–587) he became the first emperor to engage in Buddhist worship. Emperor Yomei was probably influenced by the fact that his mother and wife were of the Buddhist Soga family, but it is likely there was political pressure as well.

Emperor Yomei's worship appears to have been a personal affair. He apparently worshiped as an individual, and did not perform public ceremonies as head of state.

This was not enough to quell the Buddhists. The situation was similar to problems encountered today with the Yasukuni Shrine, where war dead are worshiped. Soga and the other Buddhists pressured the emperor to worship the Buddha publicly. Such a ceremony would amount to public recognition of Buddhism and make it the state religion. For the emperor to comply would naturally entail his discarding Shintoism.

In the third year of his reign, Emperor Yomei died with the issue unresolved. The political issue of making Buddhism the state religion became involved in the selection of the next emperor. Buddhists fought vociferously with those who sought to preserve Japan's ancient Way of the Gods by excluding Buddhism, with Soga on one side and Mono no Be on the other. It was Japan's only religious war. The overwhelming majority of the rich and powerful threw their weight behind the Buddhists, led by the Sogas. Their support indicates that the ideals of materialism typical of classical civilizations had spread widely, and that Asuka period Japanese society valued improving material productivity by introducing the technology that came with Buddhism.

As I will describe later, throughout the world we can see that there was little desire to create more material goods during the ancient age, when agriculture was first adopted and city states were born. Maintaining the community through ties of blood and ties to the land was of primary importance, and social stability and equality were more valued.

When the invention and spread of irrigation and plowing increased production levels, surplus production began to be traded, creating territorial states, encouraging land development, and fostering commerce. This was the start of the classical stage of civilization, which is characterized by a clear desire to increase material prosperity.

By supporting the economic expansionism pushed by the Soga family and the Buddhists, Japanese of the period showed an inclination to move from the reverence of myth and ties of blood of the ancient age to the desire for material prosperity and civilization of the classical age. Given this background, the eventual victory of the Buddhists, led at that time by Soga no Umako, was probably inevitable. Mono no Be and others who revered the traditional Shinto beliefs and wanted to exclude Buddhism were destined to fade from the chronicles of Japanese history. The Emperor Sushun (587–592), who was considered pro-Buddhist, was enthroned with the support of the Soga family. However, Sushun almost immediately began to feel the political danger that the Buddhists posed. The resulting period was a key turning point in establishing Japan's distinctive social climate.

CONTRADICTING THE SHINTO LEGENDS: AN IMPERIAL CRISIS

The Shinto myths are the basis for the imperial family's place at the head of Japanese society. Japan (the Yamato court) is a country that was founded by the epiphany of the Emperor Jimmu, descendant of the god Amaterasu. The imperial family ruled Japan on the basis of the Shinto myth that they were the descendants of Jimmu and Amaterasu.

Since the belief in Buddhism contradicted the Shinto system, it was a refutation of Amaterasu. The principle of the imperial family maintaining its supreme position in society by virtue of being the descendants of the gods residing in Takamagahara (the Plain of High Heaven) was also contradicted. This was naturally a major concern for not only the imperial family but also the entire system of government.

Buddhism was not the only new idea entering Japan at this time. All of the history and thought of China and Korea came with it to Japan. The presence of Confucianism has been recorded, and Taoism (belief in the Taoist immortals) was also known. Many of the other beliefs of the Confucian period— the philosophies of Guanzi, Mencius, Micius, Zhuangzi, Han Feizi, and the like—probably entered the country at the same time. The concept of the "mandate of heaven," used to justify the changing of imperial dynasties in China, almost certainly was familiar to the Japanese of the day as well.

According to Chinese theories, the emperor was a person who by virtue of his goodness was chosen by heaven to rule the country. The progeny of the virtuous emperor, benefiting from that virtue, would succeed their imperial forebears as emperors. This mandate of heaven, however, could be exhausted, and unworthy emperors could appear; at that time, heaven would destroy the dynasty and select a new person of virtue to serve as emperor. This theory was used to justify the changing of dynasties. When a person of a new family became emperor, the dynasty name would change.

The doctrine of the mandate of heaven was officially enshrined when King Wen of Zhou overthew the Yin dynasty and founded the Zhou dynasty (1027–255 B.C.). The mandate of heaven was spent because of the mad behavior of Yin dynasty King Zhou (no relation to King Wen of Zhou), whose last name became a synonym for tyranny. The Yin dynasty was overthrown by the virtuous King Wen, and the concept of the mandate of heaven was used to legitimize the founding of the Zhou dynasty. Eventually, the Zhou dynasty itself was overthrown, and the Warring States period ensued until the country was unified under the First Emperor of Qin. Emperor Qin's children were inferior, however, and Qin's family was overthrown by Liu Bang, who founded the Han dynasty in 206 B.C. By the time the Han dynasty was overthrown, the mandate of heaven had become a firmly established political concept.

This concept of continual revolution and change also provided powerful opponents of the emperors with a rationale for opposing imperial rule and led to many confrontations. The period from China's Northern and Southern dynasties (when Japan came into contact with Buddhism) to the Sui dynasty was one of China's most turbulent, when fractious fighting split China into a series of short-lived regional dynasties. The concept of the mandate of heaven was nothing if not realistic.

This concept raised the possibility that Japan's imperial family could also outlive its mandate and be replaced by a more virtuous line. Since this idea came from a more advanced country, the emperor's position became uncomfortable. The denial of the logic of the Shinto myths that gave the imperial family its legitimacy was thus an extremely dangerous development. And a powerful opponent—the Soga family—had in fact risen to challenge the imperial family. Soga no Umako may well have had dynastic ambitions.

The Emperor Sushun, whose accession had been supported by the Buddhists, swung back to supporting the Shintoists when the danger became clear. Sushun thus put off making Buddhism the state religion, seeking to protect Shintoism. Five years after he took power, Sushun was murdered by Soga. Sushun remains the only emperor in the entire dynastic line to have been clearly murdered.

Throughout Japanese history the emperor's personal safety had been sacrosanct, no matter how fierce the war. Only in a conflict over the imperial family's legitimacy could an emperor have been murdered.

How Prince Shotoku Reconciled Buddhism, Confucianism, and Shinto

The Empress Suiko (592–628) followed Sushun on the throne, becoming the first ruling empress in East Asia. Neither Korea nor China had a queen, empress, or other female ruler prior to the Empress Suiko, although the Korean kingdom of Silla would have a queen half a century later. Throughout its long history, China only once was led by an empress, Wu Zetian of the Tang dynasty (690–705), almost one hundred years after Empress Suiko.

When Empress Suiko assumed the throne, there were several adult male contenders. Many theories have been formulated as to why a woman, especially the empress of a former

emperor (Bidatsu), was chosen. First, the influential supporters of the Soga family may have thought that a woman would
be easier to sway. Suiko was also the daughter of Emperor
Kimmei and her mother, Princess Kitashi, was of the Soga
family.

What changed everything was the appearance in the imperial family at this time of a political genius, Umayado no
Toyotomimi no Ooji, better known now as Prince Shotoku.

Serving as regent for his aunt, the Empress Suiko, he discovered a way to reconcile Buddhism and the imperial system
and thus preserve a political voice for the imperial family. His
innovation was the reconciliation of Shinto, Buddhism, and
Confucianism.

Adopting a little sophistic logic, he proclaimed: "Let Shinto
be the trunk from which Buddhism spreads its branches, luxu-
riant with the etiquette of Confucianism to achieve a flourishing in the real world." He proclaimed that adding something
new did not negate the old. This was a suitable and practical
answer to a problem that was disturbing many Japanese at
that time.

"The gods must be respected," he said, "but the gods of
Japan can bring evil curses even though respected. The Buddha will allay those curses, so we must worship the Buddha as
well."

The prince's approach was ingenious. By raising fear of the
gods, he prevented their being discarded; and by emphasizing
the compassion of the Buddha, he was able to affirm Buddhist
worship as well. This approach conveniently declined to consider religions as exclusive systems.

There may not be another figure in world history who
conceived such a creative and practical philosophy and in
such a timely fashion. Hinduism is replete with examples of
gods of other religions being added to their pantheon, but
they were merely co-opted into what remained an intact pantheistic system. China has created a fusion of religions that
blends the many sects of Buddhism and Taoism with ancestor

worship. But new religions cannot be worshiped unless they are first incorporated into the religious conglomerate.

Prince Shotoku's reconciliation is impressive in that it permits monotheistic Buddhism and pantheistic Shinto each to be worshiped side by side as systems, and even recommends the practice. Theologically, it can only be called sophistry, but its practical political effect was penetrating.

The overwhelming majority of Japanese of the day were probably quite taken with Buddhism and the advanced technology accompanying it. They were probably also reluctant to discard the rituals of ancestor worship their parents had practiced. Though caught in this antinomy, the logical inconsistencies of Prince Shotoku's approach were in all likelihood not much of a problem. Prince Shotoku's reconciliation of Shinto, Buddhism, and Confucianism was quickly adopted throughout the land.

How Japanese Were Freed from Religious Doctrines

Prince Shotoku politically implemented his new ideology himself. As soon as he became regent, he built Shitenno-ji (Temple of the Four Heavenly Kings) as a national Buddhist temple at Settsu (Osaka) and began to use the state to promote Buddhism. The prince had sided with the Soga family in the conflict with Mono no Be, and the Soga victory was symbolized when he had a statue of the Four Heavenly Kings carved and worshiped it. To reflect his victory, Japan's first national Buddhist temple was named for the Four Heavenly Kings. Although they were Buddhist figures, they had a pantheistic feel to them. Prince Shotoku, who was twenty years old at the time, explained Buddhism in a form that was strongly colored by pragmatic pantheism.

He also had a second temple constructed for his personal use; at this temple, called Horyu-ji, the prince began very serious study of Buddhism, employing many naturalized Koreans in this service.

The year after the state temple Shitenno-ji was completed (609), Shotoku issued the *Keishin no Mikotonori* edict, urging the respect of the Shinto gods as before and honoring the Ise Shrine. The *saiguu* (the unmarried young women who served at Ise Shrine) were kept in service. Both religions were effectively recognized as state religions, opening up the option for Japanese to follow both paths at once. The low point for religion was the high point for politics.

Prince Shotoku's new ideology was undoubtedly a shock to Soga no Umako, who had anticipated supplanting the imperial family when Shintoism was refuted. Prince Shotoku strengthened his victory with a new system of twelve court ranks and the Seventeen Article Constitution, and even set his hand to compiling a national history. The bureaucratic system was expanded, the structure of state clarified, and the institution of imperial rule solidified.

Prince Shotoku didn't let his efforts end there. Wresting control of the routes of foreign trade through Korea from the Soga family, he opened direct contact with Sui dynasty China and created a road from the northern part of the Yamato Plain (Nara) to Naniwa (Osaka Bay). For his political and economic opposition to Soga no Umako, Prince Shotoku was killed. Even the wisdom and intelligence of Prince Shotoku could not easily control the Soga family. Their power was broken only in a palace coup d'état in 645, twenty-three years after the prince's death.

Prince Shotoku's life as a politician was not an easy one; his children and grandchildren were also murdered by the Soga family. But thanks to the creative system he devised, the Shinto shrines survived Buddhism's new status as a state religion. Thereafter, religious conflicts, such as that between the Soga family and Mono no Be, were never to recur.

And just as Prince Shotoku's reconciliation of Buddhism, Shinto, and Confucianism eliminated deep religious conflicts from Japan, fervent belief in religions themselves was also essentially eradicated. In that sense, Prince Shotoku gave Japan the world's first "freedom from religion."

The effects on the Japanese spiritual outlook were, needless to say, quite substantial. Not only did it make Japanese less inclined to accept religious precepts and teachings, it also established the habit of taking only what they considered necessary from foreign cultures. Japanese could now accept foreign cultures without having to believe the entirety of "God's words and precepts." Japanese also lost any tendency they might have had to look at cultures as complete systems, ones that had to be absorbed totally or not at all. If they could take just the good parts from religion, that strictest of social systems, then surely they could do the same to any aspect of foreign cultures.

No Sense of
an Absolute Good

Right and Wrong Are Relative Values

From worshiping multiple religions at once, the habit of taking only the needed parts from each religion was established and the tendency to believe in absolute, inviolable divine teachings eroded. Since this happened about the same time Japanese were learning to write, Shinto never developed any written holy texts or rules. Even Buddhism, which came from abroad, lost its holy texts and precepts when it entered Japan, because Japanese would pick and choose freely among them. A feeling for absolute truths embodied in systematic form never developed in Japan.

Author Shusaku Endo has noted that since there are about six hundred thousand strict Catholics in Japan and about the same number of active Communist party members, there does seem to be a threshold for such rigid foreign ideologies in Japan. Ideologies that proclaim absolute values and prohibit the sampling of other systems apparently cannot achieve more than half a percent of believers in Japan. This is not enough to cause religious wars.

Wars and deep political conflicts that have their roots in religion are found across the globe—Arabs and Israelis, Indians and Pakistanis, Irish Catholics and Protestants—but Japanese cannot imagine how differences in religion could be something important enough to fight over. Sectarian differences are simply not important. The next-door neighbor might be Christian, across the hall they might be Pure Land Buddhists, upstairs maybe they are Soka Gakkai, and downstairs they could be Moslems, but it would all be virtually irrelevant in daily life. Someone might complain that maybe the drums are too loud or too many people are coming and going, but that is about the extent of possible problems. The differences Japanese see in religions are basically the differences in the form of their rites.

The real differences between religions are in ethical views, between what is right and what is wrong. In the strictest sense, religions are ways of distinguishing right from wrong based not on objective facts or principles of cost and benefit, but on the holy books and laws of gods. Belief is not subject to debate. People with customs of religious belief have a sense of absolute right and wrong regarding secular affairs as well. Without this sense they feel uneasy, they seem to have no standards to govern their behavior.

Because of their habit of believing in multiple religions at once, Japanese do not have one absolute set of divine teachings or an unchanging set of commandments. They must rely on "everyone's opinion." In other words, the majority view of people gathered at the particular time and place is the correct opinion.

Unlike "god's teachings" recorded in holy texts and "god's commandments" stipulated in doctrines, the words and agreements of people are relatively easy to change. So if everyone's way of thinking changes, the Japanese sense of right and wrong can also change. This has occurred many times in Japanese history.

FOR ARINORI MORI, MARRIAGE WAS A VOW TO HIS WIFE AND GOD MERELY HIS WITNESS

Japanese believe in people more than they believe in gods. Japanese cannot easily understand the absolute quality of gods. There are many examples of this trait in history. The early Meiji period politician Arinori Mori was infatuated with Western ways. He left his home province of Satsuma to study in England and later served as ambassador to the United States and minister of education, making many contributions to reforming the school system. He was extremely accomplished at English and French and was universally respected for his excellent knowledge of foreign ways. He even went so far as seriously to suggest the abolition of the "barbaric" Japanese language and its replacement with French when he became minister of education. His obsession was extreme.

Naturally, he was a fervent Christian, and he married in a Christian ceremony. In front of the altar he was asked, "Do you take this woman as your wife, till death do you part?" and he answered yes. As it turns out, Mori understood this vow to be a contract between himself and his new wife.

This understanding is a clear contravention of the prohibition in the Ten Commandments against oaths. An oath to another person, with God merely as one's witness, is prohibited in Christianity. The answer given to the priest in front of the altar is historically understood as a vow to God, not the partner. The oaths sworn in courts and induction ceremonies, taken with a hand clasping the Bible, are an outgrowth of this tradition.

Since ancient times, oaths in Japan have been made to the other party, with the gods serving as witness. When the five senior ministers led by Tokugawa Ieyasu signed the oath of the Hachimandai Bossatsu (God of War) at Toyotomi Hideyoshi's deathbed, they wrote on it "we will be loyal to [Hideyoshi's son] Hideyori, and if not, may the punishment of the gods descend upon us" before presenting it to Hideyoshi. They made their oath to the other person, and the gods were merely the witness. So they would have had no objection should the witnessing gods punish them later for lying. Since the gods were witness, then if the oath was broken it was natural that the gods would mete out the punishment, sending the liar to hell. Catholics do not recognize divorce because the vow to God is considered indissoluble. If the vow was to the bride or groom, the vow could be broken with the consent of both parties. In Japan, where people swear their oaths to other people, divorce by mutual consent has never been prohibited.

Since Arinori Mori, despite his deep infatuation with things Western, was proud of the fact that he made his vow to his wife with God as his witness, it seems clear he did not fully understand the morality of the Christian church.

No matter how fluent in English, no matter how well studied in Western learning and technology, no matter how great the appreciation for the cuisine, there remains something in the European and American moral view that defies Japanese understanding. Arinori Mori was able to become fascinated by the West precisely because he did not understand Christianity. Even this learned man was so permeated by Japanese naiveté that he would probably have fled in horror had he fully comprehended the absolute nature of this monotheistic belief.

WHY JAPANESE DO NOT UNDERSTAND THE LEGEND OF NOAH'S ARK

The teachings of God are absolute values for the more fundamentalist branches of the monotheistic religions of Judaism, Christianity, and Islam, and they cannot be changed based on the judgment and situations of man. One story that illustrates this concept is the tale of Noah's ark from the Old Testament.

The tale starts when Noah hears the voice of God telling him that a great rain would fall, flooding the world. God commands Noah to build a great boat to save himself, his family, and one pair of each of the animals. When the flood receded, his descendants would multiply.

Noah builds the ark. People think he is crazy to build a boat in the desert and laugh at Noah.

Then the rains begin. The world begins to flood. Noah loads his family and the animals onto the boat, which floats above the flood. After one hundred and fifty days, the flood recedes. Every other creature has perished. The animals of the earth are replenished from the survivors on the ark.

What a horrible tale! Everyone else but Noah's family drowned, including Noah's friends and relatives. They must surely have cried out to Noah, "Let us on!"

In the Japanese imagination, Noah's boat must have been so small that to let another person on would have sunk it. And yet it was loaded with cows and pigs and horses. Someone would have called to Noah, "Throw off a pig and save your dear friend!" But Noah would have refused them all. How could he explain? There may have been violence. To Japanese, this seems an incredibly cruel tale. But it was proof that Noah was a prophet. If Noah had relented and said, "Okay, get on. We'll make this pig swim for it," he might have been sent to hell for breaking his oath to God.

THE DUTY OF THOSE WHO DO NOT PROVIDE FOR EMERGENCIES IS TO DIE

Why was such a cruel tale created and passed down in the name of God? The values of a people who were coping with a harsh climate and hostile neighbors are clearly reflected. Its lesson was that those who have provided for adversity will survive; those who have not may perish.

This is completely at odds with Japanese values. In Japan it is considered that those who have prepared for adversity must share in times of trouble with those who have not.

Aesop's fable of the ant and the grasshopper also illustrates this moral. In Japanese picture books and children's books, the fable of the ant and the grasshopper has a happy ending, with the kind ant sharing his food with the grasshopper. That's not the ending as Aesop wrote it, however, and that's not how it ends in Western children's books. The ant waits for the grasshopper to die and then eats his corpse. A scholar who researched Aesop's fables has found a happy ending, such as the one used in Japanese books, in only one of 148 versions he found published in Europe and America (the happy ending was used in a Spanish book).

While the statement that only those who have prepared for adversity may survive is by itself a problematic assertion for Japanese, the idea that those who have not prepared may die is extremely disturbing. For people who live in the environmentally harsh conditions of the desert, constantly at war with other peoples, those who don't prepare for adversity may not survive.

Building an ark is a waste of time if the world does not flood. Stockpiling food is unwise if no famine occurs. Preparing for emergencies means sacrificing today to be ready for disasters that may occur only once every ten or one hundred years. Ancient peoples were not rich, and they needed strong fear to compel them to set aside part of their meager stores. If they thought that someone would be there to help them when an emergency occurred, probably no one would bother to set extra supplies aside. The tale of Noah's ark is the religious version of this principle; Aesop's fable is used to teach it to children.

Cultures with absolutist values have repeatedly had the experience that by the time an emergency has occurred it is too late to make decisions based on the consensus of those gathered at that time. Emergencies cannot be foreseen with human knowledge. Because Japan had such a mild climate and was defended from foreign marauders by its seas, no emergency was that serious. It was more important to ensure the peace of the community than it was to prepare for disaster. Rather than setting forth strict rules governing good conduct, it was better to seek a more laid-back cooperation. This attitude helped the Japanese people embrace Prince Shotoku's sophistry reconciling the religions.

WHY JAPAN CAN PROCLAIM THE ADVANTAGE OF THE MAJORITY A VIRTUE

Since Prince Shotoku's reconciliation of Shintoist belief with Buddhist values, Japanese have completely abandoned any sense of absolute truth. This does not mean that Japanese do not believe in right and wrong. The Japanese sense of right and wrong is actually stronger than that of people in other countries. The difference is that "right" is defined as the more powerful (or majority) current of opinion at a given place and time. The Japanese sense of right and wrong is humanistic and relative. When the majority opinion changes, right and wrong also change.

In the Tokugawa period, loyalty to the shogun was the highest virtue. When the *bakufu* government of the Tokugawa collapsed, loyalty to the emperor became the highest virtue. In the first year of the Meiji period, the words *royal order* were sufficient in the Owari Fief to convince the councillors of the defeated daimyos to commit ritual suicide. Since the value structure had changed, no other explanation was required.

In the Meiji period, "civilization and enlightenment" (namely, learning from Europe and America) was the prime virtue. As the Showa period began (1926), the slogan "all men are brothers" symbolized the prime virtue, followed by "Japan is strong and good." A "good" country, at that period in history, meant one whose virtues should be spread to the world. A "strong" country was one that was militarily able to invade other countries. There was no place in this construct for anything else, not even "Japan is a rich country." By 1941, to be a "rich country" like America had become a vice, since it meant that the nation was besotted with materialism and was declining.

After the war, to be a "strong" country was no longer a virtue. The new virtue became "Japan the good country, rich country, demilitarized smart country." "Good country" now meant a country that did not engage in war.

At one point victory in war was a virtue. One of the phrases on a traditional set of playing cards *(iroha garuto)* was *"Mutsu* and *Nagato* [two battleships] are the pride of Japan." If one were to say today "F-15s are the pride of Japan," the media would erupt in a frenzy. The pride of Japan today is the world's second largest GNP and Japanese-style management, which produces excellent industrial goods.

Since Japanese feel only a relativistic sense of values, they can rapidly change their ethical views in a short period of time. In 1945, people who had sworn to destroy the American and British devils heard the imperial edict ending the war and, after a night of drinking, readied themselves to participate in the "democratic restructuring of Japan" from that day forth.

It is not uncommon to hear people in other countries expressing concern that Japan may develop nuclear weapons or suddenly re-arm. After all, only half a century ago, victory in war was the country's highest virtue, and it seems unreasonable to expect Japan to remain "weak." But nothing could be further from Japan's intentions, because the point of view that esteems a "strong" country has completely disappeared from Japan.

For Christians and Moslems, the fact that the teachings of their God are absolute is the fulcrum of their psyches, the standard they use for judgment. No matter how much they talk about "freedom," Europeans and Americans cannot easily let go of this limitation. Japanese, without such limits, are spiritually free-floating. Without an anchor to cling to, Japanese seek interaction with other humans. Japanese consequently are unable to let go of the group easily, and they find it difficult to develop as individuals.

Since Japan does not have these absolutist values, "virtue" is whatever the persons with power in a given situation or time (and usually, they are also the majority) think is "good." Therefore, virtue generally conforms to what is good for those people. If the given situation and time relate to a company, then what is good for those who have power over the company's employees becomes that which is "good for the company." The financial wheeling and dealing of the eighties and the practice of covering big customers' losses were considered appropriate practice at that time.

The ability to alter its values depending on what is beneficial makes things convenient for Japan. Japan can proclaim whatever is good for the majority to be in and of itself a virtue.

THE PROS AND CONS
OF SELECTIVE ADOPTION

THE QUICK STUDY THAT OUTSTRIPS THE MASTER IN FORTY YEARS

Judaism, Christianity, Islam, Hinduism: they all have absolute truths. Even China, which has a complex conglomerate of religions, has absolute values in the form of the "judgment of the next life." The Chinese desire is to leave one's name in history and be respected by one's descendants.

In countries where these religions prevail and in China, one must protect the teachings of the gods even when to do so is to go against the interests or convenience of the majority. New ways of thinking, new technologies, or new systems sometimes meet with the objection that they may be convenient, but they are not right. Europe and America's debate between creationists and evolutionists and China's resistance to the Westernization movement in the latter half of the nineteenth century are classic examples. In today's Iran, many object for religious reasons to women not wearing the *chador*.

Japan has lacked this characteristic since ancient times. Japanese also never thought of "cultures" as indissoluble units. They felt no need to evaluate logic, technology, or systems in religious terms of right and wrong. Japanese consequently excelled at studying foreign cultures. Beneficial technologies in particular were very easily absorbed.

Japan has generally been able to exceed its mentors in the practice of newly imported technologies within about forty years. This has been true not just of postwar automobiles and electronics but since ancient times.

For example, Japan first learned deposition techniques for making large copper statues around the beginning of the eighth century of the common era. (Unlike iron and aluminum, copper is difficult to weld. Copper welding techniques were only pioneered in the 1960s. Prior to this time, copper had to be joined by deposition.) In deposition, the copper is melted and poured into a first mold and cooled. Then a second mold is placed above that and molten copper poured into it to join the two together. The repetition of this process many times to create large copper statues was very difficult for ancient peoples.

But in 747, forty years after this technique had been introduced to Japan, the construction of the Great Buddha of Nara began. The enormous statue was virtually completed within two years. Given this speed, it may have been constructed without any mistakes in deposition whatsoever.

Creating a giant Buddha using deposition technology would not be a simple task even today. First, a rough statue must be made out of clay, then the statue covered with something like brick to create the mold. Then, more than a hundred kilns would have to be placed around the statue to melt the copper, and the molten metal then poured between the brick and clay. The very bottom portion is completed first. This process is repeated many times and the Buddha is gradually built up. The portion from neck to chin is especially difficult because the mold widens outward again. The head of the great plaster Buddha built by Toyotomi Hideyoshi at Kyoto's Hoko-ji fell off the statue after a short time. Without an iron structure reinforcing it from the inside, a plaster neck cannot support the weight of a larger head.

Deposition bonding technology enabled the Japanese to build the Great Buddha of Nara in only two years, although the touch-up work and application of gold leaf took an additional three years. The Great Buddha remained the largest copper deposition statue in the world until the 1980s, when a larger Buddha was completed in Fukui Prefecture.

Neither China nor Korea, from which Japan learned deposition technology, ever constructed such a large copper statue. The world has other mammoth copper statues, such as the one-time Colossus of Rhodes, a statue of Apollo over Rhodes harbor (which was one of the Seven Wonders of the World), and the Statue of Liberty in New York, constructed by the French. Both of these, however, used a different technique: layering copper over an inner core. There was plenty of copper available for both these statues, but even one hundred years ago France did not have the copper deposition technology needed for such a large statue.

In a span of forty years, Japan overtook its master China and achieved the world's most advanced deposition technology.

REVERSE ENGINEERING OF GUNS, SILK, AND COTTON SPINNING

The same pattern occurred with firearms. Firearms are generally considered to have been introduced to Japan at Tanegashima in 1543. Forty years later, when Osaka Castle was constructed, Japan was producing the best and largest number of firearms in the world. In his account of 1565, Luis Frois described the weapons fired at his Portuguese ship, constructed by merchants of Sakai and Matsuura Hidenobu, as "crude guns made in Sakai." Twenty years later, he was acknowledging the quality and precision of Japanese-made bird guns.

The Battle of Sekigahara in 1600 marked a peak for the use of guns in Japanese warfare. Between the two sides, a total of

60,000 guns were used. Japan is estimated to have had almost 100,000 guns at that time. Contemporary Europe's largest army, that of the king of France, had only 10,000 guns. The total for all of Europe was less than that of Japan.

By the end of the Warring Countries period, Sakai alone produced 15 guns a day. Its yearly production of 5,000 was about 60 percent of the total national capacity, which in turn exceeded that of Europe. Japanese weapons also outperformed European arms in aiming precision and all-weather use. Forty years after their introduction at Tanegashima, Japanese again had exceeded the skills of their "teacher" Portugal in both production capacity and technology.

This same pattern has been repeated many times since the start of the Meiji period. Modern silk thread technology was introduced to Japan in 1868, and the Fukuoka model factory completed in 1873. Designs, machinery, bricks for the building, and even desks and chairs were imported from France along with dozens of French technicians. Japanese copied everything down to their exact hand and foot motions. The model factory was identical to a silk factory in France.

By 1910, Japan had become the world's leading exporter of silk thread, again exceeding the skills of its "teacher" France in a short forty years.

Modern cotton spinning technology followed the same pattern, Japan building a modern spinning mill in 1882 and creating a large-scale copy of an English spinning company in 1885 that forty years later had made Japan the world's leading exporter of cotton products. Osaka, the heart of the Japanese cotton industry, had overtaken Manchester, England, as the world's largest international cotton center.

When Japan imports foreign technology it always starts with an exact replica from the more advanced country. Japan then works to improve the artifact by making its own innovations. This process is Japan's strength. In copper deposition and the forging of firearms, Japan initially mastered the technology through copies and then became the world leader.

When Japan learned copper deposition, it first made statues the same size as China did. Apparently, quite a few of them were made at that time, and several of these can still be found in Shiga Prefecture today. With guns as well, first an exact copy was made of the guns the Portuguese had brought. When the Shimazu daimyo Shimazu Yoshihiro made a trip to the capital, he brought as presents "guns from Tanegashima." Over a dozen of these still exist. Since the Portuguese are only known to have given away two guns, it is clear that test copies were already being made in quantity at that point.

Copying the master exactly is the most efficient way to acquire new skills and learning. Japan has always faithfully produced its copies and learned.

JAPANESE DO NOT THINK OF CULTURES AS SYSTEMS

The same pattern was repeated after World War II in automobiles and electronics.

The postwar Japanese auto industry started with copies of Austins and Renaults, the electronics industry from copies of transistor radios and color televisions, the synthetic fiber industry from replicas of nylon. This trend continues even to this day, when Japan is an economic power. One recent exact copy is Tokyo Disneyland, a faithful reproduction built ten years ago of the American Disneyland.

Making exact copies is a good way to learn the technology behind the artifact and also exposes any shortcoming in the original design. These shortcomings can then be improved upon using the traditional Japanese attention to detail, so Japanese progress is rapid. Who knows, maybe thirty years from now Japan will have learned and improved on the technology of Disneyland and become one of the world's leading "amusement powers."

Although this approach may strike most Japanese as being so self-evident as not to merit mention, Japan is actually the only country that can do it. The primary reason that the other countries—Turkey, India, China—that encountered Western civilization earlier have lagged in adopting Western technology is their refusal to produce exact copies.

Japan has no problem with the concept of making exact copies because it studies only the technology, ignoring the philosophical systems of the culture behind it. When Buddhism entered Japan, the custom of following multiple religions (which may not, strictly speaking, be worship at all) spread throughout the country, and the habit of selectively adopting only the desirable features of foreign cultures became firmly rooted. Religions, philosophies, and economies could all be examined in terms of their constituent elements and only the desirable features selected.

Japanese were thus able to study only physical technology and leave the philosophies and religions behind. The act of creating an exact copy of an artifact was thus completely unthreatening. The philosophies and systems that gave birth to the artifact became irrelevant to the artifact itself.

Other countries cannot do this. China, India, the Islamic world, and Europe itself developed their own independent cultural systems, so they know well how much a "culture" is a whole entity with an indivisible system. When these countries study foreign technologies, they first consider whether their culture can also accept the ideology behind the technology. They thus try to transform technologies they adopt into forms more suitable to their own culture. This prevents the building of exact copies. Even when they can reproduce the hardware, they stumble over the operational management. Copying systems of human interaction, such as organizations or personnel systems, is even harder. The introduction of foreign technology can even become a political or societal problem, often causing considerable disturbances.

China is the prime example. China encountered the military might of Britain in the Opium Wars, twenty years before the Meiji Restoration. Significant domestic voices called for

China to introduce modern technology, promote modern industry, and build a modern army, but others feared that the spread of the ideology that had produced that modern technology would have an unforeseeable impact on Chinese political and social structures. Tens of thousands of treatises debating this question were circulated between 1860 and the early twentieth century.

After China's defeat in the first Sino-Japanese War, China became painfully aware of the need for modernization. Under the young Emperor Guang Xu, Kang Youwei and his disciples pushed through the Wu Xu Reform (1894), but this effort lasted a mere one hundred days before being overturned by the conservative faction led by the Empress Dowager Cu-xi in a coup d'état.

The Japanese inclination toward cost benefit thinking might lead to looking at this Chinese example in terms of a move by the ruling class to preserve its power, but this is not entirely true. Instead, the conservative elements in Chinese society opposed reform because they saw free competition lurking behind modern technology and feared its effects on regional society and the family system.

Japanese, in contrast, hardly ever think of technology as being bound up with ideology and social questions. Since Japanese were so accustomed to selectively adopting bits of foreign cultures, they rapidly grasped those aspects of Western culture that they thought would be convenient, fashionable, or strengthen the country's position in international conflicts.

As in the Nara and Warring Countries periods, Japan was able in the Meiji period rapidly to learn new technology and to develop its industries. To achieve this, however, Japan paid a stiff price.

STRUGGLE BETWEEN
MODERN CIVILIZATION
AND JAPANESE TRADITION

MODERN RATIONALISM: HAPPINESS LIES WITH
MATERIAL ACCUMULATION

Japanese adopted the technology of modern civilization without considering the underlying ideological and ethical systems. These systems were, however, far from innocuous. Their primary feature was a belief that happiness lies with increased material wealth. This belief had been forged through the centuries of conflict that characterized Europe's political and ideological journey from the Renaissance to the eighteenth-century industrial revolution.

In its Middle Ages, Europe was under the sway of the Catholic world view and a sense of religious morality in which the teachings of God were absolute. Material wealth was held in low esteem and the pursuit of material acquisition was considered uncouth. People who elevated poverty to a virtue—such as Poor Pierre; Saint Francis of Assisi, who spoke with birds that lit on his hands; and Louis IX, who had to be ransomed by the French people after his capture in the Seventh Crusade—were typical of those revered by society. Material desires were suppressed in favor of fervent worship of God. Medieval absolutist sensibilities were completely at odds with the ideas of modern rationalism, which found greatest merit in achieving happiness through the accumulation of material wealth.

This conflict was not settled through reasoned debates. Sometimes it erupted into religious wars, sometimes into religious tribunals. Many scientists and inventors were burned at the stake as witches. To increase material wealth, reality had to be explored objectively, its mechanisms and materials accurately assessed, and machines constructed based on scientific laws and rational procedures so that production could develop. This frequently meant opposing the teachings of God inscribed in the Bible.

By watching the heavens, for example, Copernicus concluded that the earth circled the sun. This conflicted with Biblical accounts of the earth as stationary and thus refuted the "divine word." The law of inertia and the law of gravity were ultimately revealed by Copernicus's insight. As objective observation and scientific research progressed in the sixteenth century and after, absolutist moralities faded before the advance of scientific objectivity. Modern rationalism replaced absolutist religious morality with scientific objectivity.

To accept this new philosophy, Europeans had to overcome the medieval religious ideology. In short, they had to free themselves from God. Three hundred years of fighting and bloodshed were the result. Replacing God with scientific objectivity and permitting a value system that honors material acquisition is not a simple matter of metaphysics. If material acquisition is the instrument of human happiness, one must beautify the actions that go along with the creation of wealth. Morality must label those actions that increase the wealth of society "good." Free expression of ideas and competition and consumption must be recognized as good things.

Competition, of course, produces unequal outcomes. If everyone is working to increase his material wealth, there will be winners and losers. If increasing the wealth of society as a whole is a moral good, the inventors and merchants who achieve that goal deserve praise. That praise takes the form of allowing them to possess and consume more material goods since, if one believes in modern rationalism, that is what increases happiness.

Introducing the modern technology that was created by this spirit of modern rationalism meant permitting free competition and the inequalities it causes. In China, the debate over the merit of introducing foreign modern technology focused chiefly on this concern. Chinese think of cultures as systems, and so they worried that the new technologies would spread like wildfire, creating a modern society. They feared the competition and inequalities that resulted would lead to the lower classes' dominating society.

THE RESTORATION LEADERS WHO OPENED THE COUNTRY

The Japanese did not approach the situation this way. They did not think about ideology. This is quite clear in the careers of the "Restoration patriots" who orchestrated Japan's modernization.

The men now called the Restoration patriots all began as proponents of the Tokugawa policy of "honor the emperor, expel the barbarians" *(sonno joi)*. They pushed the Tokugawa government to expel foreigners and advance the prestige of the Land of the Rising Sun domestically and internationally. Only a few years later, however, these same people formed the nucleus of the new Meiji government of "civilization and enlightenment," which opened Japan to Western ways. This was an extreme turnabout. These same men, later styled the elder statesmen of the Meiji, did not seem to feel any compunction over this drastic change. Neither Takamori Saigo, Toshimichi Okubo, nor Shogoro Katsura ever expressed the slightest reservations over this sea change. Their explanation was simply that they became aware of the power of "civilization and enlightenment."

In other words, they never were believers in any system. They did not even appear to think of Japan's traditional culture and Western modern civilization as opposing ideologies. As soon as they saw the black ships of Admiral Matthew Calbraith Perry—clear symbols of modern civilization—an ethnic feeling of not wanting to be humbled before foreigners stirred within them. They pressed the Tokugawa government to oppose foreigners through military means (expel the barbarians). The bureaucrats of the Tokugawa government, however, had a far better idea of the true state of affairs outside the country, and they knew they could not hope to expel the barbarians through military power. So they stalled and did nothing. The patriots then decided the Tokugawa government was hopeless and turned to the emperor. "Honor the emperor" thus became linked to "expel the barbarians."

When the daimyo lords tried to implement the expulsion policy of the patriots, the bombardments of Kagoshima and Shimonoseki soon showed the Japanese how weak they were. So the patriots rethought their position. They needed artillery and naval vessels, not ancient swords and bows, to resist the foreigners. The daimyos began madly importing artillery and naval ships, which were very expensive. The patriots realized that to strengthen the military and keep Japan from being humbled by the foreigners, they needed to obtain foreign technology, to foster industry, and to earn foreign exchange.

The ultimate goal of the Restoration patriots was constant: to keep Japan from being humbled by foreigners. Both "honor the emperor, expel the barbarians" and "civilization and enlightenment" were means to that end. So they felt no pangs of conscience in their 180-degree turn because their goals had remained exactly the same.

The approach that the Restoration patriots formulated through trial and error was quite effective. The traditional Japanese approach of making exact copies of foreign artifacts also served them very well. Japan modernized rapidly. But since they did not understand the ideological underpinnings, before long they ran up against major contradictions.

PAPERING OVER CONTRADICTIONS WITH A
GROUP-ORIENTED STATE

The ideological underpinnings of the modern technologies that Japan imported would show up before long, regardless of whether or not the Japanese were aware of them.

The technology born of modern rationalism created free competition and an evolutionary "prosperity of the fittest," and the gap between rich and poor in Japanese society grew. Not having thought through their policy of "rich country, strong military" this far, those Japanese who dreamed only of new technologies and systems were surprised and concerned.

Somehow the ideology of individualism and free competition, which included accepting the resulting disparities of wealth, seemed to be hidden in modern technology. As modern systems took root, some wondered if the soul of the nation was not being Westernized as well. The doubts that Chinese felt prior to the introduction of modern technology now began to arise in the Japanese people too.

The formula offered by apologists for modernization was "Japanese soul, Western skills." Though they might learn the knowledge and technology of Europe and America, Japanese would retain their souls unchanged.

The "Japanese soul" these apologists referred to was group orientation. As described in Part 2, Japanese dislike relation-ships of dominance and submission and thus avoid powerful dictators and individualistic leaders. Everyone's opinion is solicited, and everyone follows the same course. Japanese are egalitarian and group oriented. Equality of outcome had been a valued ideal, particularly since the later Tokugawa period. "Vertical equality," which held that "equality" was when people maintained their social and financial position forever, was of special importance.

Inequality in the sense of differences with persons in other classes (horizontal inequality) can certainly be annoying, but not as much as the rise in status of someone who used to be at the same level as oneself (vertical inequality). Nothing is more disturbing to group equilibrium. In a group-oriented society, one who rises even a little above his fellows becomes the object of intense jealousy. A neighbor's accomplishments are resented in a climate of beggar thy neighbor.

Had Japanese known that the values of modern civilization included acceptance of disparities in incomes, they may well have refused to embrace it. Unknowing, they accepted it. Growing income disparities plunged the nation into a whirlpool of resentment, riots, and assassinations. To suppress this, the high-ranking bureaucrats and *zaibatsu* economic groupings who had profited first from the adoption of Western culture took to calling themselves "Japanese souls with Western skills."

This simplistic phrase had lost its effectiveness by the time the Sino-Japanese and Russo-Japanese wars had made Japan a major industrial nation. Modern civilization was clearly leading to "prosperity for the fittest," and farmers and commoners experienced income disparities never before seen in Japanese history.

A nativist movement that called for the nation to return to the old ways grew in strength. How to reconcile modernism with nationalism became the leading political question of the day. This was also a matter of how to get Japanese to reconcile the people's desire for greater material wealth with their jealousy of vertical inequality. The result was something that could be called a group-oriented state. Japan was declared a patriarchal state in which all Japanese were a family, headed by the emperor. A grotesque, group-oriented modern industrial society emerged.

How a Penchant for Compromise Created the Industrially Optimized Society

Japan introduced modern civilization with the intention of selectively adopting only those parts it desired. The country was infatuated with the results of modern technology and modern systems, much as Japan had been enamored of the technological fruits and grand ceremonies and pomp that arrived when Buddhism and classical Chinese civilization entered Japan about 1,500 years earlier. As we have seen, this earlier importation had caused great discomfort among many Japanese when they learned that the absolutist values of Buddhism would cause a political crisis by refuting the beliefs of Shintoism. Likewise, the Meiji period leaders were disturbed as modern civilization ate away at Japan's long-standing group orientation by emphasizing competition and disparities. The method they used to solve this crisis was to reconcile old and new forcibly into a group-oriented modern industrial state.

This method was very similar to that used by Prince Shotoku in reconciling new (Buddhism) and old (Shinto) within a new religious approach. Nevertheless, it was extremely naive, both intellectually and in its applicability to the surrounding environment. Twentieth-century Japan had no genius of Prince Shotoku's caliber.

Japan's leaders in the midtwenties and in the thirties propagated the image of a patriarchal country centered on the emperor, but it was a façade. The real government policy was to further a modern industrial society through administrative guidance and to create a standardized mass-production system. This policy was influenced in the midtwenties and thirties by the imperial loyalists, who wanted to make the imperial façade a reality, and the authoritarian faction, who sought to create a more complete mass-production society. The former was formed of battle-hardened troops and ultranationalist ideologues, while the latter was composed of economic administrators and the central command of the military. Industrialists who had profited from modernization supported the latter group, and the remaining farmers supported the former.

While these two factions contested for the most part, they joined hands to strip the Diet of power. Once the parliament had been successfully deprived of its authority and power through financial scandals, however, the stakes rose. The authoritarian faction triumphed when the imperialists were crushed following the attempted coup of February 26, 1936. The defeat was profound. The Japanese-style group orientation permeated military and bureaucratic organizations, and the entire country grew disenchanted with the patriarchal state. The army, navy, and ministries all became internally focused, self-contained communities.

After the defeat in World War II, the concept of the patriarchal state headed by the emperor was thoroughly repudiated. The occupying Americans, who imposed this rejection, were astonished by the lack of resistance, but once again the Japanese trait of making the interests of the most influential group the interests of the nation as a whole functioned spectacularly.

The tradition of Japanese group orientation survived the eradication of the patriarchal state philosophy. It resurfaced in stronger form within bureaucratic and corporate organizations. It nurtured the system of bureaucratically led industrial cooperation known as administrative guidance and then supported its further development, until a powerful industrially optimized society was created.

For many years, Prince Shotoku's face adorned the highest denomination of currency printed in Japan, moving from the hundred-yen note to the thousand-yen and ten-thousand-yen notes in turn. Since the reconciliatory ideology that the prince created—the principle of selective cultural adoption—so greatly speeded Japan's modernization, his selection was truly appropriate. The spirit and philosophy bequeathed by this man influence Japan profoundly even to this day.

4

SHADOW GOVERNMENTS AND A CULTURE OF SIMPLICITY

JAPANESE COMMUNAL GROUPS

A GENIUS FOR BEING GOVERNED: THE JAPANESE

One reason why Japan is so stable and Japanese society so prosperous is that the Japanese people are very governable. Japanese are amazingly compliant by any measure, whether it is the low crime rates, the strictness of government regulation, or the pervasiveness of administrative guidance. This docility has been very important in enabling Japan simultaneously to achieve economic prosperity and social stability.

The experience of modern Japan, especially in the postwar era, is replete with exceptions to what are widely regarded as worldwide economic rules.

For example, Japan achieved fast economic growth even as income differentials narrowed markedly. As Japanese corporations get larger, employees get more loyal. Small salary differentials and lifetime employment do not dampen competition for promotions within companies. Despite a smaller differential in incomes and in positions based on educational attainment than in any other country, testing competition is intense. As income levels rise, workers do not slack off. Increasing urbanization is accompanied by falling crime rates. A service shift in the economy does not produce an expanded underground economy. (The recent scandals with banks and securities companies are a problem of the group orientation that binds government and the population together, not of any underground economy. They are not a matter of the government's services being monopolized by evildoers, but a violation of laws and socially accepted practices that occurred against a background of tacit government agreements and overprotection.)

Japanese take these things for granted, but seen from a global perspective they are quite rare.

Two of these factors—increasing urbanization accompanied by falling crime rates and a service shift in the economy unaccompanied by an expanded underground economy—have attracted world attention as indicators of the high governability of the Japanese people and cause other countries to feel threatened. So has the lack of resistance to taxes.

Japan's extreme governability is due in large part to the physical environment described in Part 2, especially its semi-isolation. Japan is separated from other countries by a substantial ocean, and yet all domestic regions are easily accessible from one another. Japan forged its identity as a single nation long ago and is domestically very homogeneous in landscape. Japanese make strong distinctions between "Japan" and "other countries," between "Japanese" and "foreigners." Even today, when goods, money, and information cross national borders with great speed in large volumes, Japanese still find it difficult to transcend the boundaries between Japan and the rest of the world, between Japanese and foreigners.

The depth of this feeling is hard to comprehend for peoples in countries where different ethnic groups mix together, or those on or near continents where national borders shift—in short, in all countries other than Japan.

JAPANESE WAR CRIMINALS COULD NOT FLEE ABROAD

There was a young British scholar who had worked in a camp for Japanese prisoners in Burma (now Myanmar) directly after World War II. He had studied the Far East at Oxford and wanted to know all about things Japanese, so he conducted extensive interviews with the men in the camp. He was particularly interested in one prisoner, a Kyoto University graduate who spoke English well and had majored in Buddhist thought. He had served as a paymaster and currently held the rank of first lieutenant.

After a few months it was discovered that this man had been a director of a Japanese prison camp for American soldiers back in Japan before his transfer to Burma and that he had been designated a Class C war criminal, for suspicion of cruelty to prisoners. The cruelty in question actually turned out to be an absurd charge that he had "forced prisoners to eat tree roots." What the lieutenant had done was to serve *gobo* (burdock, a plant root similar to a thin, rather stringy carrot) as part of the meal. At that point, however, the substance of the charge was not yet understood.

The death penalty was then a real possibility for many war crimes. The Briton had by that time come to respect the lieutenant and agonized over whether to inform him of the changes. The British scholar felt the first lieutenant would certainly try to escape if he knew of them.

The lieutenant heard the news from someone else, however, and told the British officer that he wanted to go home as soon as possible, even if it meant standing trial for a war crime.

The Briton was impressed by "Japanese warriors, who do not fear death," and came to respect the prisoner even more. When this British officer later became a journalist, he was very surprised to learn that this reaction was not unique: not a single accused Japanese war criminal attempted to escape abroad. He decided that the Japanese were an indivisible people. This was the single conclusion that he reached after many years of studying the Japanese.

By contrast, many Nazis accused of war crimes fled abroad. Jewish organizations are pursuing them to this very day in South America and the Middle East. The Nazis were far from unique, though. French Nazi collaborators also fled abroad, as have Iranian royalists and Chinese anti-Communists and anti-Communist White Russians before them. When these people feared that the change in regime cast their lives or property in danger, they fled abroad. More recently, large numbers of Vietnamese and Cambodians, even those who were not in important positions, have fled abroad.

In Japan's case, seeking refuge abroad has been virtually unheard of, even during the Meiji Restoration and after the defeat of World War II. It is more accurate to say that the idea is not in the Japanese repertoire. The fact that Japanese war criminals did not flee abroad simply means that they did not feel they had the option to do so.

Japanese Lose Their National Identity Outside of Japan

One of the characteristics of Japan is that the area of the sovereignty of the Japanese state, the Japanese people, the Japanese language, and Japanese culture are almost entirely coterminous.

Within the sovereign territory of the Japanese state, 98 percent of all residents are Japanese citizens. And 97 percent of them are the descendants of persons resident in the Tokugawa period. Taking this as a definition of being ethnic Japanese, this means virtually all Japanese citizens are ethnic Japanese. An even higher percentage of Japanese residents use the Japanese language, follow Japanese custom, and believe in Japanese ethics and aesthetics.

Japanese sovereignty, language, ethnicity, and customs coincide to a remarkable extent. This is a rare state of affairs in a world of multinational, multilingual states.

At the same time, 97 percent of all ethnic Japanese live in the area under Japanese sovereignty. That means less than 3 percent of all the descendants of persons living in Japan in the Tokugawa period now live outside of Japan, including long-term residents such as government and corporate personnel stationed abroad and foreign students. That's even more unusual. Ethnic Japanese who at one time spoke Japanese emigrated to the United States and Brazil in the Meiji period and later. But they constitute only about one percent of the current population of Japan.

Korea is similar to Japan in the overwhelming purity of its ethnic stock, but far greater numbers of ethnic Koreans live outside the country. Considering North and South Korea as a single country for this purpose, there are many Koreans who have lived in northeast China from ancient times and many who have emigrated to Japan (some who were compelled to and some of their own free will). More ethnic Koreans now live in North America than do ethnic Japanese. There are no other examples in the world of states whose national sovereignty coincides so exactly with the site of residence of the ethnic group that makes up the nation.

Not only have the Japanese been subject to little influence of alien peoples within the territory of Japan, they have also had little contact with foreign cultures through their co-ethnics living abroad. It is thus not surprising that Japanese are a homogeneous nation with little understanding of or skill with the cultures of other nations.

The other side of the picture is that Japanese living in America and Brazil quickly forget Japanese and the ethical and aesthetic views of the Japanese. They essentially cease to be Japanese.

Almost all the descendants of Chinese laborers who came to the San Francisco Bay Area in the latter half of the nineteenth century can still speak Cantonese, even those of the third and fourth generations. By contrast, most third-generation Japanese-Americans cannot speak Japanese. Japanese-Americans are among the ethnic groups in the United States who are the fastest to lose the language of their immigrant ancestors. The use of Japanese in daily life outside the borders of Japan is extremely rare.

Losing the language is analogous to losing the culture. The descendants of Japanese who emigrated to the Americas generally lose all Japanese values by the third generation. Once Japanese leave the territory of Japan, once they leave the rule of the Japanese state, they quickly lose the Japanese language, aesthetics, and ethics. They cease to be "Japanese."

Japanese who are members of bureaucratic and corporate organizations are faithful to the customs and interests of the organization to which they belong and make no attempt to blend into local society. This trend has not been changed a whit by the growth of the Japanese economy and the consequent stationing of more personnel abroad. This tendency extends to the dependents of the employees as well. Their socializing occurs within the group of Japanese abroad—a little extension of Japan overseas.

Foreigners living in Japan, by contrast, become Japanized quite rapidly. *Enka* songs and sumo wrestling, considered quintessentially Japanese today by the Japanese themselves, have benefited from the efforts of second- and third-generation descendants of foreigners who came to Japan in the twenties and thirties. The homogeneity of Japanese culture exerts a powerful assimilating effect.

The only societies of Japanese outside of Japan—where Japanese is in daily use, Japanese customs are adhered to, and Japanese ethical and aesthetic views prevail—are limited to a very few Japanophile emigrants and government and business people stationed abroad who are smitten with foreign countries. The even smaller numbers of foreigners stationed in Japan make up the only society on Japanese soil that is not Japanese.

For Japanese, to leave the soil and organizations of Japan

and reside overseas is to cease to be a Japanese. It means that the person is living in a foreign country as a foreigner. And nothing inspires more terror in Japanese. More terror, in fact, than being imprisoned or even killed.

The first lieutenant who so calmly wanted to return quickly to Japan, where a court trial awaited him, was not a "warrior unafraid of death" but more simply a prisoner deathly afraid of the unknown.

GOVERNED OBEDIENT TO THEIR GOVERNMENT, GOVERNMENT OBEDIENT TO THE GOVERNED

To continue as a Japanese, one may not elect to live outside the land of Japan. That land, as described in Part 2, consists of fertile rice fields and steep mountain ridges. In the fertile valleys, people could not live apart from the highly concentrated village community; productivity was low on the steep slopes, and only an extremely small number of people could survive there. Essentially, Japanese could not survive outside of the community of Japanese.

It was thus natural for them to want to survive as happily as possible within this rice-cultivating village community, the only possible place to survive. It was also natural that they would fear conflict with the village community and by extension the government that ruled all Japan, their "superior."

That Japanese were an orderly people fearful of conflict with their superiors does not mean that the superior (the government) was powerful and despotic. Throughout the long span of its history, Japanese government has been "obedient to its people." The superior also feared being cut off from Japanese society and sought to be liked by the Japanese people. The Tokugawa military government, which appears extremely undemocratic when seen from a distance, was no exception.

In January 1703, forty-six *ronin* (masterless samurai) of the

Asano family of Ako fought their way into the home of Kira Kozukenosuke, a *bakufu* retainer and former shogunate liaison official, slaughtered Kira and sixteen other people, and seriously injured another twenty-three people. The breaking into the Kira compound was the climax of the story detailed in the play *Chushingura*.

The Tokugawa government struggled long and hard in shaping its response to this incident. The shogun of that time, Tsunayoshi, and his senior minister, Yanagizawa Kichibo, solicited the opinions of government and private scholars. They even investigated street rumors and graffiti so that they would be aware of public opinion in making their decision.

Based on the facts alone, the charge should have been either riot or mass murder, but there were extenuating circumstances. Kira and the previous head of the Asano family, Asano Naganori, chief of the Imperial Works Bureau, had been involved in a dispute that ended in Asano's being forced to commit ritual suicide amid great bloodshed within Edo Castle. The military government had handed down a decision on the Kira case after debate among the councillors of the shogun, deputy councillor, and the shogunate administrator. Kira had been found not guilty but was dismissed from his post of shogunate liaison and mediator. The raid on the Kira compound occurred after that decision was handed down. Therefore, the forty-six *ronin* were plainly guilty of riot, murder, and assault. Under the laws of that day, the death penalty should certainly have been imposed.

The *bakufu* military government was strongly in favor of that sentence, as were many civilian scholars. But the opinion on the street was that the *ronin* were honorable men who had avenged the wrong done to their master. Public opinion overwhelmingly regarded them as heroes.

Caught between a clash of law and order and public opinion, the *bakufu* government agonized over its decision for a full two months. They even tried to get the imperial prince in residence at Tosho-ji temple at Nikko to issue a pardon and use that as an excuse to release them. The crown prince did not do so, however. In the end, the *bakufu* government did the correct thing and forced the forty-six to commit ritual suicide. But it also cut off the Kira family, the supposed victims, from their government positions and exiled their adopted son to house arrest in Shinano for life. Law and order were thus upheld, but with many concessions to public opinion.

Shogun Tsunayoshi was a strong-willed autocrat. He was also a great patron of the arts. Tsunayoshi collected under him the greatest Confucian scholars, mathematicians, astronomers, and *go* and *shogi* players of the Tokugawa period. Splendiferous temples were built, new sea routes pioneered, and rivers tamed. During his reign, Tokugawa Japan reached the climax of its economic and cultural development. This was largely due to his gaudy, intellectually curious, boastful character.

But for that very reason this shogun has a very poor reputation in Japanese history. He exhibited too much leadership for a Japanese leader. And yet even this willful man wanted public approval so badly that he bent the law to obtain it.

WARS REQUIRE DICTATORIAL AUTHORITY

At about this same period, King Louis XIV of France was forging artillery pieces that he styled "the king's last word." It was a clear expression of the fact that royal authority ultimately rested on military power.

Louis XIV, also known as the Sun King, built the Palace of Versailles and was an autocrat who proclaimed the divine right of kings. For all his bluster, Tsunayoshi fell far short of the dictatorial Sun King. Yet in France, Louis XIV is second in fame only to Napoleon.

Why are Tsunayoshi and Louis XIV held in such different regard? One answer is that Japanese profoundly dislike strong-arm rulers and autocratic government, mainly because of the peaceful origins of the state, as described in Part 2.

War has an unfortunately important role in human history. To be defeated in war is a deeply unpleasant thing for any people. Although victory in war does not necessarily benefit the victor, the loser is always harmed. In ancient wars between different peoples, this was even more true than it is today.

In the ancient West and Middle East, defeated peoples were sometimes virtually exterminated. Any survivors were enslaved or banished to marginal regions. Even in less extreme cases, large numbers of people would lose their lives and often their culture would be destroyed. Even in modern times this is not unknown. It is natural that continental peoples, who have been through this experience repeatedly over the last several thousand years, come to prize a system that concentrates on preventing defeat in war. To avoid defeat, a ruler capable of making quick decisions and leading the entire nation is of paramount importance.

In war, plans for overall victory must include sacrificing the lives of some troops. And these plans must be carried out secretly and quickly so that they are not disclosed to the enemy. Absolute decision-making power must thus be given to one person or a very small number of people. It is difficult to preserve secrecy when many people are involved in debate and decisions are slow. Since there is no guarantee that everyone involved will be willing to die, orders must be strictly obeyed, and the purpose of the orders and expected outcome must be kept secret. Only dictatorial authority can accomplish all these things.

In continental countries that have repeated experience with war with alien peoples, the people understand that they must sometimes give dictatorial authority to capable leaders. They also become well acquainted with the grave dangers dictators pose. They thus establish clear rules for selection of government and parameters for constraining the actions of leaders. Many individuals also try to evade the orders and rule of the dictatorial power. People try to avoid detection by government.

SELF-SACRIFICE MORE IMPORTANT THAN THE RESULT

For such countries, the main qualities sought in rulers are the decision-making skills and leadership to avoid defeat in war.

Since Japan's maritime buffer protected it from violent conflicts with other peoples, wartime leadership was only rarely a skill demanded of Japan's rulers. Even in the Warring Countries period of the sixteenth century, fighting was between factions of the ruling class seeking dominion over land and people, so conflicts ended with the ritual suicide of the defeated clan leaders and several important ministers; the ordinary population was almost always spared from slaughter. Since warring parties sought dominion over the people, there was little sense in destroying their prize.

In Japan, at least from the standpoint of the common people, their rulers were not army commanders, nor did they need to be. What the common people sought from government was a coordinator who could manage a peaceful society and fulfill the public welfare. There is little need for snap decision making to assure the peace and public welfare, especially when the rice harvest on which society is centered is comparatively reliable. There is also little need for secrecy. Rice cultivation does, however, require that everyone work together diligently and manage water to assure the success of the crop. The amity, cooperation, consensus, and agreement of the members of the group become paramount.

Rulers thus need to be universally considered fair, they must be patient enough to listen to everyone's opinions and then obtain everyone's agreement. They must also be self-sacrificing, taking the initiative in working hard. This kind of character—a person good at seeking out opinions and creating consensus—is the exact opposite of a dictator.

CITIES WITHOUT WALLS

THE GREAT WALL HAD REAL USES

During a 1986 debate over the merits of the Seikan Tunnel, which now links the islands of Hokkaido and Honshu, a pundit remarked that the Seikan Tunnel will rank alongside the Egyptian pyramids and the Great Wall as one of history's most vainglorious wastes.

The Seikan Tunnel is the world's longest undersea tunnel. It took more than thirty years and great expense to construct, and the trains that run through it chalk up considerable deficits, even before taking any recovery of the construction costs into account. Virtually all travelers from Honshu to Hokkaido now go by plane, so demand is far less than was anticipated when the tunnel was planned.

While opinions vary as to whether the Seikan Tunnel is in fact a colossal waste or the greatest construction project of the century, it can be stated with certain assurance that it was not an efficient investment. But the comparison to the pyramids and the Great Wall is ill considered. And this lack of understanding illuminates precisely the characteristic Japanese attitudes toward religion and defense.

Even though the Great Wall may now be useless, it certainly wasn't in the age it was built. It may have even been the single most useful and significant artifact the Chinese people ever built.

Many Japanese, familiar with the story of the cruel emperor Qin Shi Huang building a section of wall, think of the structure as a wasteful project forced on the people by the despotic power and whimsy of an autocratic ruler. Most of the Great Wall still extant, however, was built in the Ming dynasty. Only a fragment of the wall constructed by the Qin emperor remains (in the far north). Several hundred miles of the wall were built before the Qin emperor unified China to protect the Chinese against the countries of the northern periphery in the Warring States period. The Qin emperor repaired and connected these sections.

The wall was repaired and extended in later periods—the Han, Tang, and Ming dynasties—as well. If the wall was so wasteful, why was it constantly rebuilt, sometimes even in different locations?

The Great Wall ends in the east at the ocean at Shanhaiguan; in the west, it ends in the desert at Yumonguan. At nearly 1,800 miles, it is the longest structure ever built by human beings. It may have once extended more than a hundred miles farther to the Liaodong Peninsula. It is also the only human structure visible from outer space. The labor and expense devoted to the pyramids in Egypt doesn't begin to compare. The wall was built not once, but three or four times for the sole purpose of national defense. It's not so tall that it can't be scaled by troops, but it very effectively prevents the inflow of horses and domesticated animals. And that was the best method of preventing both the uncontrolled immigration of nomadic peoples and military invasions.

ANCIENT KYOTO HAD NO DEFENSES

The Great Wall is only the most significant of many examples
of how Japanese do not understand the defensive measures
undertaken by continental peoples. Japanese basically have
no experience or even conception of military defense.

Japanese have been avid pupils of Chinese civilization since
ancient times, but they did not copy everything. There were
several aspects of the culture that were decisively rejected,
most prominently defense strategies.

In the Nara period the Japanese built Heiankyo (ancient
Kyoto) following the plans for the Tang dynasty capital of
Chang'an. As usual, it was almost an exact copy, but with
a few major differences. For example, Heiankyo was constructed on half the scale of Chang'an, perhaps to reflect the
smaller scale of the country.

Heiankyo was laid out as a grid of nine major north-south
avenues and nine major, slightly shorter, east-west avenues.
At the center of the northern edge was the royal palace; at the
center of the southern edge, the front gate Suzakumon. A
central boulevard ran between the two points. This road,
Suzaku Boulevard, was eighty-one yards wide, precisely half
the width of Chang'an's central boulevard. Despite the precision of the reproduction, one major feature was changed: the
sturdy stone walls that surrounded Chang'an were replaced
by a roofed mud wall. The Japanese figured that a mud wall
would be sufficient to control the incursions of thieves and the
traffic of the common people. It had no military function.

Defensive stone walls were never built for any Japanese
city. The Japanese are virtually the only people in the world
to have built cities without walls. All the world's other major
cities were surrounded by walls until the invention of artillery
rendered them obsolete. Athens, Rome, Paris, Baghdad,
Delhi, and Beijing were all surrounded by stone walls. Having

walls, in fact, was the prerequisite for being called a city (polis). The Chinese word for city, *cheng-shi*, includes the word for *wall (cheng)*. The Japanese version of the same word, *jo*, usually indicates a castle. The Japanese word *jokamachi*, for *castle town*, physically places the town beside the castle, rather than inside its walls.

Ancient Japanese had no experience of living within defensive structures. They had no need to. Japanese never had to use the military as the measure of all things.

The 260 years of Tokugawa reign were even less militaristic. Japan became a virtually unarmed country. Today, the strategy of unarmed neutrality is seriously debated only in Japan. In some sense it represents a return to Tokugawa period ideals.

AN ARMY IS A SELF-SUFFICIENT MILITARY GROUP

Since Japan was ruled by warriors during the Tokugawa period, how can that be considered an "unarmed country"? During the Tokugawa period, the samurai did in fact rule. However, these people were descendants of the soldiers of the Warring Countries period and they constituted a social class, not a military group. After the Ieyasu stormed and took Osaka castle in 1615, destroying the Toyotomi family, the samurai quickly lost any military capabilities, practices, and outlook.

By definition, soldiers are the members of military units. Military units are groups organized to have the capability to wage war. To perform, they must meet two conditions.

The first is that they must be able to deploy, as a group, weaponry powerful enough to overcome others. A group of unarmed people cannot wage war. Simply possessing weapons is also insufficient. Police and criminal gangs carry weapons, but simply possessing such material is obviously not a sufficient condition for defining a military unit. Military units must possess weapons more powerful than those of police and criminal gangs, must have a clear command structure, and must be trained to function as a group.

Yet even these are not sufficient conditions. Possessing powerful weapons and having a clear organization do not create a military unit. Many dictatorships and socialist countries have or had national police forces and interior ministry troops that met these criteria, equipped with quite powerful arsenals. The Soviet secret police even had fighter planes and tanks. Toward the end of the Stalinist period, they were armed as well as the army. But they were still a police force, not a military unit.

The American National Guard, on the other hand, though armed only with small arms and machine guns, is considered a military unit. So is the Swiss Navy, though it functions only on Lake Constance. Their naval vessels are smaller than those of the Japanese Maritime Defense Force, yet they are clearly a military force.

The difference between such groups and the Soviet Interior Ministry troops is the second condition that military units must satisfy: they must be fully self-sufficient. They must be independent. To be a military unit, a group must be able to fulfill within its internal organization all the functions it must perform.

The transport of supplies is the duty of the transport corps. Private transport companies are not employed for this purpose. Building bridges, constructing barracks, and laying roads are the responsibility of military engineers. Military doctors care for the sick and injured. Military chaplains conduct religious services and minister to the dead and dying. Military police enforce military regulations; violators are never sent to civilian police or courts. Military organizations are able to provide for all of their own needs if not indefinitely, then for at least a certain length of time.

This clearly sets military units and police apart. The primary purpose of military units is to achieve victory on the battlefield, which may well place them in circumstances where corporations and civilian organizations cannot function. A region experiencing war conditions will find construction companies, transport companies, hospitals, and courts all shut down. Residents may well flee. To maintain their effectiveness, the military must have a full range of primary capabilities.

Military units thus have organizations and the authority to ensure self-sufficiency in emergency situations. To activate these functions, a declaration of war or emergency (martial law) must be proclaimed.

Police are an armed group for protecting the residents' personal security, business operations, and administrative functions during peacetime. It is assumed that construction companies, transport companies, and courts are all functioning. There are consequently no such things as police engineering corps, police supply corps, or police courts. In some countries there are police hospitals, but these are social welfare facilities for the benefit of police officers, not emergency facilities.

To guard against the possibility that transport and administrative functions are disabled during an emergency, military forces are stationed on bases, where they live in groups able to function under any circumstances. They must keep arms and vehicles ready for use and must live together. Police activities are based on the assumption that society is functioning normally. Police return to their homes at the end of the day, going on duty when needed.

A military unit is thus one that meets the two conditions outlined above. These criteria must also be considered in determining whether Japan's modern Self-Defense Force is a military force. The Self-Defense Force is clearly an organized group equipped with weapons powerful enough to overcome others, but its self-sufficiency is open to question. Its regulations for courts-martial are not clearly defined, and it does not have exceptional powers in times of emergency. Japan's Self-Defense Force is sufficiently organized and equipped to comply with American military needs but still lacks some degree of self-sufficiency and a legal role in emergency situations.

In 1990 and 1991, the dispatch of Self-Defense Force troops to the Persian Gulf was debated. The lack of self-sufficiency was raised by the uniformed groups and was a major hidden problem. When participation in United Nations peacekeeping operations was debated in the Diet after the war, this point received little attention. It may well be dangerous to send a group of people that lacks sufficient capabilities and authority into a war zone.

TOKUGAWA PERIOD SAMURAI WERE NOT SOLDIERS

How do the Tokugawa period samurai measure up under these criteria? They have extreme difficulty measuring up to even the first of these two conditions, that they be sufficiently armed to overcome others. They showed their spears in the household *tokonoma* (display alcove) and carried swords, but even the *yakuza* (Japanese mafia) were that well armed. The spears and lances of the samurai were hardly better than the pikes of farmers.

The most powerful weapon of the day was the rifle. Samurai skills with guns declined rapidly after Ieyasu took Osaka Castle, and by the Kan'ei era (1624–1630) the daimyo lords had very, very few operational guns.

In his novel *Wow! Cannons!*, Ryotaro Shiba tells the following story. The Uemura family, rulers of Yamato Takatori Castle, were granted by Tokugawa Ieyasu six cannons that had been used in the siege of Osaka Castle. The Uemura family guarded these cannons as family heirlooms, they were known as "imperial bequest cannons of Tokugawa Ieyasu." A magistrate responsible just for the cannons was appointed to keep them polished and shining.

Toward the end of the Tokugawa period, the Heaven's Wrath Brigade *(Tenchugumi)* advanced on Takatori Castle. The old reliable cannons were brought out and lined up, but they hadn't been fired since the storming of Osaka Castle, 240 years earlier. A firing was attempted using the "secret arts of artillery," but only one actually was able to fire. But that was enough. The Heaven's Wrath Brigade was frightened by the sound and ran away! What wonderful things the "imperial bequest cannons of Tokugawa Ieyasu" are, they said!

This amusing story was hardly unique to the Yamato Uemura clan. Before he was killed, Asano Naganori, the famous model for the character in the play *Chushingura,* was charged by the military government with seizing Bitchu Matsuyama Castle. The castle lord, Mizunoya, had died intestate. Anticipating someone would try to resist the seizure, several hundred warriors were called up. The Asanos had no working guns or gunpowder, so they hastily borrowed gunpowder from relatives in Hiroshima and ordered six new guns in Sakai.

Weapons were not the only thing lacking from Tokugawa period warriors. By the Genroku era (1688–1703), the military also lacked skill, organization, and practice performing as military units. This was a big problem for the Asanos. While there were "units" that had survived on their fame from the Warring Countries period, they had not been called up for three generations; in addition, many of the men had become officials who, when the order came, could not easily leave their posts. One member was a seventy-eight-year-old man, one a seven-year-old.

It took two months simply to reassemble the unit. When they finally were mobilized, they did not know how to march. Advance guard Oishi Kuranosuke sent a letter to a martial artist in Kyoto named Shindo asking about the "secret traditions of martial organization." The reply that came was "the first secret tradition is to start the march with the left foot. The second secret tradition is to unfurl tents to the southeast when the army is encamping." If this was the level of discussion, Japanese of this period evidently never thought about organized military action at all. It's evident that the Tokugawa military failed to meet the condition that they be a group able to use weapons in organized fashion to overcome an enemy.

They were even further from meeting the second condition. Samurai did not live in military encampments during the Tokugawa period. They commuted from home. Many lived in "dormitories for officials," also called "samurai houses," with their wives and children. There was no corps of engineers or supply corps. Japan had army engineers and supply corps—the Kurokuwamono engineers and Nidamono transport corps—only from the days of Oda Nobunaga to the storming of Osaka Castle, when they were disbanded.

The Tokugawa *bakufu* military government suppressed the military power of the feudal daimyo lords, keeping them whenever possible from possessing guns and abolishing the Nidamono transport and supply troops. Samurai were allowed to use swords and spears to maintain order within their domains, but transport of significant quantities of grain for troops for local operations was forbidden, since it was unnecessary unless a daimyo intended to invade a neighbor.

Since construction of military facilities was forbidden, the Kurokuwamono, or military engineers, disappeared naturally through the inertia of the samurai. In the early days of Tokugawa rule, around 1630, samurai did castle repairs and built roads, but thereafter these tasks were turned over to civilians, and samurai did no civil construction whatsoever.

In Tokugawa period Japan, there essentially were no military units. The warriors of the period were descendants of soldiers or members of that class, but by the time of the Kan'ei era, they had no military capabilities whatsoever, only police and administrative functions.

During the Tokugawa period, or at least during the more than two hundred years from the Kan'ei era (1624–1629) to the Kaei era (1848–1853), Japan was a demilitarized country in the strictest sense. The Tokugawa *bakufu* government's first move after it took Osaka Castle and extended its rule over the entire country was to reduce the military power of the daimyo lords. When the daimyos lost their military capabilities, the *bakufu* itself drastically built down its own military forces. The *bakufu* continued to maintain relative superiority within a completely demilitarized country.

There are few examples of such successful military deescalations in human history. The military deescalation that is occurring with the end of the Cold War may be aided by the experience of the early Tokugawa years. Rarely have multiple opposing powers been able to negotiate military forces downward. An authority in a position of overwhelming superiority must compel others and exercise self-restraint over itself.

TOKUGAWA PERIOD ORDER WAS MAINTAINED BY HARMONY BETWEEN GOVERNMENT AND GOVERNED

Tokugawa Japan was unusual in that the country stayed completely unified and peaceful for more than two hundred years without the existence of a military, a truly freakish event in the annals of world history. The special governance technology Japanese developed in this period performed very effectively.

The way the government responded to farmer uprisings probably best demonstrates this. Although history textbooks write now that the farmer uprisings were "suppressed," the meaning is different from European and Chinese history, in which military force was used to quell peasant uprisings. In Japan, there were almost no massacres of farmers by large numbers of samurai armed with guns. The samurai did not have sufficient military power, and the *bakufu* had forbidden it anyway. Revolts were resolved through negotiations with local magistrates and ministers. The demands of the revolt were heeded, and the road of cooperation and compromise was used.

In most cases peasant requests were accommodated to a degree and the daimyo's minister and the chief magistrate of the problem area were forced to commit ritual suicide. The idea was that it was these daimyos' ministers and chief magistrates, not the daimyos themselves, who were at fault. Like a lizard losing its tail, the system offered up a sacrifice and adopted a conciliatory posture to end the uprising. Then the peasant leaders of the uprising would be put to death because it had been standard practice since the Warring Countries period to punish both parties to an argument, regardless of fault.

There were many cases of revolt leaders who were put to death unjustly because the apologies and flattery of the governors was believed. But Japanese are such pragmatists that revolts were rarely rekindled by such injustices. Since Japanese have no absolutist beliefs, once their economic grievances are addressed, their rebellions tended to die out anyway.

After this pattern was repeated a few times, revolts would not happen as easily. The village headmen and elders who would naturally become the leaders of a revolt began to suppress rebellious urges in the farmers and were co-opted into the governing structure of their social superior.

The daimyo's minister and the chief magistrate also tended to lend an ear to the grievances of the farmers, since their lives were at stake should a rebellion occur. So although they were part of the governing structure, they tended to fuse into the farmers' community and were zealous in relaying farmers' concerns to their own superiors. Order in the demilitarized Tokugawa period was maintained by this fusion of the governed and the governing.

The relationship between governing and governed in Japan is markedly different from the clear split between rulers and ruled in most other countries. As a result, Japanese taxes became quite low. As previously described, the only Japanese tax formally collected during the Tokugawa period was a yearly in-kind land tax. This land tax was virtually never raised throughout all the years of Tokugawa rule. It declined from about 40 percent when the Tokugawa reign began to only 20 percent in the latter half of the period.

When *bakufu* and daimyo finances began to suffer in the

Genroku and later periods, miscellaneous taxes were levied on a variety of items and monopoly systems were instituted for special products, but the rates were very low and the revenue was not steady. Other forced contributions, such as a special surtax *(myogakin)*, were placed on ordinary commerce and industry, but their total was small, the amount generally being determined through discussions.

A survey of one typical set of merchant records shows that ten thousand *ryo* (an ancient Japanese monetary unit) was levied by the *bakufu*, but the merchant applied to pay five hundred *ryo*, because of losses in the period, and one thousand *ryo* was ultimately paid. It was a donation based on consent.

The samurai, nominally the ruling class, gradually became impoverished. In most fiefs, the total amount of rice dispensed to samurai as stipends remained the same throughout the Tokugawa period; samurai pensions rarely increased. Even though the stipends were paid in kind (rice), in over two hundred years official salaries did not rise. As living standards rose, the samurai were subjected to a natural salary reduction. But what more could the toothless ruling class expect?

An ascetic life-style was forced on the samurai, as was a code of values in which simple living was highly regarded. The Shogun Yoshimune and his councillor, Matsudaira Sadanobu, who presided over a drastic decline in living standards but were themselves extremely self-sacrificing, were thus seen as very honorable and wise men.

The image of samurai as impoverished became fixed in the general imagination in the Kyoho era (1744–1747), and Japan developed a class structure in which the upper classes had low incomes but high status. This in turn affected the way Japanese affix value to people and professions, engendering a spirit in which people engaged in diligent work without regard for compensation.

SYSTEMS THAT SEPARATE
APPEARANCE AND REALITY

THE SAME LOGIC AND AESTHETICS THROUGHOUT SOCIETY

Separated from other countries by buffering seas yet internally very cohesive; small but very productive fields in valleys between steep mountains; early development of communities based on rice cultivation; a pragmatism that does not view cultures as indivisible systems; a homogeneous society where governing and governed are ethnically the same: the combination of this unusual set of conditions characteristic of Japan led to a peaceful country with a fusion between the government and the general population. Even more important, Japan developed an information environment that was shared by the entire country, in which all social classes and regions shared the same ethics and aesthetics.

The inhabitants of the village communities in Japan's densely populated narrow valleys developed very close interpersonal relationships and had few encounters with peoples of other cultures. The Japanese early on developed a longterm perspective and came to understand one another very well in any kind of dealing. They came to discern qualities of character by watching behavior over long periods of time rather than analyzing a person's words and actions of the moment.

This custom gradually extended to larger and larger areas, and finally to the whole country. In that process, several historical influences were important. The first was Prince Shotoku's reconciliation of Shinto, Buddhism, and Confucianism. This settled Japanese in the habit of selective adoption of features of religion and religious texts. Parts of holy texts could be ignored while other parts were focused upon, remaining true to the perceived spirit though not necessarily the letter. For example, though one might not follow the letter of Buddha's teachings, if one believed in the Love of Amidha, things would somehow work out in the end. Without this flexibility, Japanese could hardly have embraced multiple religions at once. Prince Shotoku's philosophy of reconciliation encouraged people to formally subscribe to one set of standards, the religious texts and sutras, while actually following another, traditional Japanese custom.

About one hundred years after Prince Shotoku, the *ritsu-ryo* system of law was adopted from the Tang dynasty. It had a similar effect. At that time China was far more economically, culturally, and technologically developed than Japan. Consequently there were many aspects of the Tang system that Japan could copy but not really implement. Japanese were thus forced to accept that actual legal practice would vary quite a bit from the official rules adopted in the *ritsu-ryo* system. This variance caused few problems in Japan, because most people already were living a common life-style and possessed a common ethical and aesthetic outlook. These common values were further solidified by a common language.

There was also declining contact with the outside world during the Heian period, which strengthened the common values shared throughout the country. In the Nara and Asuka periods, when Japan was in contact with Sui and Tang dynasty China, informational exchange had to be accurate and specific for Japan to absorb the alien culture. When such contact diminished in the Heian period, communicating by "atmosphere" was sufficient. Japan developed the cultural habit of distinguishing external appearance *(tatemae)* and underlying reality *(honne)*. Communication through atmosphere and the avoidance of direct expression became Japan's preferred mode of transmitting information.

CEREMONY IN KYOTO, AUTHORITY IN KAMAKURA

Human beings are social animals who live within a complex world of information from the moment they are born. In the process of living, human beings develop certain assumptions and knowledge that allow them to understand the world about them, what we sometimes call "common knowledge."

People who lack a common informational context must spell out everything explicitly. In the Roman Empire, many different cultures and peoples intermingled, so it was important to have a detailed written law. In Europe and America today, weight is placed on written contracts; because their expectations are formed within this informational context, Europeans and Americans have faith that contracts will be executed. Japan has had a single informational environment since ancient times, so such explicitness is not only unnecessary, its avoidance is actually prized.

If someone does not follow through on his word, Japanese thinking goes, it is foolish to abuse him with language that will offend him. Better to keep words short and pleasant and act in accordance with the new situation. This type of policy was formally and publicly embraced as an administrative and political system in the late Heian period, when Japanese culture began to crystallize. This embrace took the form of the *bakufu*'s extralegal officials *(ryogenokan)*, ruling officials whose posts did not exist in any formal government system like the *ritsu-ryo*. Minamoto Yoritomo was the genius who expanded this system to the central core organizing the Japanese state.

Minamoto Yoritomo established the first *bakufu* at Kamakura when his armies defeated the forces of the Taira clan. Yoritomo had no *ritsu-ryo*-sanctioned status as grand minister of state *(dajo-daijin)*, as his enemy Taira Kiyomori had; he was neither a regent representing the emperor nor an imperial adviser. But he was a *seii taishogun*, a barbarian-quelling generalissimo. (This office was originally one of two equal ranks that stood atop Japan's military hierarchy; the *chinzei taishogun* was supreme commander of western Japan, and the *seii taishogun* was the commander of the east.)

Because Taira Kiyomori had been made the chief power of the land as grand minister of state, Yoritomo knew that the retired emperor, the reigning emperor, and all the retainers of the Heian Court aristocracy had supported the Taira family. He thus felt a keen need to separate political power from the traditional authority of the capital and used the position of *seii taishogun* to accomplish this.

As a *taishogun*, Yoritomo had the power over the military. All warriors in the country, he proclaimed, were obliged to obey his commands. So he made all soldiers in the country members of the eastern command (including all of what we would today call reserves), and as *seii taishogun* took commanding authority over everything relating to soldiers' salary, wealth, deployment, and social position. The Kamakura *bakufu* was formally the commander, judicial official, and paymaster of the entire military of the country.

Because most of the land and villages of the country were then under the power of the samurai, having the power to command them effectively meant the ability to rule the country. It was a bizarre type of regime, but in logical construction it was a very creative political stroke.

There were groups that the samurai did not control, namely the imperial court nobles and the temples and shrines. Yoritomo left some of these intact, placing them outside the formal control of the *bakufu*. Unlike the later Tokugawa *bakufu*, the Kamakura *bakufu* had no temple magistrates. Their function was performed by the imperial court under the supervision of the army headquarters in Kyoto. Although it lacked total political control, the *bakufu* was firmly established, and its actual political and administrative power extended over the entire country without so much as touching the existing *ritsu-ryo* system.

All the imperial positions—regent, imperial adviser, grand minister of state, minister of the left, minister of the right, and on down to captain of the imperial guard—continued to exist in Kyoto. They simply had minimal jurisdiction and no power. Even so, since the emperor had the nominal power to appoint the *seii taishogun,* the imperial court was able to retain a modicum of dignity and social standing.

In any other country, anyone taking political power through military might would simply have abolished the imperial court. Minamoto Yoritomo would have founded the Minamoto dynasty. Though the emperor might have been retained as a religious figure, his governing structure would certainly have been abolished. The *bakufu* would simply have had its own grand minister of state, minister of the left, and minister of the right.

Yoritomo, however, made no such drastic changes. Instead, the Kamakura *bakufu* established its own extralegal officers not provided for in the *ritsu-ryo* codes. Japan now had one set of formal officials and a separate set of shadow officials, who held the real power.

THE COMMON CULTURAL CONTEXT CAUSED A SEPARATION OF OUTER APPEARANCE AND INNER SUBSTANCE

This separation was possible in Japan because of the common informational environment. Everyone in the country could readily understand that while there were still various ministers in Kyoto, the real power was held by the Kamakura *bakufu.*

One can imagine that if something similar had happened in Europe or China, there would have been confusion as people tried to figure out whose orders to obey. Foreign ambassadors would also have been confused. Someone would undoubtedly start plotting to take advantage of the situation. In fact, European and American ambassadors coming to Japan in the nineteenth century were very confused about the relationship between the Tokugawa *bakufu* in Edo and the imperial court in Kyoto. The anti-*bakufu* movement took advantage of this to achieve their aims. Back in the twelfth century, Yoritomo felt at ease leaving the semblance of imperial officials because no one in the country would misunderstand the situation.

Once this separation was established, yet another separation occurred within it. Within three generations, the position of shogun itself had become a showpiece, and real power was held by the regent Hojo Tokimasa (1138–1215). Once again, everyone in the country knew that the regent was the real power, even though there was still a shogun.

The regents exercised power vicariously through the *seii taishogun*. This pattern became institutionalized, and by the time of Tokimasa's grandson Yasutoki (1183–1241), the regent had assumed dictatorial powers. Hojo Tokimasa's formal position was merely that of "protector of Sagami"; his grandson Yasutoki was "protector of Musashi," equivalent to a present-day prefectural governor. As regent for the *bakufu*, that "protector of Musashi" exercised the power of the shogun, commanding the entire country's samurai. It is as though the current governor of a suburban Tokyo prefecture also acted as commander-in-chief of all armed forces, ignoring the prime minister and all other government officials. The orders of the governor would immediately overrule the decisions of the cabinet in the minds of all police and all administrators.

This worked rather well in Japan. There was no need to go to the significant trouble of abolishing all positions of the imperial ministers. As long as they made no trouble, they could continue in their positions. Minamoto Yoritomo and Hojo Tokimasa were quintessential Japanese pragmatists.

This system endured for hundreds of years, so Japanese

ceased to place much faith in superficial appearances. Written contracts and laws were reinterpreted to fit the situation. Sometimes they were applied beyond their intent, sometimes ignored altogether. The only criteria were that actions conform to the "common knowledge" of the Japanese information environment and to the current context. This ambiguous fluidity was relied on to provide justice.

Today's Japan has extralegal officials in many positions. The influential politician Michio Watanabe is said to have told a foreign head of state that "there are at least ten men in the Liberal Democratic Party more powerful than the prime minister." Such men are the epitome of the extralegal official. The factions within the Liberal Democratic Party and other groups of friends unknown to the public exert more influence than the prime minister. Recently, discussions between the secretaries of the factions have been said to be setting the most important policies. Japanese society consents to this state of affairs without the slightest hesitation because everyone in society shares the same basic assumptions.

This climate applies not only to politics but to bureaucracy and corporations as well. In some large corporations, the board of directors is led by consultants who do not even have the right of corporate representative. Sometimes vice department heads have the real power. A woman not even in the company might be controlling personnel policy. In the thicket of interpersonal relationships within the Japanese workplace society, that hidden power can be clearly identified by everyone.

Consultation Decides What Contracts Really Mean

When the Japanese exchange rate shot up in 1986, foreigners whose salaries were dollar denominated felt a real contraction in their pay. For a foreigner working and living in Japan, the damage was vastly accentuated by having to pay living expenses in yen. Foreign professional baseball players were notably affected. Not all were very highly paid, so some of these players certainly experienced difficulties maintaining their life-styles. But of the thirty-odd foreign baseball players in Japan, not a single one asked to have his salary reconsidered. They figured it was their bad luck, since they had signed dollar-denominated contracts. It is not that baseball players are particularly prone to honoring contracts; this is just how Americans think.

In Japan, however, the underlying intent of a regulation or agreement is considered to be the real contract and that intent must be implemented in keeping with the changing situation. Little weight is given to the actual written word. In 1973, for example, prices for petroleum products and building supplies shot up after the oil crisis and virtually all building contractors began renegotiating their construction prices.

The provisions of contracts and laws can be disregarded when situations change and actual problems arise, relying on "common knowledge" to illuminate the new course of action. Contingencies need not be explicitly written down. Japanese contracts always contain the provision that "doubts arising as to this contract be resolved through negotiations between A and B." This allows many particulars to be omitted. Even items that are explicitly stated within a contract often become the subject of further discussion. For example, subcontractor agreements for construction projects always have penalty clauses for delay of completion, but these are rarely enforced unless there are compelling circumstances. While Japanese do enter into contracts for appearance's sake, the real intention is often different. This custom is completely opposed to European and American practice, where the contract is supreme. It is also different from China, where the real intentions are acted on without resort to even the appearance of a contract.

Continental countries see many different peoples and ideas. Customs of ruler and ruled can vary, as can races, languages, and religions. Ethical and aesthetic views cover a wide range, and information environments are diverse. In such environments, unspoken understandings are not common. There are no extralegal officials, and rulers take great pains to declare their authority. Systems of power are clear.

Chinese history has known political power to be exercised from behind the cover of an emperor at the end of dynasty. Cao Cao of Wei, who appears in *The History of the Three Kingdoms,* is one such figure. Such power never lasted long. Either the power holder or his or her progeny would establish a new dynasty, or the behind-the-scenes power would dissipate within a few generations.

In modern European and American society, this is even clearer. The contract has been a sacred concept since ancient times. Europeans and Americans even have religions that start with a covenant with God. In modern times, this attitude has permeated the political and business worlds. Non-Japanese think of contracts as promises that must be carried out. Europeans and Americans thus make very detailed contracts and Chinese try to avoid such agreements altogether.

For Japanese, a contract is merely a document prepared to record the outward appearance, more like a record of how the parties feel at the time the joint endeavor is begun and a goal to be worked toward. If conditions change later, it is natural that the deal will change also. Trying to enforce the letter of a contract when the conditions have changed is the height of bad form.

Take an employment contract, for example. If Japanese believed in contracts, an employee signing an employment contract with a company would not be able to sleep at night, because nowhere in the document does it say anything about lifetime employment. The same applies to civil servants. If a company were to start dismissing employees with the three-months' notice stipulated in the contract, however, it would meet with a firestorm of disapproval.

This becomes a real problem when foreigners hire Japanese. A foreign priest I know who works at a Catholic church in Japan used an employment contract for a church worker. The contract was a standard one for Japan, with a two-year term of employment. The priest, after two years, naturally assumed that the term of employment was over and dismissed the person, because the person in question had said nothing about wanting to continue in the job. The Japanese who heard of this thought the priest brutal and cruel. The priest was surprised. He did not understand why they were so upset. He did not know that Japanese expect that even though the contract states "two years," it will be renewed unless there is a compelling reason otherwise. An understanding between minds takes precedence over the written word. The employer should understand by looking at the employee's attitude and finances that he is interested in continued employment even if the employee does not request that the term be extended.

VAGUE EXPRESSION IS CULTURED

If one does not hold to contracts that are clearly spelled out, how much less important are the conversations of daily life or business meetings. They are used to establish an atmosphere, not for their literal content. Japanese dislike someone who says something that is accurate but spoils the mood. In Japan, speaking frankly is discourteous. Japan has developed techniques for communicating intentions through attitude and expression, what Japanese call "gut-to-gut transmission." The words themselves are window dressing and not to be believed.

The story of the Kyoto tea rice (hot tea poured over rice) illustrates this point. A host greets a visitor at the door to his house. The host says, "Well, why don't you come inside and eat a little tea rice."

If the visitor then said, "I think I'll take you up on that" and stepped in the house to eat, that person would be considered uncouth and ignorant. Even if the invitation is pressed quite strongly, the words are pretense only and the real desire is that the visitor leave quickly.

If on the other hand circumstances indicated that the visitor should say, "Well, just one cup of tea rice," then the last thing the host should do is give the guest one cup of tea rice. The guest would feel that the host doesn't know how to treat guests. If the guest felt it was permissible to accept the invitation in the first place, he would expect the best treatment.

This manner of interaction became firmly established in Kyoto residents long ago. In *Reflections in Hours of Idleness,* Yoshida Kenko (1283–1350) notes that "the people of the East [Tokyo area] say exactly what is on their minds, unlike the people of the capital [Kyoto]. They are uncouth barbarians and we should overlook their lapses." Indirect speech was already the "culture of the capital."

When *Reflections in Hours of Idleness* was written in the early fourteenth century, the Kamakura *bakufu* with its extralegal officials had already been a fact for 150 years, and the system was about to collapse into the upheaval of the northern and southern dynasties. The custom of not speaking directly had become thoroughly rooted even as the entire country was becoming accustomed to a clear separation of surface appearance and underlying reality.

LEGAL SYSTEM ALLOWED ROOM FOR DISCRETION

Gut-to-gut transmission of information has always had a place in the governance of the Japanese state. The assessment of the yearly land tax during the Tokugawa Period as described in Part 2 is a prime example. On the surface, the rate was six parts for the government, four parts for the farmers, but the effective rate was lowered to only 30 percent for the government through the connivance of local officials.

So why was this not just placed into law as 30 percent rather than going through all the complex maneuvers required to achieve the same effect? It could never happen. The legal requirement was high, the actual requirement low; leaving room for official discretion is an integral part of Japanese public order and morals.

This approach was even more prevalent in criminal law. The social status of samurai was quite distinct from that of farmers or townsmen in the Tokugawa period. Were a farmer or townsman to be disrespectful, the punishment was beheading. While that was the literal law, in practice any samurai cutting off someone's head was also in principle expected to commit ritual suicide. What's more, when a samurai's sword was drawn, someone's head was expected to fall, and to threaten someone by drawing a sword was strictly forbidden. So a samurai had to be ready to commit suicide to draw his sword.

Samurai thus lived in fear of getting entangled in altercations with farmers and townspeople. They were even pushed around by *yakuza* and robbers.

Differences like these between the appearance and the reality of politics and government often occur today. To operate a gasoline station, all one legally needs is a simple registration, but in practice this becomes a permit system because city officials do not necessarily accept registrations. Financial assistance to private schools is likewise forbidden by the constitution, yet it is still done publicly. The state gives a grant to a private school promotion association, and this is then distributed to individual schools as stipulated by the state. The existence of the Self-Defense Force is only the most prominent of many current policies that are not strictly in keeping with the Japanese constitution.

In Japan, operation or management practices are often changed without changing the law. In many cases, reading laws and regulations gives little information about actual practices. And for the same reason, many "reformed" laws and ordinances remain effectively unchanged. Revision of laws becomes more and more difficult.

When the Kamakura *bakufu* was established, the *ritsu-ryo* system lost its legal force, but it remained in place for another six hundred years, until the Meiji Restoration. Most of the laws of the Tokugawa *bakufu* were "ancestral laws of Ieyasu Tokugawa" enacted in the early 1600s, but they remained unchanged until the end of the government in 1868. The Meiji Constitution was kept untouched until the defeat in World War II. It comes as no surprise that the current Japanese constitution, which has drifted away from actual practice in many areas, remains completely unrevised.

In the almost fifty years since the end of the war, few other countries have kept a single constitution, unaltered. Japan has not changed its constitution because discrepancies between form and substance are completely acceptable. The Self-Defense Force and financial aid to private schools are the extralegal officials of the twentieth century.

This method is possible because superiors and the ordinary population (officials and civilians) share an informational context that is exactly the same.

A CULTURE OF SIMPLICITY
THAT ESCHEWS
THE "UNNATURAL"

THE CULTURE OF SIMPLICITY AS A SYSTEM

In April 1992, Spain opened Expo '92 in Seville. It was the first international exposition held under the provisions of international treaties since the Japan Expo in Osaka in 1970. Spain poured the nation's energies into this Expo. I personally worked as the executive producer for the Japanese Hall at the fair.

The theme of the fair was "discovery," marking both the five-hundredth anniversary of Columbus's voyage to the New World and Spain's entering the European community. MITI set up a committee to devise a theme for the Japanese Hall that would fit with this theme. After various proposals were discussed, the committee settled on "discovery of Japan." This would not display Japan's culture and industry but trace the reasons that Japan became a "faceless economic power." The committee felt that the many previous displays focusing on Japanese culture and daily life had not mentioned Japan's origins or future and so had left much open to misinterpretation.

It is not an easy task to pick out what has been characteristic of Japanese culture through history. As I have already described, Japanese culture and society are complex and multilayered. In the ancient age, Japanese worshiped primeval nature and their ancestors; in the classical age, Buddhism entered the country and a grandiose culture developed. The Heian period was a dynastic culture, but during the Kamakura and Muromachi periods Japan was a warrior culture. The splendor and show of the Azuchi Momoyama culture of the Warring Countries period was followed by the "culture of form" of the Tokugawa period. The Muromachi and Tokugawa periods exhibited an attention to detail, but the Nara and Warring Countries periods did not. Japan embraced Shinto and Buddhism. The cultures of the court aristocrats, the warriors, and the commoners all remained distinct. Even if Japan could be explained with reasons and theories, it would be difficult to create a display that the crowds of Europe could view and understand in a relatively short time.

One of the features often used to characterize Japanese culture as a whole is the so-called culture of simplicity. Simplicity refers here to things as they are, in their natural state, unvarnished, undisguised. The use of plain wood in Japanese architecture and the techniques used to bring out the natural qualities of materials are most often cited as examples of this aesthetic. Research on this point, however, has never dealt with the systematic extent of the aesthetic or its genesis. It is my contention that simplicity is a feature of the entirety of Japanese society, not just of a few isolated fields like architecture and crafts.

Japanese dance, for example, is composed of a series of "natural movements" taken from ordinary life. Except for a very small influence from Chinese dance, heels are never raised above shoulders and there is no rapid spinning. There is never anything as flashy as the pointe work of Western ballet or the somersaults of Beijing Opera. Japanese dance can be called a "dance of simplicity" that consists entirely of a series of natural movements.

Waka and haiku are likewise natural forms of poetry without rhyme. The influence of China is pronounced in every aspect of Japanese literature, from characters to subject matter, but the studied rhymes and fixed meter of Han poetry were not embraced. So haiku and *waka* represent in some sense a "poetry of simplicity."

In Japanese cuisine, too, food is eaten in its natural state in dishes like sushi and sashimi. In music, techniques of projecting through the Adam's apple and falsetto are not used. Undecorated, natural vocal techniques have been used in Japanese music from ancient times.

The culture of simplicity is a basic, systematic characteristic of the entirety of Japanese culture, not just architecture and crafts.

EXTREMES OF EXPRESSION AVOIDED

The birth and development of a culture of simplicity in Japan, and only in Japan, was a result of the common informational context prevailing throughout the country.

With this strongly shared, single informational context, information about atmosphere or mood gained from long-term observation was more important than the words and actions of the moment, and a custom of avoiding direct expression developed. In time, any kind of extreme expressiveness, not merely in words, came to be avoided, and an aesthetic that regarded powerful colors, dramatic shapes, and unnatural postures as low class spread throughout the society.

In the Nara period, Chinese culture flooded the land. Massive temples with Chinese-style lacquered columns were constructed and gold-leafed Buddhas forged. These temples and Buddhas, however, were then allowed to age. They lost their color and gold foil plating and no attempt was made to repaint or restore their surfaces. Japanese placed some distance between themselves and the Chinese in the Heian and later periods, feeling that it was uncultured and unnatural to make old things look new, thus creating the aesthetic of simplicity.

Horyu-ji temple is the oldest wooden structure in the world. The second oldest wooden structure is in China's Shanxi Province. Unlike Horyu-ji, that building is even now painted in bright vermilion. It has been repainted dozens of times, each time keeping the colors and patterns it had when it was built. Chinese like clarity of expression, and a temple that does not "look like a temple" has no value.

The same applies to statues of the Buddha. When the Great Buddha of Nara was completed, every square inch of it was plated with gold leaf. It must have shone like the sun. Now, all of it is gone and the statue is coated in the soot of many years of incense. And it is precisely because of that quality that Japanese today feel so touched by its beauty. In 1990 the Nara Museum displayed a reproduction of the head of the Great Asuka Buddha plated with the same kind of gold foil used at the time of construction. The effect was, if anything, humorous.

Japanese who enter ancient Chinese temples are inevitably dumbstruck by the shiny gold Buddhas they encounter. The glittering gold leaf renewed many times on a Buddha statue hundreds of years old feels to Japanese like an aesthetic assault. Old buildings and statues left in their natural state give Japanese a sense of beauty and holiness because they so clearly indicate their age. The glitter of a Buddha kept in its original condition strikes Japanese as an attempt to convey in the twinkle of an eye an insight that should be gained through long years of observation.

The Japanese attitude appears in daily social conduct as well. Chinese consider it proper to wail at the funeral of an acquaintance. In Europe, people embrace and press cheeks to express welcome. In Russia and the Middle East, men even kiss each other. In interactions between peoples of different cultures, such extreme expressions are needed.

Japanese, needless to say, have always lacked such demonstrativeness. Everyone assumes that the other's reactions are the same as one's own, so there is no need to cry to indicate the sadness one feels at losing a friend, since everyone else understands. The intention to welcome is understood without being expressed in a hug. In Japanese social conduct, a simpler method is seen: the use of more natural (ordinary) words and expressions.

"Nature" Means "As the Human World Goes"

I just wrote "more natural." My meaning, however, is not that of the word *nature*. In the Japanese, the word for *nature*, *shizen*, comes from the meaning "as the human world goes." My emphasis of the word *natural* should not be taken to imply that Japanese are a nature-loving people.

But it is often said that Japanese love nature. To interpret nature as meaning mountains, fields, oceans, and wetlands untouched by the hand of man, and to proclaim that if the whole world had the sensibilities of Japanese culture the global environment would be safe is to invite a backlash of world opinion. Japan today is the object of considerable criticism for its role in the destruction of rain forests, its opposition to the banning of whaling and catching of sea turtles, for its profligate use of pesticides, for anchoring its coastlines with giant concrete tetrapods.

One can almost sense an antinature sensibility when mothers scold their children for playing in the "dirty" sandbox, shriek at snakes and caterpillars, and discard vegetables showing the slightest signs of insects. Japanese are, in fact, pro-urban: when a worker is to be transferred from the countryside to the city, the family will move to the urban area well in advance. Many rural governors and professors move to Tokyo after they retire.

In fact, Japanese have never been a nature-loving people. In the Japanese language, the prefix *ya* means "wild." Grasses not planted by people are "wild grass." Nondomesticated birds are "wild birds," undomesticated animals are "wild animals." A person who acts "naturally," unfettered by education and manners, is a "wild person." Any word in Japanese that contains the prefix *wild* is without exception a pejorative. The Japanese word *yabanjin* is far harsher than the English equivalent, *barbarian.*

In Japanese children's stories, a happy ending is usually, "then they went off to the city." Going off to the mountains or to an outlying island is reserved for tragic endings. Cities are, for Japanese, the places where riches and beautiful people gather.

This is the opposite of Europe, especially northern Europe, in which happy endings often have the heroes disappearing off into the forest. After William Tell overcame the villain in the town, he returned to the forest. Living in towns that were surrounded by walls, rife with strict regulations and prying eyes, Europeans found the forests a place of romance where sleeping beauties and frog princes were found.

Even today, many Europeans and Americans retire to the countryside, the mountains, or the coast as a reward for a lifetime of hard work. This tendency is strongest in writers, scholars, and artists. Japanese who meet with success—winning the Akutagawa Prize, Japan's most prestigious literary award, for example—inevitably respond by moving swiftly to Tokyo.

This misunderstanding about Japanese and nature arose because the meaning of the word *shizen* was expanded. The word *tennen* is a better equivalent of the English word *nature,* which seems obvious when one considers that it is the word used in the Japanese phrases for "natural resources," "natural color," and even "natural beauty." The distinction in use was quite rigidly adhered to up until the beginning of this century. The word that is now applied to nature *(shizen)* literally means "things as they are" and was originally applied to the affairs of human beings (although sometimes it was used in place of *tennen*). It means "naturalism," as it is applied to the works of Maupassant and Zola. These authors wrote not of the world of nature but of the very human goings-on of the townspeople of Paris. This kind of "nature" is something Japanese dearly love. From their roots in the very communal rice culture, Japanese came to despise and fear anything that disturbed the flow of the human world. Only in the twenties and thirties was the meaning of the word *shizen* expanded to include "nature," and Japanese thereby gained the reputation of being a nature-loving people.

Japanese are said to love the changing of the seasons, but true love of the natural world was a characteristic only of the Kamakura and Muromachi periods. What Japanese really love is a facsimile of nature tamed by human hands and presented in a garden. This is another reflection of a culture of simplicity that enjoys reproducing everyday scenes.

DEFORMING THINGS TO MAKE THEM "THE WAY THEY ARE"

The culture of simplicity that builds with unfinished wood, reproduces everyday movements in its dance, composes poetry without rhyme, and finds beauty in temples and statues allowed to weather is seeking beauty in the materials themselves. When one avoids colorings and surface alterations, the selection of the materials themselves becomes far more important. Straight grain cedar without knots and pure white silk are prized.

Techniques for exploiting unfinished materials developed, and the culture became laden with abstraction and symbolism. Use of symbolic expression and the omitting of words in conversation are examples of these tendencies, as are the stylized movements of *No,* the tea ceremony, and the abstract shapes used in theaters and gardens. Since all Japanese came from the same cultural context, everyone had the background knowledge needed to understand subtle movements and expressions fully.

Origami, the indigenous Japanese paper craft, is a typical

example. To Japanese, a square shape is considered natural for paper. Folding is also considered more natural than cutting and pasting. The joy of origami came from creating animals and objects solely by folding square pieces of paper. Since complex curves could not be made by this method, the animals and objects portrayed were altered in their representation. Because of the common information context, these altered shapes were easily understood, just as the mere seventeen syllables of haiku were enough for everyone to understand the actions and settings that came before and after.

Symbolism and abstraction worked through simplification and abbreviation, creating a characteristic style of Japanese design and painting. The family crest designs that were developed in the Muromachi period and the use of empty spaces in Japanese art raised this sensibility into the world of art.

The Japanese Hall at the Seville Expo '92 was a systematic representation of Japan's "culture of simplicity," illustrating its origins and future. The building was built of unfinished wood, and origami was used in the exhibit of the Japanese climate and terrain.

Japanese were so enamored of Western civilization at one point they were ashamed to be living in "houses of wood and paper" and thought of steel-reinforced concrete boxes as "modern living." The massive housing projects constructed on this model looked to Europeans and Americans like rabbit hutches. As in ancient times, Japanese are good at the details, but less skilled at overall coordination and unsuited to extreme expressions and dramatic shapes.

5

RESOURCES
AND
POPULATION
AFFECT
CIVILIZATION

Societies of Shortage and Abundance

The Three Formative Factors of Civilizations

It is an age-old question why different areas of the world produce such vastly different civilizations and why human cultures change through the ages. In my book *The Knowledge-Value Revolution*, I identified three factors I termed "disrupters of civilizations" and described how they work to create these differences.

The first of these is the resource environment, which in a larger sense is synonymous with the "climate" and "physical environment" I discussed in Part 2. The physical environment—abundance or shortages of resources, topography, temperature—and the changes within it are important factors in determining how cultures and civilizations manifest themselves in a given age or region.

The second factor is population. Demographic changes in the population—its density, growth rate, and ethnic composition—have major effects on the character of the civilization.

Technology is the third factor. Joseph Schumpeter has indicated the potent influence of technology and ideology on the form that a civilization takes. The level of technology does more than merely affect the supply and cost of resources—it is decisive in determining how people think, work, and live.

While there are other factors affecting human cultures and civilizations, these three are very important, basic elements that influence how people think and live.

A fourth significant factor is social organization. History shows that when the mode of social organization changes, culture is significantly affected. Whether these organizational changes are autonomous or simply a reflection of changes in environment, population, and technology I am not yet prepared to say. Research in the history of organizations is the least developed of historical disciplines, and accurate materials and analyses are scant.

Different cultures and civilizations also influence one another both geographically and temporally. Culture can spread between regions, and older cultures can persist under the overlay of new cultures. A stable and nonmobile culture in proximity to a mobile and violently aggressive nation can become very defensive, which of course dramatically affects the shape of communities and their ways of thinking.

Part 2 described in detail how Japanese culture was shaped by the rarity of wars with alien peoples. The major factors that prevented such wars were the physical environments of Japan and neighboring nations and changes in the technology and populations of those countries. Japanese history would undoubtedly have been quite different had there been a seafaring people like the Phoenicians or the Vikings close to Japan. Conditions in neighboring countries and in earlier ages must be considered in any investigation of resources, environment, population, and technology.

To help the reader gain a better understanding of Japan and the Japanese, I now turn to a consideration of cultures and civilizations of different peoples throughout world history.

Design and Planning Started with Agriculture

When did humanity become humanity? When did people become the creatures whose exploits are tracked by what we call history? Opinions vary quite a bit, but the age when people first began to engage in agriculture must be included in the history of civilization.

The hunting and gathering societies and nomadic societies that predated agriculture also had their own civilizations, but their influence on modern civilization is open to debate. If we go back far enough, historically ascertainable facts begin to disappear. The civilizations of these early periods are too distant for modern people to accurately reconstruct using imagination alone because when agriculture began, the way people lived in their societies was fundamentally transformed.

There is a consensus that humanity began to engage in agriculture between six thousand and ten thousand years ago. The earliest agriculture is generally believed to have started along the banks of the Tigris River in Mesopotamia and the Nile in Egypt, although more recent research has shown that agriculture was probably contemporary or even older along the Indus River in Pakistan, North China's Yellow River region, and Yunnan Province in the far south of China. And when agriculture began, we can be sure that the ways humanity associated, lived, and thought were profoundly affected. People began to settle in certain defined locations and began to introduce planning into their work and lives.

Stone and clay implements have been found that predate agriculture, and preagricultural mankind already used fire and drew skillful cave paintings. Tools and the use of fire were landmarks that distinguished humanity from other animals, but they did not lead to spatial design or temporal planning in either work or life.

Agriculture did. People began manipulating the spaces in which they lived, defining agricultural plots, and building structures for fixed residences. Production and living were planned around the progression of the year. These developments set humanity more apart from other animals than the use of fire and tools had.

Possibly because we live in an industrial society, most historians have sought to understand changes in historical ages and the progress of society in terms of material objects. This has left an impression that when humanity began to engage in agriculture the material quality of human life changed dramatically, attaining a level of prosperity very different from the style of life that preceded it. The reality was probably different. The agricultural productivity in the ancient age, which lasted thousands of years, was very low, and early agricultural technology allowed for the cultivation of only a very limited stock of land.

Agriculture today is far more productive than hunting and gathering. Cultivation technology has advanced, fertilizers are used, and techniques exist for weeding out unwanted plants, so a single planted seed will yield a harvest of dozens or hundreds of times as much grain. The agriculture of thousands of years ago was far less productive. Records as recent as those from thirteenth-century France show that grain harvests were only triple the amount of seed sown. Although riverbanks and oases are very fertile, it is unlikely that thousands of years ago they were yielding very much more than thirteenth-century Europe.

The amount of arable land was also very limited in these ancient times. The land had to either receive sufficient rain, be watered by natural springs, become flooded before planting, or otherwise be naturally irrigated. It also had to be soft ground with few trees, so that it could be opened to cultivation with the primitive stone and wood tools available to early man.

The people who lived off the harvests of these limited agricultural sites were materially poor. For them to reserve one-third of the harvest for the next year's planting required great self-control. It seems unlikely that they achieved this through the individual self-restraint of all members of the community. More likely, they had to plan as a community and exert some kinds of pressures on one another. I have already described how this need to reserve part of the harvest for seed is closely linked to initial development of a ruling authority.

In its earliest stages, agriculture was important not for materially bettering life for humanity but for enabling people to reside in one place and necessitating the planning of both living and production. It made groups stable. I have termed the age when this happened the "ancient age."

The civilization of this ancient age was a culture of material shortage. Arable land was limited; agricultural technology was in its infancy. For one person to monopolize and consume large amounts of resources was to deny them to others, threatening the others' very lives. Disproportionate consumption would have caused intense conflict within the group and threaten its stability.

Actions that harm the stability of the community have been avoided in every age. In the ancient age, a fascination with the material and the desire to create things and use them up was dangerous to the health of the community. Hard work to this end was also dangerous. Virtue in the ancient age was to pray that the harvest obtained from the limited land and limited agricultural technology would be great. In the earliest days of agricultural technology, the efforts of man were no match for the whims of the gods.

ANCIENT CULTURES VALUED THE SPIRITUAL

Relics of ancient cultures that have been excavated in modern times have shown a tendency to abstraction and symbolism. Realism is virtually absent from the stone statues, woodwork, and copper figures of these early periods. They were often female symbols unlike anything that ever walked the earth, sporting horns and many breasts, or monsters with strange horns and wings, or totems that combined the characteristics of multiple animals.

As time advanced, the designs became more abstracted. Religious implements excavated from ancient-age Yinxu in China (the onetime capital of the Yin people, inhabited before 1200 B.C.) are extremely complex and abstract. Clay pots for daily use exhibit splendid swirling patterns. The fantastic imagination and creativity of primitive man are a worthy competitor for modern artists and designers.

The exact and uniform replication of precise patterns shows that ancient-age humanity had the skills and ability to create realistic art. They did not seem to consider accurate reproduction of natural, existing things and creatures either beautiful or of value. They honored instead the life force or supernatural spirit within the things themselves.

Japan's ancient-age culture was no different. As I described in Part 2, the Japanese archipelago lacked open plains suitable for hunting and nomadic cultures, so its preagricultural culture was primitive and its population low. Around the first century A.D., however, Japanese began cultivation of rice in Japan's many small alluvial plains. Village communities developed rapidly. These communities were similar to those in other countries in that their harvests were felt to be dependent more on the whims of the gods than on human effort. Like other early peoples, Japanese directed their creative impulses toward the interior aspects of things, finding life and the presence of the gods in everything. Japan's indigenous religion, Shinto, arose from this sensibility.

In Japan's case, people felt little interest in animals because they had never had a full-fledged hunting or herding culture. Since they early on developed a rice culture that was highly dependent on the weather, they were extremely conscious of the rains and river flows. They were keenly aware of the life forces of plants, water, and the earth. This is the probable genesis for the pseudo-nature-loving characteristic that has long been considered a defining feature of Japanese culture. Japanese culture changed profoundly in the fourth through sixth centuries, when the technology and ideology of classical Chinese civilization entered the country through the Korean peninsula. The islands of Japan had been isolated, and the country was a thousand years behind China in its development, but when the waning flower of classical Chinese culture arrived, it bloomed anew.

THE AGRICULTURAL REVOLUTION GAVE BIRTH TO CLASSICAL CULTURES

I call the phenomena that transformed the ancient age into classical civilizations the "agricultural revolution." At the start of the first millennium B.C., humanity developed technologies for improving the land. Irrigation canals were built to open up previously unsuitable land to cultivation. Technology for crop selection and deep cultivation also improved. The insight that weeding improved yields probably occurred in this era as well.

These advances became gradually established and trusted, and were then spread by spontaneous discovery or trial and error. This slow process undoubtedly required hundreds of years.

While agricultural technology was progressing, metallurgy was also making dramatic advances. First bronze and then (hundreds of years later) iron implements were created. The use of metals made it easier to clear forests, break ground, and build irrigation channels. The use of iron, which began in the highlands of Asia Minor and Iran in the eighth century B.C., decisively changed the nature of land development and agriculture.

New agricultural techniques expanded the amount of arable land in the middle of the eleventh century B.C. in Mesopotamia and by the end of that century in China, so agriculture spread out from oases and riverbanks. Work became more planned, organizations grew in size, and ways of thinking changed. The advance of agricultural technology changed the way people produced, which then changed the basic organization of society. This was more than a simple improvement in technology, it was an agricultural revolution.

Once it became clear that people could increase production by increasing their own efforts, society began to honor people with the skills and knowledge to achieve this gain. Those with the ability to organize gathered authority. Observation of the existing world and discovering the rules by which it could be manipulated came to be a virtue.

This approach caused a further advance in technology and encouraged development of land. City states sought more land to develop and expanded into territorial states; commerce sprang up as people exchanged surplus production; and "empires" that had the aggressive military power—cavalry and ships—to secure the routes of commerce appeared. Trade with distant regions thrived, currencies spread, and civil and criminal codes were drafted to protect the fairness of transactions. The civilization of this developing classical age was completely different from the ancient age that had preceded it.

The most important change was the large-scale development of a system of slavery. Technological progress and the expansion of arable land meant that one person could produce more than he needed to survive. The slave system was developed to make others work and capture their surplus production. Slaves were treated as animals, as powered tools, rather than as individuals with unique characters.

When the advanced regions of the early world—Mesopotamia and China's Yellow River region—were at their height, Japan had just barely begun practicing agriculture and was developing an ancient-age culture. Rice cultivation entered Japan sometime between the end of China's Warring States period and the early years of the Han dynasty, as China's ancient period ebbed several centuries before Christ. Technology for land improvement did not come with it, because either few people were familiar with the technology or those bringing it were from marginal, outlying areas of the culture. These technologies were not to enter Japan until the second and third centuries A.D. and did not become widely practiced until the fifth century. By this time, the materialism of the advanced areas of the world—the Mediterranean, the Middle East, China—was already coming to an end as forest resources were depleted and energy became scarce.

Where Did Hannibal's Elephants Come From?

Scholars have asked the question of where the elephants came from that Hannibal brought across the Alps during the Second Punic War.

Hannibal was a general of Carthage, an ancient city near the site of modern-day Tunis in North Africa. He trained his soldiers in Carthage's colony in the Iberian peninsula and from there marched across southern France before crossing the Alps into the Italian peninsula, where he repeatedly defeated Roman troops. Along with his army he brought dozens of war elephants.

Today, elephants are not found in Iberia. Nor are there any native to Tunisia or even Egypt. North Africa has none of the forests where elephants typically range. Were they African elephants from south of the Sahara? It is absolutely impossible to conceive of elephants being brought from Tanzania or Kenya across the Sahara to North Africa. Elephants eat and drink a great deal. They could not have survived the barren Sahara.

One would not think to use elephants in battle unless one were around them on a regular basis, nor would one develop the skills to work with the huge beasts, let alone guide such unusual creatures across the Alps.

Conto's theory is that elephants lived in Tunisia during Hannibal's day. He hypothesizes that in ancient times Tunisia had the forests in which elephants would have thrived.

Conto went to Tunisia to investigate his theory. He discovered a valley filled with the buried tusks of elephants. He confirmed that there used to be a smallish elephant—the Tunisian elephant—that lived in North Africa and other places along the Mediterranean coast that are now desert. In ancient times the coast was covered in dense forest, a perfect environment for elephants. In the three centuries after Hannibal, this forest was completely destroyed.

The cedars of Lebanon, with which the Phoenicians built sturdy boats that traveled from the Mediterranean to the Atlantic, have also been largely lost, as have the forests of Mount Olympus, where the gods were said to reside, and the mountain forests of Iraq and Turkey, which were nourished by the headwaters of Mesopotamia's Tigris and Euphrates.

The same phenomenon of rapid forest depletion is found in northwest India and the Yellow River region. The bald mountains of the modern Yellow River region were apparently verdant forests in the days of the Spring and Autumn period (722–484 B.C.). They began to shrink in the second and third centuries B.C. and had reached their present state by the time of Christ.

Several explanations have been advanced as to why the world's forests were so depleted during this period. In the Greek myth of Icarus, a young man steals a pair of wax wings and uses them to fly to the sky but gets too close to the sun. The wings melt and he falls to the earth and a huge forest fire results. This myth points to the destruction of forests through slash-and-burn agriculture.

Another explanation that has been offered is that overgrazing by sheep caused the deforestation. As population increased, more forest was harvested, and then sheep were grazed on the land. Unlike cattle and horses, sheep eat tough young tree saplings, so trees cannot reclaim the land. When enough land is deforested in this manner, a desert may be created.

A third explanation is that world climate conditions changed, evidenced by the speed and severity of the depletion of forests. But even if this were the case, the development of classical materialist civilizations and the increase in human population must have played a part, because the destruction of forests was most conspicuous in precisely the areas of advanced classical civilization.

Several studies have been done of changes in human population on the planet through history. Villerain concluded that population was relatively stable until 1000 B.C. and thereafter began to increase. Its swell was markedly rapid on the Mediterranean shores and in India and China from about 700 B.C. By the time of Christ, world population had reached about 500 million people.

The rapid expansion of population and the economy caused a corresponding increase in demand for building lumber and fuel wood, and more forests were felled. Probably additional destruction was caused by slash-and-burn agriculture and climate changes as well. Grazing by sheep after the forests were cut down prevented the forests from reappearing. Land that lost forest covering was subject to surface erosion and became desert. At a certain point, climate conditions changed, rainfall decreased, and destruction of forests accelerated. The repetition of this cycle depleted forest resources, and the ancient world faced an energy crisis.

ANCIENT POPULATIONS BEGAN SHRINKING

Another characteristic of the declining years of the classical civilizations in the first three centuries A.D. was a decrease in population. Villerain's research has indicated that the earth's population decreased by 30 percent between the third century and the eighth century. This varied by region. Around the time of Christ, the advanced areas of the ancient world—the Mediterranean coast, northwest India, the Yellow River valley—experienced a marked decline in the birth rate and a simultaneous influx of peoples from peripheral regions. By the third century, the population of the peripheral regions had begun to shrink as well, and total world population began to decline.

Ideologies of materialism require constant increases in the amount of material consumed by each person. When agricultural land is being expanded and resource supplies are increasing, people can believe that there will be increasing material happiness for everyone if they continue to work, increase the amount of land, and develop resources. Population increases rapidly.

Faced with the energy crisis that resulted from depletion of forests, it was soon obvious that the supply of goods could no longer be increased. When income does not grow, the most efficient way to assure an increase in supply of goods per person is to reduce the numbers of persons.

This is precisely what happened in Europe and China in the first century A.D. The Roman Empire was gripped by a fervor to control births. Many of Rome's most famous citizens of this period were childless. Of the famed Flavian emperors, all except for the last (Marcus Aurelius) were childless. (Because the emperors adopted children, a succession of emperors was possible.) Marcus Aurelius did have a child, but he was an imbecile, and the age of the Flavians ended. The idiot child, Commodus, was also rumored to be the child not of Marcus Aurelius but of his empress, Faustina, and her soldier lover.

If even emperors, who could easily afford to raise a child, had this much aversion to doing so, how much more powerful would the aversion have been for the common citizens? The Roman population began to decline in the second century, even as the population of the peripheral areas under Roman influence, such as the poor northern reaches inhabited by Germans, began to increase.

Imbalances in wealth and population lead naturally to migrations. At first, the surplus population of the backward peripheral regions was useful to the Roman economy for slave labor, but as the military power of the empire declined, immigrants swelled the lower classes. With the availability of cheap slave labor, Roman citizens moved from physical labors like farming and building to sedentary occupations. The supply of superior soldiers declined.

The barbarians who came to Rome before long built houses and started families, and the ethnic composition of the Roman Empire changed. In the end, Germans poured into the empire, attracted by the experience of their compatriots, and the Western Roman Empire crumbled.

The same trend was happening in China. China has long had a strong family system and maintained strong family ties, but during the Later Han dynasty, restrictions on giving birth increased, the population began to decline rapidly, and family ties loosened. The three blood brothers Liu Bei, Guan Yu, and Zhang Fei who appear in Chen Shou's *The History of the Three Kingdoms* are well known, but their actual brothers and sisters are never mentioned. There is no indication that they were all only children. The family system was in such tatters in this period that people didn't even know who their real siblings were.

The decay of the family system indicates a system of sexual mores in disarray. In Rome during the empire, people were very promiscuous, and the divorce rate was high. Women took as many lovers as men did. After the era of the Flavian emperors, a man whose wife had only two lovers was considered a lucky husband. The absence of any birth siblings in *The History of the Three Kingdoms* is also an indication of the decline in sexual order.

Classical civilizations pursued material wealth and had their shining moment of glory. But the aftermath featured lower birth rates, so that each person could be wealthier, the abandonment of any kind of sexual morality, and a population decline. There were many things about this era that are echoed in modern industrial society's unabated pursuit of material prosperity.

SHORTAGES PRODUCED THE MIDDLE AGES

Human beings have a tendency that encourages us to use up materials in surplus and conserve materials when they are in short supply. Once it became clear that forest resources had become depleted, that energy was in chronic shortage, and production capacity had reached its limits, conspicuous consumption came to be considered uncouth and antisocial. People lost their interest in material things, becoming inner directed and fascinated with spirituality. The rationalism of the classical civilizations gave way to the very religious culture of the Middle Ages.

Art is always the harbinger of social change. The realism that marked the classical age began to decline in Europe in the fourth century. Realism declined even sooner in China, dying by the second century.

Art historians have long considered realism to be a feature of Greek art, found only where the influence of the Greeks was also felt. It has been my contention for many years that realism can also be found in Indian and Chinese art, which was not influenced by Greece. For early civilizations to enjoy material prosperity, they first had to develop an aesthetic based on accurate observation of natural phenomena and have the inclination and technology to copy nature. This theory has been dismissed by both art critics and historians.

However, stunning examples of realistic art have been discovered in China. The clay statues of troops in the tomb of the Qin emperor, discovered in the 1970s, included eleven thousand decidedly realistic statues of soldiers and horses, proving convincingly the large role of realism in Chinese art of the period. The vast scale of realistic statues produced during that period is evidence of the maturation of a conducive aesthetic and technology.

Realistic art was a characteristic not only of Greece and Rome, but of all classical civilizations. In the second century in China and the fourth century in the West such art went into decline and art became standardized into formal abstractions that were about as distant from realism as art can be.

The precision of realistic art practiced in Greece and Rome has long been said to have been lost in the chaos that was created by massive migrations of peoples, but this is inconceivable. There were many regions that were stable after the fourth century both politically and militarily. Conversely, Greece suffered great political confusion and military defeats in the second century B.C., but much realistic art from that period survives. Art created by individual artists is not readily influenced by war or politics; rather, it is a leading indicator of changes in the world's psyche.

The shortage of energy sundered expectations of continuing increases in material production and caused people to become more introspective. They began to explore the supernatural and the mystical. Those who avoided worldly excess such as China's Seven Wise Men of the Bamboo Grove came to be admired. Long hours of elevated conversation became the fashion. This prepared the ground for Buddhism to enter China from Central Asia. Religions from the Middle East likewise spread into the West, and before long Christianity had become the state religion of the Roman Empire.

Religion begins with belief in a "god" that cannot be known with the senses. It emphasizes not what can be seen or heard in daily life but pursuit of those mysteries latent in the soul. Artists began to consider not what could be seen around them but the form that the sacred should take. Realism was left behind. The sacred gradually became formalized into standard shapes and forms.

Byzantine art is the prime example of this trend. The ways

in which each saint could be depicted were rigidly pre-scribed. Human forms had nine levels of body sizes that could be used. They had unnaturally small heads on long bodies, forms that could not possibly stand in life. Adherence to form was the standard of beauty. Artists who drew more realistic work were considered to have not yet mastered the art.

Science followed the same pattern. The classical age valued a scientific mind that accurately observed natural phenomena to discover its principles. That spirit was lost in the fourth century. Observation of the existing object was thrown over in favor of discerning an inner reality. Existence in the world was no longer real; everything was considered in terms of religious right and wrong.

A collection of illustrations of plants produced in thirteenth-century France shows only plants and flowers that do not exist. The stem of the mandrake plant is shaped like a human body and little dogs hang down from the leaves. The camas plant has a four-legged animal where its root should be. Thou-sands of such plants are depicted, all represented as being actual existing plants; their harmful or beneficial qualities are described in detail.

The collection contains not a single plant, such as wheat or the pine tree, that exists in the real world. Such plants were treated as false forms that the eye perceived, not the true forms.

The worldview outlined in the Bible, positing that man is the crown of creation and that the earth is the center of the universe, was accepted as incontrovertible. Everything was explained by religious authority: it was written in the Bible, it was the word of God, it was the word of the church.

As Buddhism spread in China in the Eastern Jin dynasty (317–420), the formalization of art and the abandonment of the scientific mind were clearly in evidence. Buddhism was not perceived as coming from India, an advanced nation, but as a mystic religion from the peripheral regions of Central Asia, which lagged far behind China itself. During China's greatest period of political turmoil, the Northern and Southern dynasties period, the great caves of Dunhuang and Datong were constructed, and temples appeared throughout the land. Priestly orders flourished and were protected by the emperors themselves. Japan adopted in earnest the advanced civilization developed by China during precisely this period.

When Japan adopted this culture, however, it was just at the end of its ancient age of civilization, and the classical period when the state becomes consolidated over a large territory was just beginning.

The discrepancy between the culture and ideas that flooded Japan and Japan's own stage of history was a profound shock to the way Japanese thought.

FORMATIVE FACTORS OF
JAPANESE CIVILIZATION

SELECTIVE ADOPTION FROM FOREIGN CULTURES

This survey of the transition of world civilizations from the ancient age through the classical age to the medieval age is intended to show what role the agents of change—resources, population, and technology—have played in shaping the character of Japanese culture and of the Japanese themselves.

As I have noted many times, Japan is an island nation. It is separated from its neighbors by a substantial, semi-isolating sea that until modern times allowed small numbers of individuals bearing culture, civilization, technology, and information to enter Japan but prevented the transport of large quantities of resources and large groups of people. Silk and pottery could be transported in ancient times, as could copper and silver, but the import of significant quantities of fuels and foodstuffs became possible only in the nineteenth century. Japan's resource and population movements have been, by and large, a domestic affair. In a sense, Japan has been a closed system.

Japan did rely on foreign countries for technology and ideas more than most nations have. Japan thus has tried to apply technologies and ideas developed in places where resource and population conditions were different. This is a defining characteristic of Japanese development.

Advanced technology and culture has been flowing into Japan since the country's early history, but it first reached significant levels in the fourth century.

Prior to this time, Japan had localized regimes. Recent excavations have traced the Yamato Court to the third century, but its authority extended only to the Kochi plain and Yamato Valley. The surrounding areas had not been opened to cultivation at that time. Small governments also existed in north Kyushu, Izumo, and Echizen. Rice cultivation was limited by natural water flows, so these regimes all had limited resources and small populations.

Immigrants from Korea in the Asuka period (late sixth to early seventh century A.D.) brought Chinese technologies for irrigation, plowing, metallurgy, crafts, and building, as well as the ideologies of Buddhism and Confucianism. Land and resources then developed rapidly, and the state was formed. Japan experienced an agricultural revolution that changed it from an ancient to a classical society, albeit a little later than its neighbors. Soon, all of Japan from the Kanto plain (present-day Tokyo) to the west was unified. Japan was for a time quite prosperous relative to its population. By the early Nara period, this development had reached a peak.

The Nara period was glorious and imposing. Its achievements can still be seen in the form of the Great Buddha of Nara, built in 747, until recently the world's largest copper deposition statue. Todai-ji temple, which was built at the same time as the Buddha, was much larger than it is today. The Great Buddha Hall was twice the size of the present structure, and seven-story pagodas three hundred feet tall stood on either side. For a country with a population of less than five million, these were huge structures. The vermilion-painted buildings and gold-plated Buddha statues were in direct stylistic opposition to Japan's older culture. Nara period Japanese were as fond of ostentatious display as any classical people.

The classical civilization of more advanced China was already well on its way to becoming a religious society. It had entered its Middle Ages. The technology entering Japan was therefore never superseded by newer Chinese technologies. The ideologies that came with it were also more typical of the Middle Ages. In their newfound infatuation with classical culture, the Japanese did not take to these medieval ideas. Although Japanese felt that these ideas must be worthwhile (because they were prevalent in more advanced China), Japan remained resistant. A few of those most familiar with Korea and China adopted these medieval attitudes, but they never took root with ordinary people.

This was Japan's first experience of selective adoption, taking those parts of a foreign culture they admired and refusing to accept the rest. Ancient Japanese copied Chinese civilization assiduously and studied much of China, but they stubbornly refused to adopt what they didn't want.

Eunuchs, for example, were an important part of Chinese society. The practice of castration spread to Korea, central Asia, and even as far as Persia and the Byzantine Empire, but Japan never adopted it. One reason given for this is that Japan was never a pastoral society and lacked experience in gelding animals, but there must have been more to it. Japanese were quite good at learning techniques, as evidenced by the construction of the Great Buddha of Nara within forty years of encountering copper deposition technology. It is not possible that the techniques of castration defied their mastery. It was the custom itself that ancient Japanese rejected.

Japanese also did not adopt Taoism, changing of dynasties, prohibition of marriages between persons of the same surname, the merit-based civil service system, Northern Song painting, or meat eating. If Japan had encountered China and had its agricultural revolution five hundred years earlier during the Han dynasty, when the ancient civilization was at full flower, it might have adopted more Chinese ways.

JAPAN'S CLASSICAL PERIOD WAS BRIEF

China and the other advanced countries were already in their Middle Ages when Japan began its agricultural revolution. This established Japan in the habit of selective adoption, and accustomed Japanese to Japanicizing whatever features of foreign culture they did adopt. Nara period Japanese fully believed that happiness came from material abundance. They could not accept the ascetic forbearance of Sui and Tang China's Buddhism and Taoism without first altering it.

At the end of the Nara period, Japan increasingly selected only those features of Chinese culture it could easily digest and Japanicized them, giving birth to a distinctive Japanese culture. Japanese were not satisfied to use Chinese characters to sound out Japanese words, for example, so they created simplifications of the characters that became an indigenous phonetic syllabary.

The huge discrepancy between China's and Japan's stages of cultural development also made Japan's classical age very brief and glorious. New technology ceased coming from the Chinese masters, so once the old technologies had been mastered the pail was empty. China was then developing an inward-looking society that was incomprehensible to Japanese.

In 849, Sugawara Michizane ordered the destruction of the ships Japan sent to the Tang court, stating "there is nothing more to buy in China." There was no new culture to learn. The major cultural appropriation from China over the next three hundred years was the antimaterialist religious thinking of Chan (Zen) Buddhism.

During this period, the Japanese population was growing rapidly. By the early Heian period it had reached eight million, doubling from the early Nara period only a century earlier. When technological progress stopped and all arable land had been developed, Japan faced a shortage of resources. As the Heian period progressed, the culture became increasingly downscaled.

The Heian period is renowned for its glorious court culture, but this culture was also characterized by a highly nuanced, exceedingly subtle world of human interaction. The Heian aristocracy was not materialist and made no effort to increase material production. Most of the high officials of the *ritsu-ryo* system of government poured their attentions into a subjective world of aesthetics instead.

The main character of the *Tale of Genji*, Hikaru Genji, was a typical member of the aristocracy of the period. He held the office of minister of the right but was addicted to an indulgent world of aesthetic pursuits and was given to elegant conversation. If the classical age and the Middle Ages are distinguished by the cultural modes and people's attitudes, Japan had already entered its Middle Ages by the first part of the Heian period.

The next time Japan was in a situation of material abundance was during the Warring Countries period of the sixteenth century. New technology began to arrive from China in the middle of the Muromachi period, around the middle of the fifteenth century. These were the technologies of the Song dynasty, which has been called China's "little modernization."

The first of these technologies were techniques of draining swamps to turn them into rice fields and advanced irrigation methods to supply hillsides with water. The next were new crops like sweet potatoes, cotton, vegetables, and soybeans. The combination of the two opened up much land that had previously been unsuitable for cultivation. Arable land expanded dramatically.

With this new productive power, the aristocrats of various regions attempted to extend their power, setting up autonomous regions. The medieval system of military government crumbled and powerful lords battled to overthrow the dominance of their Muromachi rulers. This strengthened local militaries and governments and provided people with greater training, leading to a further burst of growth for the economy.

By the sixteenth century, regional aristocracies were competing to introduce new technology, develop land, and build waterworks. Bracing mine shafts with wood allowed deeper mining than ever before. Smelting and metallurgic technology made great strides. By the second half of the century, Western technology was being added to the mix, the most important element of which was a mercury refining technique called gold-silver amalgamation. This allowed Japanese gold, silver, and copper production to increase dramatically and monetary metal to be stockpiled. With the increase in agricultural production resulting from the newly arable land, commerce was given a major boost and crop production became more efficient.

In the latter half of the sixteenth century, Oda Nobunaga's disbanding of the old official markets in favor of free markets was a response to this increased commercial activity. The Kinai area merchants, who at first feared the destruction of the old system, became fervent partisans of Nobunaga within a few years, because they had profited greatly by the formation of a unified market. Shogun Ashikaga Yoshiaki and the Hongan-ji temple priests opposed this move because Nobunaga's revolutionary policy ate at the foundations of the traditional power structure.

JAPAN'S RENAISSANCE: THE WARRING COUNTRIES PERIOD

The phrase "warring countries" conjures up weak countries being devoured by strong countries and marauding warriors pillaging the helpless common people. There was more to the period than this. The economy was expanding, new technologies were being introduced, and the land was being developed, so relative power was shifting within society. People's living standards were improving, and the population was growing.

There was a lot of war. Homes were burned, fields ruined, and farmers murdered, but overall, people were safer than they had been from the roaming bandits of previous ages. The common folk and farmers were not innocent bystanders. They were sometime warriors themselves and often formed fierce vigilante groups to hunt down fugitive warriors. When Oda Nobunaga died in the Honno-ji Incident (1582), the landed samurai and farmers of the land rose up and wiped out the assassins led by Anayama Baisetsu as they tried to escape from Sakai to Ise. Kawajiri Hidetaka was besieged in his castle in Kai and killed. The class distinction between farmers and warriors was not yet hard and fast.

Economic development led to an increase in population. The Japanese population had not grown much between the early Heian period and the middle Muromachi period. It was still at about eight million during the chaos of the Onin era (1467–1468). In the Warring Countries period it began to explode and had doubled to sixteen million by the time of the Battle of Sekigahara in 1600. Productivity had also increased so much that the average person was living half again as well.

These changes caused the rise of a specialized warrior class, an explosion of commerce and industry, and Japan's return to a state of material surplus. Oda Nobunaga and Toyotomi Hideyoshi were both acquisitive men and symbolized a turnabout in Japanese metaphysical attitudes from the asceticism of Hikaru Genji.

The powers who captured control of this surplus production encouraged a grand cultural explosion. New buildings were larger, artwork incorporated more gold leaf, and weaponry was embellished with personalized flourishes. The ensuing era of gaudy glory is now called the Azuchi Momoyama period.

In the sixteenth century Europe experienced the Renaissance, when the ancient spirit of rationalism and realism staged a resurgence. Politically, however, states fractured into chronically warring principalities in Italy, the site of a flowering of realistic art, and in Germany, the scene of religious revolution. Renaissance Europe was engulfed in cruel destruction and unscrupulous intrigues far worse than what Japan saw. Even though Japan experienced something similar during the Warring Countries period, the economic development, technological progress, and cultural transformation of the period were more noteworthy. Perhaps the civil strife of this period has figured more strongly in the country's imagination because war has been so rare in Japanese history.

THE TOYOTOMI ORGANIZATION WAS BASED ON EXPANSIONISM

The people of the Warring Countries period felt that material prosperity was the guarantor of happiness, and they sought to increase their prosperity and power. The newly powerful formed strategic alliances. Most successful of all was Toyotomi Hideyoshi. His organization was the Toyotomi clan.

No other organization in Japanese history has grown as fast as the Toyotomi clan. The impoverished farmers of the Nakamura county of the Owari region were the foundation of this organization. Under Oda Nobunaga's leadership they conquered all of Japan in barely thirty years.

As the organization grew, the members of the organization also advanced. Hideyoshi and the members of his organization all burned with the desire for expansion. They started out as poor foot soldiers under the command of head footman Hideyoshi. Many were promoted to generals, each the lord of a castle and a fief. After Hideyoshi became the daimyo of a large fief that produced fifty thousand *koku* of rice each year (one *koku* is five bushels), his men began to win battle after battle, so advancement seemed to be constantly dangling before their eyes. Once they'd experienced this as young adults, they naturally came to expect that they would succeed at whatever they set their hands to. Hideyoshi's retainers had numerous anecdotes they used to illustrate the importance of expansion.

One such story is the tale of Ishida Mitsunari, who at that

time was called Sayoshi. Sayoshi was a farmer for Hideyoshi
at the age of fifteen or sixteen, but by his twenties he had
become the lord of a fief producing forty thousand *koku* of rice
each year. At this time Hideyoshi figured that the very able
Sayoshi would have gathered an interesting group of retainers.

After Sayoshi had been lord for a month, Hideyoshi asked,
"Have you collected your retainers yet?"

"Thanks to you, I finally have one," Sayashi replied.

"You are a lord of a forty-thousand-*koku* fief but you have
only one retainer? Who is he?"

Sayashi puffed out his chest. "Shima Sakon," he said.

Shima Sakon had been the councillor of Tsutsui Junkei of
Yamato, but after Junkei's death he had become a masterless
samurai. He was considered a superb warrior, and many
daimyos had attempted to enlist him with promises of up to
one hundred thousand *koku,* but he had refused them all. And
he was twenty years older than Ishida.

"A young man like you did well to get such a famous man
with only the forty thousand you have. How much did you
give him?"

"Twenty thousand," he replied.

Of course this only left twenty thousand for Sayoshi. This
surprised even Hideyoshi. "I've never heard of a retainer
getting the same as his lord."

"With Sakon, I'm going to expand my domain to one hundred thousand, then we'll get a proper balance."

This story illustrates not only that Sayoshi placed a great
deal of importance on gathering good people to him, valuing
them more than his fief income, but also that his personnel
strategy required expansion to keep everyone happy, as did
Hideyoshi's.

Sayoshi was not alone in this approach. It was widely used
by Hideyoshi and Nobunaga's retainers. One source of
strength for Hideyoshi's organization was that it could gather
in more people than it could support based on the expectation

of future growth. In modern terms, he was like an aggressive forward investor.

KOREA WAS INVADED TO DEFUSE PERSONNEL PRESSURE

Once Hideyoshi's forces had taken Odawara Castle, suppressed the Kunohe disturbance, and pacified the entire country from Kyushu in the south to Tohoku in the north, there was no more room for Hideyoshi's samurai to expand. The daimyo houses who had used this growth-dependent strategy and their retainers were suddenly confounded. Like an employee who borrows against future expectations of salary increases, a sudden stop to growth can bring the whole structure crashing down.

The Toyotomi family and retainers debated a variety of responses. Much like a forward-investing corporation with saturated domestic markets turning to exports, their final conclusion was that if Japan was full they would go to Korea.

This is the trap many expansionist organizations fall into. They venture into new endeavors for internal personnel reasons. They will attempt an ill-advised project if there is even the slightest prospect of success.

The experience was similar to the long-awaited collapse of the bubble economy in Japan in 1991. Corporations accustomed to high growth had focused their extra capital and personnel on investment in real estate and stocks and lavished money on slipshod development plans. They needed something to do or corporate growth would end and the rotation of personnel would stop.

This phenomenon will likely happen to Japanese corporations again in the future. Corporations are drowning in internal staff and their college-educated employees are getting older. Growth is imperative to give employees new posts and higher salaries to be promoted to. So they chose projects that are the least of several evils. And in most cases they try to apply old methods to new situations.

Hideyoshi's new trial project—the invasion of Korea—followed his tried and true method of expanding territory militarily, but it ended in disaster. The organization of family and retainers fell apart and the Toyotomi family was destroyed. After one hundred years, the warrior society could no longer grow.

IEYASU CRUSHED EXPANSIONIST DAIMYOS

In a zero sum society, anyone looking for growth upsets the equilibrium. Knowing this, Toyotomi Hideyoshi's successor, Tokugawa Ieyasu, acutely felt the need to communicate to the warrior classes that they should no longer expect growth. He taught them by crushing any daimyo who showed a desire to expand.

The first to be crushed was Fukushima Masanori. As the greatest participant in the Battle of Sekigahara, Masanori had become the immensely powerful daimyo of Aki and Bingo. Ieyasu's ostensible reasons for crushing him were quite trivial. The real reason was Masanori's intense desire for expansion. Ieyasu had to make an example of him.

Most of the daimyos of the west were on the losing side at Sekigahara and had already been crushed. A few were allowed to survive with reduced fiefs, which were thereafter left in peace. The daimyos of Uesugi, Mori, Satake, Tachibana, and others had their fief allotments lowered a single time; these fiefs thereafter remained intact. Nabeshima and Shimazu were allowed to keep their entire fiefs.

After Sekigahara, Ieyasu and his son Hidetada, his successor as shogun, crushed not their enemies but their firmest allies.

If Ieyasu had destroyed the daimyos who initially opposed him, it would have looked like revenge and nothing more. By crushing some who were faithful, he made everyone stop to think. Thus Ieyasu chose to show the daimyos how dangerous expansionism was for them.

To give a modern parallel, if the government were intent on ending the bubble economy and wiping out inflated land values by letting a few small or medium-size corporations go bankrupt, it would hardly be cause for alarm. If, however, the government permitted the bankruptcy of a first-rank corporation, a large one that had been considered absolutely safe and government protected, solely because it had speculated in land, the entire business community would be so shocked that no corporation would ever engage in land speculation again. Ieyasu's reasoning was similar.

Ieyasu destroyed the Mogami family, despite their great loyalty, simply because they had the typical ambitions of a warring country. They were expansionist.

Ieyasu even opposed warriors growing beards, because beards were seen as a way of appearing stronger, and the desire to look strong indicated a desire to engage in feats of arms on the battlefield and was thus expansionist in implication.

The daimyos all shaved off their beards and tried to look unthreatening and even stupid. The third-generation Maeda lord Toshitsune of the million-*koku* fief Kaga even let his nostril hairs grow long and tied dragonflies to the ends as he walked around.

When expansionism was prohibited, many warriors began to wonder why they were needed at all. Suzuki Shozo (a writer of the early Edo period) was the first to answer this question. His philosophical answer was that warriors must discard material lusts and foster their spirituality.

This approach was probably gleaned from Confucian teachings. Confucianism, following the commentary of prominent scholar Zhuzi (1130–1200), encouraged hard work, so long as it was not to increase material production. It promoted non-material works, such as scholastic diligence and faithful adherence to polite conduct. Zhuzi lived toward the end of the Southern Song dynasty (China's "little modernization"), when it had become obvious that China could expect little future growth.

Suzuki Shozo's approach was one answer for the warrior class under the Tokugawa *bakufu* system. They had never been a productive class. They could achieve a certain honor within a warrior society without competing for material wealth if they used martial skill and Confucian training as their standards for excellence instead. To comply with this system, the *bakufu* separated material wealth (fiefs) from exercise of authority (government) and social standing (rank). They created a system that balanced satisfaction and dissatisfaction among groups. The more independent "allied" daimyos had the greatest wealth, the *bakufu* retainers had the greatest power, and the Kyoto court officials had the greatest rank. The warrior class prepared itself to convert from a period of material prosperity to an age of poverty.

JAPANESE CULTURE OF
DILIGENCE AND SOFTWARE

MERCHANTS IN THE ZERO SUM SOCIETY

As it turned out, the economy was still growing rapidly at this time (early Edo period). With the end of the wars and the stabilization of society, the capital and manpower that had been invested in arms was now invested in land development and commerce. The economy and population increased. In the hundred years between the Battle of Sekigahara in 1600 and the middle of the Genroku era, the population almost doubled, and the country's gross national product tripled.

This growth came to a rapid halt after its peak in the Genroku era. Technology suddenly stagnated and resources reached their limit, so there was nothing to invest in. The economic world (the merchant society) entered the zero sum world that the warriors had encountered a century earlier.

The first thing to happen was that there was excess money and interest rates declined. High-interest loans were common during the Tokugawa period, but if the object of investment was trusted, loan rates were very low. After the Kyoho era, the rate charged by the daimyos (the prime rate of its day) stayed under 3 percent, at times dipping under 2 percent. There were no more projects left that promised high returns.

Society had returned to a state of too many people and too few things.

The second thing to happen was a deep depression. Economic conditions declined from the end of the Genroku era through the Hoei era (1688–1709), and full-blown optimism gave way to abiding pessimism. The plays of Chikamatsu Monzaemon, which centered on lovers' suicides, were popular throughout the country. This downturn hit bottom with the intense famine in the Kyoho era (1716–1735).

The third factor was the crushing of expansionist tendencies in the merchant society. Nouveau riche men like Kinokuniya Bunzaemon and Naraya Shigezaemon went bankrupt and were imprisoned. The entire estate of Yodoya Tatsugoro, whose family had been in business since the Warring Countries period, was confiscated on the vague charge of "intolerable luxury."

Since merchants basically seek to enrich themselves and rate their success on how many assets they accumulate, their entire way of living is called into question when society as a whole stops growing and enjoyment of the fruits of their efforts is labeled a social evil. This shakes them to their very foundations—not just as businessmen, but as human beings. What are they working for? Why are they in business at all? In the fifty years from the start of the Genroku era to the end of the Kyoho era, the Japanese commercial world struggled to answer these basic questions.

Many commercial houses instituted "family precepts" during this period. The precepts of the Konoike and Mitsui families were drafted then. Their primary aim was maintenance. These precepts were the rules that good merchants had to follow to survive in a zero sum society. The most important of these were the avoidance of luxury and procrastination and the treasuring of interpersonal relations. These were means of keeping fortunes, maintaining discipline, and ensuring loyalty during hard times.

This approach can certainly work for individuals or families, but when everyone is working hard and being frugal, the macroeconomic balance of the economy is clearly thrown out of kilter. Nationwide, supply increased and demand shriveled. What seemed to be virtues on the microeconomic level spelled macroeconomic disaster for the economy as a whole.

Through some kind of wisdom, Japanese became aware of this contradiction and sought a means to rectify it. It was in fact the same problem that the Mediterranean and China faced at the end of their classical periods, between the third and fifth centuries of the common era. In those cases, they turned from an outward material focus to a religious, inward metaphysical approach. Japan initially did the same. The prime example was the Fuji Society of Ito Shinroku.

THE ISHIDA SCHOOL OF PHILOSOPHY RECONCILED THE CONTRADICTIONS OF DILIGENCE AND FRUGALITY

Ito Shinroku came from the same Matsuzaka area of the Ise peninsula as the Mitsui family and moved to Edo where he became a very successful merchant. He was a very hardworking and frugal man. One characteristic setting him apart from his fellows was his realization that the macroeconomic balance would be destroyed if everyone worked as hard and saved as frugally as was his practice. His solution was to preach purification of the self through detachment from the senses and the climbing of Mount Fuji. He founded the practically minded Fuji Society.

"Money is the boat in which we sail across this transitory world," he proclaimed in a very realistic affirmation of the importance of money. But if industriousness and frugality were to be kept from drowning the society in overproduction, the only answer was to engage diligently in unproductive activities. This radical answer illustrates the depths of merchant concern during this period.

The Fuji Society had many sympathizers and was at one

time very powerful. It also had its critics. Such clearly wasted efforts were not a very positive solution to the problem.

The ultimate answer to this dilemma was developed by Ishida Baigan (1685–1744). He was born in Tanba and went to Kyoto as an apprentice at a dry goods store, but the store went under.

Ishida Baigan's father was a farmer. When Baigan was a boy, he found a chestnut and brought it home. His father asked him which side of the mountain boundary line it was on, left or right. Baigan replied that it was from the right. Then go put it back, his father commanded. That's not our part of the mountain. And he made Baigan go back in the middle of the night to return the chestnut.

When Baigan went off to his apprenticeship, his father told him to treat the shop as though it was his parent and do nothing to cause it embarrassment. Baigan kept to this instruction so rigidly he didn't even tell his father that the shop had gone bankrupt. Several years later, his parents came to visit him. The shop was closed, with Baigan living a life of poverty. This aroused even his father's compassion and they took him home. Baigan worked as a farmer in Tanba for a while after that, but when he reached his twentieth birthday he returned to Kyoto to again become an apprentice at a dry goods store.

Apprentices customarily started at the age of twelve or thirteen, working their way up to clerk at the age of twenty, and finally manager at the age of thirty, so Baigan came to the second store at the age by which he should have already become a clerk. This would be like a high school dropout today being employed in an entry-level position at thirty.

Baigan worked long and hard as an apprentice and finally at age forty he became a store manager. At that age, any ordinary person would resign as store manager to build a house and start a family. In commercial houses of the day, store managers lived in the shop and could not marry.

Since the expected lifespan of the day was fifty years and

only when approaching the age of forty could one take a wife, the merchants of the Tokugawa period were phenomenally abstinent. This was the kind of life-style suited to keeping a zero sum society with material shortages in balance.

Unsurprisingly, prostitution was a booming business. Single samurai assigned to distant posts were the typical customer of Edo brothels, but clerks and managers of the merchants were more typical Osaka customers. Osaka had little playhouses in the southern district of Dotonbori and brothels in the north at Shinchi. Having the entertainment districts in the center of town would have tempted the clerks and managers to dally whenever they had a moment's spare time, so they were placed on the outskirts of town.

Ishida Baigan spent his long youth in this world of forbearance. After he finally became a manager, he retired and started a preparatory school. During his long apprenticeship he had many revelations that became the basis of the Ishida school of philosophy.

THE JAPANESE WORK ETHIC IS BASED ON THE ISHIDA PHILOSOPHY

The foundation of the Ishida school is the phrase "all work is the pursuit of knowledge" *(shogyo soku shugyo)*. Working with all one's heart at any occupation—agriculture, commerce—was a means of training one's character. Work was primarily seen as a means of building character and only secondarily as a productive activity.

Human beings must therefore be first and foremost hardworking. A sterling character cannot be forged except through industriousness. If work then is character building, there is no need to be particularly concerned about productivity. By turning the qualities of diligence and frugality into an educational philosophy of character building, economic productivity could be ignored.

This provided Japanese with suitable answers to their problems, and it spread like wildfire. When Ishida Baigan opened his school in Kyoto, at first he lectured to passersby on the street. Baigan himself wrote that the only person who listened to him then was a single farmer standing on the street with horseradishes hanging over his shoulder.

His message was quickly heeded, however, and three years later he was setting up another school in Osaka. In the blink of an eye, his schools had spread throughout the country, and his thinking developed into the systematic Ishida philosophy.

My description of Japan's history since the Warring Countries period has been written with the aim of illustrating the genesis of the Ishida school of philosophy because it is the philosophy that today informs the unique Japanese work ethic. It is a major influence on modern Japanese commerce and service markets.

Max Weber (1864–1920) attributed the capitalist spirit of Europe to Protestantism. The Catholic ideology that dominated medieval Europe was crafted for a world of material shortage and is shot through with a philosophy of honorable poverty that takes no interest in material prosperity. The Protestantism of Martin Luther also started with an antimaterialist attack on those who used the authority of the Catholic church to enrich themselves. But, with the rising interest in the things of this world that was growing in Renaissance Italy and Spain and the realistic art and the geographic discoveries of the era, Luther's Reformation gave birth to Calvinism, which valued efficiency of production and affirmed the virtue of hard work. Linked to the honorable poverty of the Middle Ages, it in turn gave birth to the diligent and frugal Puritans.

But widespread diligence and frugality are not conducive to a macroeconomic balance either in Europe or Japan. The Puritans at one time were powerful enough in England to succeed in a religious revolution, but in the end many were unable to live in Europe and exiled themselves to the American continent. The diligent and frugal Puritan spirit could prosper only in an environment of plentiful natural resources and land.

Japanese townspeople could not emigrate to a new continent or increase their exports, so they sought relief from the dilemma by adopting the Ishida philosophy. Europe's diligent workers and frugal souls removed themselves to America to carve a life from its primeval forests even as Japanese townsfolk were affirming the character-building nature of hard work and devoting themselves to a lifetime on their limited land and resources.

The French Huguenots, another Protestant group, took a different course. These religious reformers of the sixteenth through eighteenth centuries affirmed hard work but disavowed poverty. Hard work and the creation and use of capital were for them virtuous activities. The Catholics found this ideology intolerable and chased the Huguenots from France to Belgium and Holland. They were the clearest expression of Max Weber's link of Protestantism to capitalism. Under their influence, Holland became very productive, developing its maritime trade and creating a wealthy urban culture.

The Ishida philosophy emphasized the importance of hard work and equated frugality (honorable poverty) with virtue. This was quite different from Weber's Protestantism. Since hard work also built character, the Ishida philosophy engendered a work ethic and criteria for judging one's fellow man unlike any other. In Zen practice, for example, one first must sweep the floors every day. If that work is performed rigorously, the heart of Zen can be understood. This was not the original thrust of Zen Buddhism. The change occurred when the Ishida philosophy was incorporated into it. Ishida Baigan was a Zen practitioner, and his philosophy radically altered Zen as it is practiced in Japan, so much so that it became a religion with virtually nothing in common with Kamakura period Zen.

The Zen that was brought to Japan as the medieval Chinese

Chan sect of Buddhism was extremely ascetic and metaphysical. The Bodhidharma sat facing a wall for nine years meditating, and that was considered a great act. Laboring in the fields was not a respected task. Chan was a medieval religion that valued not hard work but honorable poverty.

European and American scholars of Zen have caused a great deal of misunderstanding about Japan. They focus largely on Kamakura period Zen, which was a medieval creed that pursued spiritual elevation and despised productive activity. These Zen scholars misunderstand the Japanese attitude toward work, so they can see the long hours that modern Japanese work only as a compulsion forced by Japanese government and business.

The Zen that modern Japanese know is completely different from Kamakura period Zen. It is a Zen that reflects the admixture of the ideas of Ishida Baigan. The same name continued to be used and the organization endured, but the contents were very much changed.

JAPANESE EVEN WORK AT PLAY

As material shortages continued, the impact of Baigan Ishida's precept that "all work is the pursuit of knowledge" permeated every aspect of Tokugawa period society. Farmers would go to the fields to work even when they had free time. Why not a little weeding, since today is free? Why not prepare a little wheat for harvest, since there's nothing else to do? Recreation was believed to be a waste of time, so people worked even when it was not productive. If they didn't, they would be suspect.

Even today, fruit shops will stay open late seven days a week, including holidays. They might have only two or three customers who come after nine at night, but still they stay open. Subtracting lighting costs, there is very little profit in such sums. But the merchants feel that being in their private rooms at the back of the store is not much different from being in the store, so they might as well stay open. In the Japanese value system, time spent without a purpose is disliked, and time spent doing nothing is a waste.

Japanese find such time meaningless. The same can be said of leisure time and vacations. The word *vacation* (the Japanese word is derived from the French *vacances*) is derived from the concept of vacancy. For Europeans and Americans, without that vacant time a holiday is not a vacation. For Japanese, a vacation has to be filled with some defined activity, like sports, travel, theatergoing, or listening to music. "Time" is time spent doing something. A newspaper survey on the subject had the wretched complaint that "I have more days off, but I still end up lazing around." "Lazing around" is a vacation in the true sense of the word. But for Japanese, spending some meaningless time in a cabin, at the seaside or in the mountains, is not a vacation.

During their short holidays, Japanese play diligently. A survey done by a Hawaiian tourist board showed that Japanese spend as much money in a stay of three nights as Americans from the mainland do in a stay of two weeks. Americans spend a couple of weeks lazing at the beach, but Japanese ride in taxis to see all the sights, they go shopping or to play golf, and they spend much more than Americans each day.

This tendency is even more pronounced in young people. They train hard to play. Personal tastes are ignored. "No one will like me if I don't ski." "You look dumb if you don't know how to scuba dive." Trend magazines inform young people what is fashionable to do. For them, "play" is "training" to look good and attract friends.

GOOD AT DETAILS, INEPT WITH THE BIG PICTURE

When people are constantly working diligently in a resource-poor society, large amounts of labor are inevitably poured into limited resources and scarce land. To cope with this problem, Japan developed an aesthetic of devoting great labor to details. Concentrating hard work on a limited object proved that a worker was a good person.

Attention to detail became intense, even when the results could not be seen. Workers became obsessed with parts that had nothing to do with either the function or the appearance of the product. Unlike the "meister" tradition of Germany, in the Japanese "craftsman art" or "artisanship" tradition the creator points to some utterly meaningless feature as evidence of his hard work. Even today, the finish of the inside of a garment, the wood grain of a dish, or the reverse side of a weld are important in the Japanese market. Many foreign products deficient in these details cannot be sold in Japan.

Once a television station sold an American pot made for American homes by showing it on screen. It was deluged with complaints when it sent out the pots. The pots were enameled around the sides but were not enameled on the bottom, where the fire contacted the metal. The complaint its purchasers had was that the boundary between the enameled area and the nonenameled area was not a neat circle but had paint runs and spots. The television station that sold them requested the American company to repair the defect. The American company was surprised. It was dangerous, they said, to raise a pot full of hot food to eye level. In other words, since the area could not be seen, what did it matter? For Japanese, such areas are important precisely because one *cannot* see them.

Japanese artisanship extends to unseeable areas, which are the proof of the artist's diligence and even proclaim that person's nobility of character. They prove that the person is a specialist. Japanese specialists so emphasize the details that they tend to ignore the item as a whole.

In buildings, the quality of the finish is spectacular. Paneling is glued on very neatly, floor tiles centered to leave exactly the same space open on either side. In other countries, tiles are usually laid starting on one side, so that only the far end is left with a partial tile. In a wide-enough room, the two sides cannot be seen at the same time, so the discrepancy cannot be seen. For Japanese artisans, such "laziness" must be avoided. When one looks at the building as a whole, however, foreign buildings win hands down. For cities as a whole the effect is even more pronounced. In Japan, the intentions of the persons responsible for the details are hard to ignore, hampering coordination of the project as a whole.

This affects organizational modes also. Japanese organizations are weak on top-level control, and section or department chiefs have considerable authority. The closer the department is to the detail work, the more authority it has. In the Tokugawa period, especially after the Kyoho era, materials were relatively scarce and labor was used lavishly. This tendency is still reflected in Japanese organizations today.

The secret of Japan's modern competitiveness in exporting industrial products lies in these impeccable details. The overall designs are imported from abroad and then the detail work is done with characteristic Japanese diligence to produce a high-quality product. One reason it is so hard to sell foreign goods in Japan is that their detail work is often poor; in addition, they are plagued by minor breakdowns. For Japan to become an international marketplace in the future, the world must become more aware of this peculiarity of the Japanese market. This is not a recent development, either. The world must know that it has evolved through a long period of Japanese history.

The economic friction Japan is now experiencing is not caused solely by the country's group orientation and expansionism. The special aesthetics of the Japanese consumer also play a large role.

LACK OF RESOURCES CREATES A SOFTWARE SOCIETY

The length of this period of material shortage and labor surplus had another very important consequence. "Software," which exploited the value of human effort, came to be considered more important than "hardware," which consumed material.

Japan lacks two things found elsewhere in the world: city walls and handcuffs. I have covered the first in depth already, but the lack of the second is equally revealing.

In human society, there are always those who must be secured bodily, such as criminals and prisoners of war. Instruments for this purpose, such as handcuffs, shackles, and collars, were among humanity's first inventions in many countries. Except for a very few manufactured during the Warring Countries period when Japan was imitating Western civilization, the pre-Meiji Japanese never made such imprisoning implements. Until as recently as the twenties they were still quite rare. Policemen usually carried a rope for binding prisoners. This lack does not imply that Japan had no criminals to lock up; they simply used general-purpose ropes rather than manufacturing specialized tools. It is not easy to tie people up so that they are not injured and yet cannot escape. And when the person being tied up is a professional thief or spy practiced at escape, the task is even more difficult.

Japan devised special techniques of tying people up. These were formalized in the Tokugawa period into thirteen types based on the subject's occupation, social position, gender, and age. Different tying styles were devised for soldiers, townspeople, priests, women, and so on. They were so complex it took three years to master them all. And yet no one ever thought to manufacture something as convenient as handcuffs. As specialists, the policemen were embarrassed to rely on mere hardware.

The approach can be seen in every field. In non-Japanese houses, areas for eating, living, and sleeping are generally separate. In Japan, a single type of room is used for all of these purposes. Doors can be removed to create larger rooms so that weddings and other ceremonies can be held in private dwellings.

There is only one implement used for meals: chopsticks. This is quite different from Western cuisine, which in addition to knives, forks, and spoons, has even more specialized serving implements. Japan instead developed elaborate forms of conduct, such as tea ceremony. Problems were solved not by creating specialized objects but by using specialized behaviors. These were the marks of learning and nobility.

EDUCATION FUELED BY A CULTURE OF FORM

In the West, specialized tools can be manufactured by experts and supplied to ordinary people who then use them with relative ease. In Japan's software-oriented culture, consumers themselves had to learn all the techniques of use. Instruction and education were naturally required for this purpose. Many teachers had to be trained. To make this possible, "software" began to be formalized in the Tokugawa period and the "culture of form" was created. Forms and models have been established for martial arts, tea ceremony, flower arranging, *go, shogi,* and even the instruction of reading, writing, and abacus. Once one masters the forms, a basic level of knowledge is attained, so persons who learn these forms can themselves quickly become teachers for initial education. In the latter half of the Tokugawa period, temple schools and martial arts schools were found in villages throughout the country.

Since ordinary people placed more emphasis on software than on material possessions, they became passionate about educating their children rather than bequeathing them gold, silver, or jewelry. At the end of the *bakufu* government in the mid-1800s, Japan was already among the best-educated countries in the world.

Education increased equality among the people and gave them a single cultural context. It was also useful in distilling the "culture of simplicity," since if a form is taught to everybody, more creative activities that require special techniques become difficult.

This concentration on form suppressed individuality and creativity. First the forms created by the pioneers are taught, then straying from them is prohibited, then egotistical style becomes scorned. "Egotistical" style is the source of individuality and creativity.

The formalism of Japanese education is also intimately bound up in the creation of a society of industrial mass production that began in the Meiji period and became firmly established after World War II. Japan was able to train great numbers of the engineers who could copy the technology and knowledge of the advanced countries of the West and stay true to the form.

6

THE
LIMITS OF
PROSPERITY
IN THE
ULTIMATE
INDUSTRIAL
SOCIETY

THE ROAD TO
THE ULTIMATE
INDUSTRIAL SOCIETY

THE JAPANESE WAY TO WEALTH

In the five preceding parts I have described how environment and history combined to make Japan in many ways unlike any other country on the globe. I wanted to show that characteristics peculiar to Japan have played a large role in creating the rich Japan we know so well today.

But these factors are not enough to explain how Japan became so prosperous. Japan's environment predates written history, and the Japanese quality of pragmatism dates back at least 1,400 years. Other typically Japanese characteristics—the group orientation of the culture, the strong sense of belonging to communal groups, the homogeneous cultural context—are also very old. Even the more recent Ishida philosophy of diligence and the aesthetic valorization of attention to detail are more than two centuries old. And yet throughout these long stretches of history, Japan remained poor. Only in the latter half of the twentieth century has Japan ranked among the world's rich nations. And this status has only been truly secure since the seventies.

So even though Japan's physical environment and historical culture may have contributed to the nation's rise to wealth, they are clearly not direct causes. Japan was able to attain its postseventies wealth thanks to a mechanism for growing rich that combined all these disparate elements. This final part will examine this mechanism, summing up the relationship between it and Japan's climate and historical culture. Before we can begin, however, we must examine modern Japanese social structures, character, attitudes, and mores. If we do not accurately grasp what Japan has come to be, we will never understand why it has become a wealthy society.

Producer Heaven, Consumer Hell

Surely everyone will agree that Japan is a very wealthy country. As described in Part 1, its per capita GNP is among the world's highest, the wealth of its individual citizens is second to none, and its international balance of payments is strongly in surplus. Japan also leads the globe in foreign investment and is among the largest donors of international aid. Its prices are stable, unemployment is low, and the crime rate is low. If there is one single factor responsible for these achievements it is Japan's success in centering its society on that defining characteristic of the modern age: standardized, mass production. The industrially optimized society made Japan wealthy.

But Japanese perceptions tell a different story. Virtually all Japanese would agree that Japan is vastly wealthier than it was before World War II or in the immediate postwar years. Most people would also agree that the country is better off than it was even ten years ago. But an assertion that Japan is the richest country in the world is met by skepticism among Japanese.

Japanese reputedly have higher incomes than Americans but have little sense of it. Tell a Japanese person that she is one of the wealthiest in the world and she will become gloomy. Tell her that her house is one of the world's most spacious and she will angrily think you a fool. The Japanese way of life is overflowing with uneasiness and irritation completely incongruous with this supposed wealth.

Why do Japanese feel so pressed and insecure in their lives even as they are surrounded by such abundance? Precisely because they live in an industrially optimized society. By optimizing its society for mass production, Japan has mandated that everyone live with standardized products. Modern Japan allows no room for choice.

Human beings are producers; they are also consumers. From their standpoint as producers—as workers—modern Japanese are truly blessed. They receive high pay and have few worries about unemployment. Corporate and commercial stability is assured. The workplace is safe and clean and the labor market very orderly. Companies foot the bill for entertainment that provides considerable enjoyment for many. In fact, businesses spend about $40 billion yearly on entertainment in Japan. This figure is far higher than total dividends paid to shareholders. As a share of GNP, it is six times higher than similar spending in the United States or Great Britain and eight times higher than in the former West Germany. Japanese workers ought to be happy.

But if they are blessed as producers, as consumers Japanese are cursed. Prices are high. Rents are high. Trains and airports are packed with people. To get a good bed in a hospital you need connections. Governmental bureaucratic procedures are complex. Red tape abounds. But most unpleasant of all is the poverty of choice. Primary and middle schools are strictly bound to demarcated catchment areas: site of residence absolutely compels a student to attend a certain school even if he or she dislikes it. There are few types of hospitals and little variety in stores. Leisure activities are relentlessly regulated by safety standards and myriad rules. For a little carefree shopping and relaxation one must spend hundreds or even thousands of dollars to leave the country. In Japan, even if you have money, you cannot do what you want. That is the reality of Japan: producer heaven, consumer hell. And it all flows from the industrially optimized society.

Why did Japan become this kind of place? How did Japan, alone among the two hundred plus countries of the world, manage to create this most rigorous, industrially optimized society?

All the Japanese characteristics I have described in this book so far are bound up in the answer. The Japanese climate, the absence of both animal husbandry and walled city states in Japanese history, the pragmatism that does not look at cultures as organic systems, the group orientation nurtured by long traditions of rice cultivation, the culture of form that expedited the diffusion of primary education—all these factors had undeniably major influences on the formation of the modern ultimate industrial society.

But then we must confront the fact that through its long history Japan was never such a society until now. Barely twenty years ago Japan became a relentless productive and technological powerhouse ready to flood the world with automobiles and electronics. The suitability of Japan's climate and traditions, of the group orientation and pragmatism of the Japanese, important though they are, cannot sufficiently explain this transformation. There must have been some crucial element that catalyzed and harnessed the venerable traditions, attitudes, and spirit of Japanese society. And that element must be found in the period that saw the dramatic growth of Japanese industry—the twentieth century.

I believe it can be found in the year 1941. In that year, a new policy was established by the military government. They called it the system of administratively guided industrial cooperation. Most people know it simply as administrative guidance.

THE NATURE OF THE INDUSTRIAL REVOLUTION

Modern industry began in what is called the industrial revolution, a phenomenon of radical transformation from preindustrial to industrial economies that began in Britain in the late eighteenth century and spread to western Europe and North America in the nineteenth century. This revolution came to Japan's shores in the late nineteenth and early twentieth centuries, when Japan adopted the modern industrial technology and modern systems of Europe and America during the Meiji Restoration. Japan absorbed this revolution by copying it extensively over a period of thirty years.

Three hundred years of religious and social ferment ensued after the Renaissance, and it took the West all that time to develop the systems and organizations that produced and exploited the technology of the industrial revolution, so Japan's adoption of the revolution's tangible results in a mere thirty years seems too fast for belief. In fact Japan's modernity was extremely superficial. And yet seventy years later Japan somehow exhibited a modern industrial society more nearly perfect than any other country's.

In many ways, this paradox is understandable. Since Japan was a late entrant to the ranks of industrial nations, it was free to create an uncompromisingly modern society in many spheres. Japan bypassed much of the turmoil that other nations experienced.

The industrial revolution was basically a series of technological advances that established industrial production using banks of large steam-powered machines as the dominant means of production. There had, however, been similar technological breakthroughs in the past, and they occurred thereafter as well. The late-eighteenth-century innovation of the steam engine is uniquely characterized as a revolution because it was accompanied by thoroughgoing transformation of not only industry but economy and society as well. Only this particular series of technological innovations created modern industrial society.

Once industry was driven by steam-powered heavy machinery, it was no longer possible for individual workers to own their means of production. It was also impossible for individuals or even families to operate such production facilities. This led to a bifurcation of the workforce into capitalists, who owned the means of production, and workers, who supplied the requisite labor without any ownership stake.

Prior to the industrial revolution, workers had owned their means of production. Peasants had possessed rights to work the land and owned their plows and hoes. Blacksmiths owned their tools and forges. Drivers owned their wagons and raised their horses. Merchants had their wares and shops and rights to sell. Once the factory system of production was born, however, large numbers of workers who did not own their means of production appeared. Not tied to such means, they could work and live anywhere. They were the "free laborers" of Karl Marx. A modern industrial society is one in which such free laborers constitute the majority.

As machine capabilities increase, so do the benefits of replacing human workers with machines. Machines are far more powerful and precise than human beings. But they can do only simple work, and they lack powers of judgment. To replace workers with machines, then, products must be standardized and the element of judgment removed from the production process. Only a standardized product can be made by the simple operations of which machines are capable. To fully exploit machinery, material inputs must be standardized as well.

Standardization is indispensable to mass production. All products must be broken down into simple standardized components that can be produced in large scale. Set assembly procedures allow machines to be introduced in more applications, further reducing the need for human labor. Labor productivity increases and product quality and uniformity improve. The modern industrial society is the society best suited to this kind of mass production.

Japan created an industrially optimized society when it turned mass production into the focus of its culture. The fields in which Japan boasts world-leading international competitiveness are without exception areas in which mass production can be employed. Japan's productivity and competitiveness in traditional crafts that cannot exploit mass production and in modern products that are produced one unit at a time (such as large aircraft and nuclear power plants) is not great. Computers provide another example. When the trend was toward large mainframes that are not as receptive to mass-production techniques, Japan performed poorly. When smaller, mass-produced machines became the norm, Japan immediately became supreme. In agriculture, services, and knowledge-intensive creative fields, Japan is weaker because its talents in mass production cannot be applied.

Japan has been trying to build a modern industrial state on par with Europe and North America ever since the Meiji period. In the attempt, Japan has created a culture optimized for mass production. Japan succeeded in terms both of volume and quality in the postwar years and has been particularly successful since the seventies. Since World War II, not only has Japan mobilized all its policy toward that goal, it has also subordinated its informational, educational, and social systems to that goal. In contemporary Japan, no other goal is conceivable.

THE PRIME VIRTUE CHANGES FROM STABILITY TO EFFICIENCY

Modern industrial society was born of rationalism, a combination of an aesthetic that finds the greatest good in the greatest amounts of material with a morality that equates efficiency with virtue. These were not time-honored beliefs in Japan.

In Tokugawa period Japan, the greatest virtue was not efficiency, but stability. The *bakufu* government founded by Tokugawa Ieyasu in the early seventeenth century was designed to suppress the expansionist tendencies of the day by pursuing stability, even at the expense of efficiency. For more than two hundred years, no bridge was built over the Oi River in the Tokugawa domains and the construction and operation for transport of multiple-masted sailing ships was forbidden because it was feared that easier (that is, more efficient) movement of people and material would destroy population equilibrium and regional markets and thus harm stability.

Under the Ishida school of philosophy, frugality and diligence were emphasized as a means of establishing macroeconomic balance and microeconomic stability. Labor efficiency was ignored, since labor was considered only a tool to improve one's character. The acceptance of this philosophy by Tokugawa period society is evidence that the people had already embraced stability as the preeminent social value.

The black ships of Admiral Perry, which sailed into Tokyo Bay from the United States in 1853, represented a different, more modern paradigm that valued efficiency more than stability. Japanese society was utterly transformed. Suddenly, stability was repudiated and the pursuit of efficiency became the prime virtue. This change transformed everything. Slogans played an important role in early modern Japan, and the isolationist slogan "revere the emperor, expel the barbarians" *(sonno joi)* was replaced by "civilization and enlightenment" *(bunmei kaika).*

The ferocity of this change was something virtually unparalleled in human history. This period, the Meiji Restoration, was perhaps the finest hour for the relativistic Japanese attitude that permits the culture to valorize whatever is beneficial for the majority of its people.

Resistance to this upheaval was weak. Within ten years of the appearance of the black ships, both the Tokugawa shogun, who had held presumably unchallengeable power and authority, and the many daimyo lords who had sworn loyalty to the shogun had relinquished their power. Few rallied to the cause of the *bakufu* government. Even the direct retainers, whose very existence was predicated on maintaining the shogunate, made no attempt to protect it. Of all those sworn to loyalty to the Tokugawa family and the *bakufu*, only a very few retainers, the daimyo lords Aizu and Kuwana, and the hired bodyguards remained loyal.

When change occurs in Japan, it occurs completely, because Japanese fear being different from the group.

SOCIAL ISOLATION: A FATE WORSE THAN DEATH

Everyone wants to be liked by others, but nobody wishes for approval as intensely as the Japanese. The Japanese fear of being disliked by the peer group is extreme, greater than the fear of death.

Non-Japanese (and sometimes Japanese as well) think of Japanese as a people fearless in the face of death. This is a grave misconception. In reality, Japanese are more afraid of death than most other peoples. Take, for example, the case of a diagnosis of terminal cancer. While the Japanese medical community has often debated whether the cancer patient should be informed of the diagnosis, in most cases in Japan, the patient is not informed. By contrast, in most other countries, adult patients are usually informed of the prognosis for life expectancy. It is reasoned that the patient needs time to prepare a will and reconcile himself or herself religiously and philosophically to the coming death. The Catholic extreme unction is a ceremony performed before dying. A cross is traced in oil on the forehead, confirming to the person that he or she will soon die. By contrast, Japanese Buddhism addresses its final words to the deceased's spirit at the funeral. The dying person would be shocked indeed were the priest to come while he was still alive. Likewise with terminal cancer, the patient is rarely informed in Japan. A significant number of people die intestate, leaving issues of inheritance unresolved. Japanese doctors, however, have a very good reason for this approach: informing patients can kill them.

Statistics of countries other than Japan indicate little difference in lifespan of patients who are informed and those who are not. Knowing that death is a certainty does not cause life-shortening worry. Japanese statistics tell a different story: the lifespan of the average Japanese told he or she has cancer is one-third the length estimated by the doctor based on symptoms alone. When informed of a terminal diagnosis, patient lifespan decreases markedly. In one particular case, a renowned Japanese priest faced with this dilemma told the doctor that he had been spiritually trained in the ways of Buddha since he was very young. He said he faced the prospect of cancer with equanimity and requested the truth. The doctor informed him he had cancer and had six months to live. The priest lost his appetite the very next day. Two weeks later he was dead.

Japanese are in fact quite afraid of death; they have a strong attachment to life and invest themselves in the desires of the here and now, not the hereafter.

So why, then, were there so many young volunteers for the kamikaze squads? The tales of Japanese committing seppuku or volunteering for kamikaze squads have given non-Japanese the impression that Japanese are unafraid of death. The reality is, again, quite different. In interviews with kamikaze squad volunteers who were saved from death by the end of the war moments before they were to be sacrificed in battle, less than 10 percent said they had felt a desire to die for their country. All the others said they had not wished to go, but everyone around them was constantly urging them to join and they felt unable to refuse. They felt they had no other option.

For Japanese, death is preferable to going against the expressed wishes of their group, of "everybody." In a water-intensive agriculture such as rice, falling out of favor with the village group meant one would not survive, so centuries of Japanese tradition has discouraged Japanese from going against the group.

This vigorous group orientation, when combined with the relativism that permits Japanese to worship both Shinto gods and the Buddha, enables Japanese society to transform its attitudes and mores dramatically, as occurred in only a decade when the *bakufu* was ended by the Meiji Restoration.

How "Civilization and Enlightenment" Became Administrative Guidance

When the American black ships first appeared, the cry of "expel the barbarians" was heard loudly and clearly throughout the country. The society of stability fought to survive. This was more because the populace did not want to comply with foreign demands than because they wanted to preserve the *bakufu* government. When the extent of the losses from the bombardments of Shimonoseki and Kagoshima sank in, however, the mood shifted swiftly.

Everything about the prevailing system was discarded. No Japanese can resist such a tide. The Tokugawa *bakufu* collapsed without offering the resistance one would have expected of a system that had maintained absolute authority and power for 250 years. But the effects went even further. The daimyo lords and the samurai class suddenly lost their prestige and authority as well. Temples and shrines were reorganized along European patterns. Land-holding patterns and occupational groups were reformed along the lines of modern capitalism. Even history and language textbooks were rewritten to conform to modern paradigms of Europe and North America.

"Civilization and enlightenment" became a widely heard slogan, and "leave Asia, join Europe" another. Its implication of abandoning all the learning and customs of the Far East was extreme. This was a more radical change than even Prince Shotoku had dreamed of when he reconciled respect for Shinto gods with state support of Buddhism.

In the twenty years after the Meiji Restoration, Japan introduced concepts, systems, and organizations copied from European models. Factories and railroads using modern technologies were built. But Japanese society could not be made into a real industrial society merely by changing moods and reproducing artifacts. Japan had to accumulate enough capital to build large modern factories, construct organizations big enough to manage investment efficiently, create a large unified market to sell large amounts of the standardized goods, and provide the masses of suitable labor needed to work at these large production sites.

Once the modern spirit of bigger is better had truly taken hold in Japan, the country pressed forward by nurturing corporations, unifying the market, and training the masses of labor that would be required. Parts of society resisted these transitions, but Japanese traditions helped the country complete a successful transformation in a relatively short time. Particularly important were the tradition of bottom-up organization (which respected the wisdom of experts), and the universal acceptance of a difference between appearances and underlying reality (which enabled dramatic reforms to be adopted behind a façade of continuity).

One of the characteristics of modern civilization is specialization, of which the mass-production workplace is the epitome. A concept is developed, then broken down into constituent components; optimal components are created and then assembled into the best possible product. In mass production, a relative few determine concepts that inform the overall product, and then a multitude of personnel in various departments produce according to that scheme. Within the departments, the task is further subdivided, each group seeking to perfect its part, thus reducing costs and improving quality.

For mass production to work well, there must be a few geniuses producing the original concepts, a substantial number of middle managers to refine the concept within the departments, and a large number of loyal workers to carry out their directives. Japan's group orientation served to produce the massive number of loyal, diligent workers while the attention to detail inherent in the custom of bottom-up management and the "culture of form" supplied the required cadre of middle managers. And while there was a deficiency of geniuses to create the overriding concepts, Japan was luckily able to import these ideas wholesale. So with its masses of loyal diligent workers and cadre of middle managers already basically in place, Japan was able to industrialize rapidly.

PREWAR MANUFACTURING INDUSTRIES RAN ON CASUAL LABOR

Alone among Asian countries Japan was able to industrialize rapidly. In the late twenties and early thirties, this process was still in its infancy. Silk production and spinning had reached world levels in terms both of quantity and quality, but other industries, especially the heavy and chemical industries that are the backbone of an industrial economy, were small and technologically backward. Heavy industry had problems developing because work in modern industry was not yet socially considered a reliable form of employment.

To build heavy industry, Japan relied on casual labor to an extent that the lifetime employees of contemporary Japan would find difficult to believe. In the thirties, Japan had the highest rates of labor turnover in the world. Employees were fired regularly and had no legal protections. Academics even advanced the notion that Japan had no need of firing restrictions or advance notice. A theory of a casual labor economy was developed.

According to this theory, since workers in Japanese factories and shops were generally the younger sons and the daughters of farmers, they had rural families to fall back on for emotional and financial support. If they were let go, they could easily return to the farm to lend a hand and were in no danger of going hungry, let alone starving. When the economy picked up, they could be rehired at a local job, or head into the city to save money for a few years. At the next economic downturn they could once again return to the farm, perhaps buying a new field and assisting their parents and older siblings in agricultural work until the economy picked up again. When they returned to the city they would lend their field to the parents or siblings as thanks for the aid rendered during the downturn. And when the time came to settle down—at marriage in the case of women, at the age of forty for men— they could return permanently to the rural community with a solid foundation upon which to build a life. This was the model of the ideal, healthy life.

Europe and North America had restrictions on firing and developed labor and management confrontations, the theory went, because they lacked this system of welcoming rural families. When Western laborers were fired, parents and children could be thrown onto the streets. Japan was more secure. The entire nation was considered a large extended family headed by the emperor, composed of smaller extended families centered on a core family. Japan thus had no need of either restrictions on firing or union/management confrontation. Japan's traditional, extended family–based welfare system was widely praised by Japanese as superior to European and American societies with their guiding principle of rationalism.

Naturally, laborers felt the system left something to be desired, but for the most part they acquiesced. Few desired an identity as a factory worker or shop clerk, and given the short lifespans of the time, the possibility of being able to take over the farm in middle age was indeed high. Tuberculosis was widespread and the older son might easily die. Adoption of younger sons into other families without sons was also common.

Up until the thirties, not only was manufacturing *not* the core of the social economy, it was not even considered a safe place to earn one's livelihood. Working for a salary was called "the precarious trade," even for college graduates working white-collar jobs. Japan had at that point merely traveled to the threshold of industrial society. It was standing on the doorstep.

There were three reasons for this backwardness. The first was the lack of capital. Although the European and North American system of technology was studied and industrial production promoted by main force from the early Meiji period, Japan could not catch up with the West's centuries of preparation and achievement in a mere fifty years.

The second reason was the immaturity of the market for the products of industry. The Meiji government simultaneously modernized the military and expanded industry. This pumped up military and public sector demand, but it also kept down the living standards of the civilian population and constrained the domestic market for durable consumer goods. In 1926 there were only 40,000 passenger cars in Japan, 338,000 radios (according to Nihon Hoso Kyokai figures) and 628,000 telephones.

The third reason was Japan's relative lack of the material inputs that industry requires and the global shortage of resources in the thirties. Japan is a cramped and mountainous country, so it is not suitable to producing the cash crops that feed industry. Japan had no history of animal husbandry to produce wool and leather, and even the production of cotton, which flourished during the Edo period when the country was closed, was not internationally competitive. Although mines produced a variety of minerals, the quantities were small and the mining labor intensive. The only competitive industrial materials prewar Japan produced were labor-intensive raw silk thread and copper, with which it was comparatively well endowed. Having to rely on high-priced imports for other industrial materials hindered both the development of industry and the accumulation of capital.

After World War I the Japanese government thrust into Asia in search of markets and raw materials, fomenting tensions with Asian countries, Europe, and America. The military bureaucracy used the search for markets as a pretext for military expansion, but that expansion further stunted the consumer market at home by depriving it of resources. To overcome this dilemma, the system of administrative guidance was created, despite much resistance.

THE EARLY DAYS OF
ADMINISTRATIVE GUIDANCE

INDUSTRIALIZATION REQUIRES STANDARDIZATION

The system of administrative guidance was not created over-night. Conservative members who represented the more rural regions in the imperial Diet resisted the military and bureau-cracy's attempt to create a mass-production society in the midtwenties and early thirties. The bureaucracy and military thus began working to strip the Diet of authority.

From the days of early Greece, the strategy of destroying parliamentary democracy has remained constant: accuse politicians of graft. The pay and peerage income of the army generals was far in excess of the wealth of even the elder statesmen of the Meiji period like Aritomo Yamagata, who lived sumptuously with scores of servants in the luxurious Tsubakiyama Villa, yet the huge fortunes of the generals did not become a major political issue.

In the twenties and thirties, however, the enemies of de-mocracy regularly publicized scandals to defame their parlia-mentary opponents. The media relentlessly pursued financial scandals even as the politicians of the period were virtually exhausting their personal fortunes in electioneering and gov-erning.

The biggest scandal was the Teijin Affair, a fabricated affair in 1934 concerning the sale of shares in the textile company Teijin; these shares were held by the government as collateral for Bank of Japan financing in the wake of the 1928 bankruptcy of the Suzuki Company—a rival in size to Mitsui and Mitsubishi.

It started with a scoop by the *Jiji Shinpo* newspaper. In the following six months, the dailies competed to publish very specific information about who attended which meetings and where, so the reports were widely believed. With the consequent swell of public opinion, dozens of politicians, bureaucrats, and financiers, including sitting ministers, were arrested and tried. The entire cabinet of Prime Minister Makoto Saito resigned, and a new cabinet was formed under Admiral Keisuke Okada as prime minister.

A three-year-long trial ended with the conclusion that the entire incident was baseless; verdicts of not guilty were handed down for all defendants. By that time, however, the attempted military coup of February 26, 1936, had already provoked the enactment of the National Mobilization Law and the war ministers (minister of the army and minister of the navy) had been placed on active status, giving them veto power over the formation of cabinets. The Diet would not recover its authority and powers until World War II ended. The trial preserved the reputations of the defendants, but it did not protect democratic government. The incident served much the same purpose as the burning of the Reichstag did in bringing the Nazis to power.

Once the military and bureaucrats had suppressed the Diet and passed the National Mobilization Law (1938), a series of new laws was enacted, revised, and strengthened until the system of administrative guidance was completed in 1941.

It had three primary aims. The first was standardization to push mass production.

The Japan Industrial Standards were promulgated for industrial products, establishing standards for everything from screws to radios to furniture. Standardization became one of the primary tasks of the Ministry of Commerce and Industry (later, the Ministry of International Trade and Industry). Grades were established for agricultural products. Rice, for example, had five grades. Japanese sake was classified into three permissible grades—special grade, first grade, and second grade—by the Alcohol Tax Act. Public facilities were also subjected to code regulations and safety regulations. Strict building codes and electrical structures standards were enacted, and a single gauge stipulated for all railroads in the country. In 1940, train stations in different regions had distinct regional characteristics, but after the single-gauge regulations were passed, the only differences to be found among stations were those of scale. Standard medical treatments were also established. In 1941 even clothing was standardized for the entire country by the National People's Clothing Ordinance. Adult male clothing was to be restricted to two grades, A and B. The Nazi-style designs were astoundingly unpopular, however, and the effort was dropped.

Standardization gave the government a way to present the country with a unified ideology and aesthetics. It was part of the reason that wartime Japanese followed government direction even without a strong organization like the Nazis or a clear ideology like communism, and that they acquiesced to a deification of the emperor and distortion of history that they knew to be irrational. Since noncompliance with the standardizing directives of the bureaucracy would result in material harm to Japanese, standardization also gave Japanese incentives not to dissent.

Once the war ended, the trend toward standardization picked up. After easing up during the American occupation, the effort resumed full force the instant that full independence was recovered. The label "Japan Industrial Standards" was simplified to "JIS." Corporations were given nominal discretion in the adoption of JIS standards, but since public enterprises and governmental purchasing were restricted to goods bearing the JIS mark, the standards were effectively strengthened. The grading system for rice was enlarged to a full set of Japan Agricultural Standards covering all agricultural products. Medical treatment was further standardized to include restrictions on hospital charges greater than insurance coverage and prohibition of nonstandard hospitals. As late as the seventies, the Japanese bureaucracy was even trying to select a "national people's car" and standardize housing.

Parallel to these efforts (or in some cases, preceding them), corporations were forcibly amalgamated by mergers. Regional banks were consolidated so that each prefecture would have a single bank, power companies were consolidated into the Japan Power Transmission Corporation, Nippon Steel was created, regional railroad companies were merged—the list goes on and on. This was part of an overall plan to increase the fruits of mass production by reducing the number of corporations and limiting the number of products.

This policy was likewise interrupted by the occupation. Several corporations were broken up, and large conglomerate groupings dissolved. But when independence was regained, mergers and consolidations resumed. By the sixties, financial groups were even stronger than they had been before the war. The government deemed them useful for achieving postwar Japan's goal of the industrially optimized society.

NATIONAL SCHOOL SYSTEM STANDARDIZES CHARACTER

The second goal of the system of administrative guidance on its path to producing the ultimate industrial society is the standardization of people: the training of a standard level of human capital suited to the mechanism of mass production. This effort reached its pinnacle in the 1941 National Schools Ordinance.

The phrase "national schools ordinance" was a direct translation of the Nazis' *Volksschule*. The Japanese progressive bureaucrats of the day, called the "reform bureaucracy," were filled with admiration for the Nazi *Volksschule* methods and faithfully translated the Nazi laws into the National Schools Ordinance.

The National Schools Ordinance created a system with two main thrusts. First, new facilities for private education were prohibited. Private schools were abolished at the slightest pretext, gradually transforming the primary grade education into a completely public system. This aspect of the system was scrupulously maintained after the war as well, and it remains exceedingly difficult to build new private primary school, middle school, or high school facilities today.

The second thrust was to create strict catchment districts so that all children within the area's boundaries were compelled to attend that district's school; the compulsory district schooling system determined the school to be attended solely by residence. This aspect, too, has been strictly preserved in the postwar era. Today, the system is so solidly established that its existence is unquestionably accepted as a natural state of affairs, but the only nations in the world that use it are Communist countries and Japan.

When these two features are combined, the students and their parents (the sources of educational demand) are deprived of the freedom to choose. The construction of private schools is prohibited to eliminate a route by which students could avoid attending their designated schools. In today's Japan, transgressing boundaries to enter school is looked at socially as a crime.

The aim of this system is to balance student groups in all schools. It is absolutely impossible that the Higashi Ward of Osaka, for example, would produce only musically inclined students, or that only mathematically gifted students would live in the Setagaya Ward of Tokyo. The system suppresses any distinctiveness in the student population. Schools become unable to provide education that is in any way distinctive.

Were a particular school to emphasize music, those students who enjoy music would be quite happy, but the other students would be dissatisfied. If another school decided to emphasize English language from the primary grades, the children who hate English would be angry indeed. The end result is that schools teach only the standard course of instruction set out by the bureaucrats.

This educational system, dreamed up by the Nazis, is very good at robbing citizens of any individuality. Once schools are no longer able to offer anything but standardized education and the state-stipulated curriculum is instituted throughout the land, education becomes completely standardized and uniform. The wartime Japanese bureaucracy aimed for a totalitarian system when it adopted this method. After the war it was pursued, and even strengthened, ostensibly for the lofty-sounding goal of equal education for all, but in reality it continued because it was advantageous for the pursuit of mass production.

Since the war, Japan has debated many aspects of education—such as the contents of textbooks and teacher qualifications—but the crucial matter of the National Schools Ordinance organization has escaped criticism. Under this Nazi system, student individuality has been excoriated and education directed at producing an idealized mass of students, each one the same.

EDUCATION EXPUNGES BOTH DEFECTS AND INDIVIDUALITY

In Japanese schools, the less the student knows about the subject, the greater the teacher's fervor in teaching it. If a child is good at sports but bad at math, the teacher will provide supplementary coaching in math. If the student is good at English but at a loss in science, the teacher will give homework in science. The last thing the teacher will do is to give additional instruction in a subject a student can do well.

The education system does not work to strengthen the strong but to shore up the weak.

The result of this approach is that students all come out like little rounded balls, lacking both strengths and weaknesses and varying only in skill level. The ideal top student gets all fives, the highest grade available, the ideal average student gets all threes. Those are good students. A student with a five and a two is a bad student. Such a student is not serious; he or she still has a trace of individuality.

Another result is that the time spent on the subjects one is bad at becomes longer and longer, even as the time spent on the subjects one excels in shrinks. People dislike what they are not good at, so unpleasant time grows and enjoyable time shrinks. Finding a child who enjoyed going to school would be cause for alarm. Japanese education emphasizes enduring long distasteful hours and patiently doing unpleasant tasks for protracted periods of time. It also fosters a spirit of cooperation so that everyone achieves the same knowledge and skills, because that is the type of person best suited to the mass-production workplace.

When education is standardized and student abilities are uniform, it is easy to train new workers. Knowing that a certain employee was a good student in a certain college gives the employer a grasp of what level of ability to expect; if the employee is an average high school graduate, the employer knows how much learning to expect. These expectations are useful guides in designing company training regimes. Since the employees are highly patient and cooperative, the employer knows they will diligently and accurately perform their assigned tasks.

When education is standardized and homogeneous, when student abilities are all little round circles, it is easy to sort the circles out by size. Universities that have groups of students who are superior when measured according to such rules (that is, by deviations from mean) are thus superior universities. A pyramid hierarchy was established among universities after the war with Tokyo University at its apex. Those students who would go on in their studies were selected solely by their deviation above the mean. This induced students to study ferociously to pass exams, which were the single measure of their competitive fitness. When the Nazi education scheme outlined in the National Schools Ordinance was instituted in 1941, the foundation of postwar education was laid, creating the examination hell that has become the great leveler of the modern Japanese nation.

Educational reform has been debated many times since the end of the war and several reforms have actually been implemented, but because the National Schools Ordinance has always been left intact, these reforms have inevitably made the examination hell even worse. The system survives unchanged for one single compelling reason: it is perfectly suited to a standardized industrial society of mass production.

TOKYO: THE HEAD OF THE JAPANESE BODY

The third guiding precept of the system of administrative guidance was to transform Japan into an organic entity with Tokyo its only brain.

In this conceptualization, the nation functions as an organism much like the human body. And like a human body, it can have but one head. All of the nation's higher functions must be located in that head, that certain city where the government is also located, the capital.

What are these higher functions? To the bureaucrats of 1941, there were three: economic regulation, information transmission, and cultural creation. They developed clever plans to concentrate these functions in Tokyo.

First, to draw all economic regulatory activity to Tokyo, industrial organizations were created for all fields and their national headquarters were located in Tokyo. Former government officials were appointed the representative directors and heads of secretariats. These organizations included everything from industrial groups such as the Japan Iron and Steel Federation and the Japan Automobile Manufacturers Association to professional groups such as the Japan Doctors Association and Cultural Performers League.

The result was that corporate managers, prominent doctors, and artists became officers of national organizations, frequently called to the group headquarters. The government bestowed honors and decorations only on officers of these groups in order to encourage managers and professionals to move to Tokyo and become officers of the organizations. And so as they became officers of these national groups, corporate heads and notables increasingly moved to Tokyo. Corporate headquarters and cultural activities soon followed.

Business convenience is usually cited as the reason that most corporations have their headquarters in Tokyo, but a closer look at how companies move their headquarters functions from the Kansai cities or Nagoya reveals that the first to be moved to Tokyo are the president's office and secretarial functions. This is because presidents or chairmen who are officers of national organizations (or are attempting to become officers) end up spending more time in Tokyo. The next to move to Tokyo are the financial and advertising departments, the former because the world of finance is regulated by the Ministry of Finance and the latter because information transmission is concentrated in Tokyo. The last to leave the home region are sales and general affairs departments, because there is little reason for commercial and personnel matters to be handled in Tokyo.

Government bureaucrats were extremely passionate in their drive to concentrate the headquarters of industrial organizations in Tokyo. This effort picked up in the sixties, when mass production started becoming established as a way of life.

But not all the industrial community went along with this effort. The textile industry, for example, had long roots in the Kansai region, where it had been developing since the Meiji years. Most corporate headquarters were in Osaka, as were industry organizations. MITI had been working to get these organizations to move to Tokyo in the beginning of the sixties, but at the end of the decade increasing trade friction with the United States in textiles led them to force a move. Some MITI officials even branded Osaka the enemy rather than the United States, feeling the textile industry organizations would never adopt any responsibility toward the negotiations with America so long as they stayed in Osaka.

In the end, the textile industry created a new superorganization, the Japan Textile Industry League, over all the other subindustry groups (for spinners, synthetics makers, and the like) and established its headquarters in Tokyo. But the "guidance" from the government was unrelenting, and most of these subindustry groups as well in the end moved their headquarters to Tokyo.

INFORMATION TRANSMISSION CONCENTRATED IN TOKYO

The government found an even better means to bring information transmission to Tokyo.

Broadcasting was the first target of this effort. In 1941, the regulations of the sole broadcasting organization, Nihon Hoso Kyokai (NHK), were revised, and it was stipulated that the transmission of national broadcasts had to originate at the Tokyo Broadcasting Station.

Until that time, the Osaka Broadcasting Station had been responsible for 35 percent of national broadcasting; thereafter, it was responsible only for regional broadcasting to the six prefectures of the Kinki region, the Iga area of Mie Prefecture, and those parts of Shikoku that would naturally be covered by these broadcasts anyway.

With the birth of private-sector broadcasting after the war, this concept lived on when the key station system was devised. Under this system, unlike any other in the world, only the station within each of the private networks that was licensed for the largest broadcasting capability, the "key station," was given rights to create programming for the entire country. Of course, no key stations were permitted outside of Tokyo. Resistance was strong from Osaka, which had developed the nation's first private sector broadcasting, and four "subkey stations" with rights to broadcast nationally were approved for Osaka (and another two for Nagoya). But the right to produce national programming remained exclusively with Tokyo. Thus for an Osaka or Nagoya station to produce dramatic programming for national broadcast, it must first petition a Tokyo key station to accept the programming, which means subjecting the project to strict review and accepting guidance from Tokyo. The only programs accepted are "regional" programs, which focus on traditional industries or local events. Even scripts and casting are subjected to strict review and a distorted view of the outlying regions is imposed. The regions are portrayed exclusively in terms of industries in decline, scandals, and accidents.

The guidance of the Ministry of Education's prewar Bureau of Thought Control was used to deal with the other primary means of information transmission, print. Book distribution was consolidated into four companies located in Tokyo, and all sales of books across prefectural lines were required to transit Tokyo at least once. Even today, for a bookstore in Amagasaki to sell a book published in Osaka, only a bridge away, that book must first be transported from Osaka to Tokyo and then shipped back to Amagasaki. All this does is raise the cost of books from regional publishers and move up their shipping deadlines. For magazines, which operate on strict time deadlines, this makes publishing outside of Tokyo impossible and concentrates absolutely all of their publishing activities in Tokyo.

Why was it necessary to pull the nation's information transmission capabilities to Tokyo? The idea sprang from a desire to create a common information environment that unified the country into a single market for standard goods. All information on national networks originates in Tokyo, so it is the same throughout Japan. This unity of information transmission is extremely helpful in selling standard, mass-produced items. A commercial produced in Tokyo can be used nationwide from the far north in Hokkaido to the far south in Okinawa, so the same standardized product can be sold nationwide. Information can be completely controlled from Tokyo.

Since the body has only one head, designing and planning capabilities also came to be concentrated in Tokyo. The result is that designs now all resemble one another and information is standardized at the conceptual stage. The perfection of the industrially optimized society was thus made all the easier.

CREATIVE CULTURAL ACTIVITIES HAPPEN ONLY IN TOKYO

Creative cultural activities are the third element in the nation's trio of "mental" functions. To bring these to Tokyo, the government constructed the specialized facilities required for such activities and their organizations exclusively in the capital.

Only Tokyo gets facilities with a specific cultural function and purpose. The National Theater (for Kabuki), the Second National Theater (for opera), and the National Stadiums (for track) were all constructed in Tokyo. What the regions get are multipurpose halls, museums that are also used for fairs and exhibitions, and the like.

What exactly are these numerous multipurpose halls? In prewar days they were called, in Nazi fashion, "total theaters." As the name implies, they are halls in which symphony orchestras, kabuki troops, operas, and ballet companies perform. Even lectures are held there. In fact, any event can be held there. But they are optimal for none. The name "no-purpose hall" would be just as descriptive.

Kabuki, for example, requires an elevated walkway placed

through the audience a little to stage left. For a symphony hall, no curtain is required. For an opera, the stage should have ample height, but rotating stages are best avoided.

Each type of performance has its own peculiar requirements and no facility can meet them all. Multipurpose halls can offer a reasonable facsimile, but they cannot offer the real thing. Artists who aspire to doing "the real thing" in music or theater have little choice but to base themselves in Tokyo, where the proper facilities and, not surprisingly, the top-flight musical and theater groups can be found.

Behind the policy of building only multipurpose halls outside of Tokyo is the guiding hand of a bureaucracy gathering all culturally significant activities to Tokyo.

As with the centralizing of economic regulation and information transmission, this policy became stronger after the war. Grants to autonomous bodies were strictly tailored to this aim. Were a prefecture to construct a single-function opera or kabuki hall on its own (without financial assistance from the national government), the central bureaucracy would curtail other grants to the prefecture based on the reasoning that the prefecture is so flush with cash it needs no government assistance. The end result is that the prefectural bureaucracy then inevitably "corrects" its plans to a multipurpose hall. Facilities built for a single purpose are absolutely impossible to construct outside Tokyo. Japanese bureaucrats carry on negotiations and decision making on a plane removed from the stipulations of law, as they have since the shadow government was set up behind the façade of imperial order in the days of Minamoto Yoritomo.

REGIONS PERFORM THE MANUAL LABOR

So if mental functions are concentrated in Tokyo, what remains for the other regions to do?

Manual labor. The outlying regions are the arms and legs

of the Japanese body, limited to the role of production sites. Actively supported by the theory of the industrially guided economy that the bureaucracy developed for the high-growth days, regional development efforts consist entirely of luring factories. According to this theory, mass-production facilities are the only type of production facility that is able to choose its siting autonomously, and the ripple effects on the surrounding locality are profound. Tertiary industries and higher-level economic activities merely follow industrial economic activity. Thus, the only way to develop a regional economy is to encourage factory production.

Not only is this theoretically unsound, it is not even borne out by objective experience. It is, however, a natural and even inescapable conclusion when one starts with the basic concept of the nation as an organic entity. And so manufacturing was sited in the regions. After the war, "regional development" came to mean enticing factories; facilities for tertiary industries were thought of merely as a way to provide services to the local populations who worked in factories. Educational institutions were created to educate the children of local workers. Medical institutions were built for the local population. And multipurpose halls were built so that the local populations could sample the musical and theatrical creations of the Tokyo cultural community a few times each year.

The Japanese government followed up the 1961 Comprehensive National Development Plan with the New National Plan and the Third National Plan. Although these appeared to embrace regional decentralization by building new cities, factory zones, and "technopolises," in actuality, the ultimate goal was the fulfillment of the organic entity model, since the only thing slated to be decentralized to the regions were the same old manufacturing facilities. The Third National Plan added the goal of augmenting "urban functions" outside of Tokyo, but it again followed the multipurpose hall model of providing services; it was merely a means of improving living conditions near the factories to aid in attracting workers.

This regional development policy was intended to create an ultimate industrial society in which a standard model would be devised at the center and doled out to the rest of the country.

THE JAPANESE ELITE CANNOT PRODUCE NEW IDEAS

The system of administrative guidance developed in 1941 marshaled industrial policy, educational policy, and regional development policy toward creating the ultimate industrial society. Standardization helped the wartime bureaucracy introduce a degree of efficiency into the grossly complex distribution system and also increased government control over wartime assignment of personnel. After the war, these efforts accelerated. The result today is a Japan that is optimally suited to mass production of standardized products, an industrial monoculture. Japanese sensibilities and attitudes shaped by environment and history made it extremely easy to implement this form.

The ultimate industrial society has made today's Japan an industrially developed nation—statistically, a rich society. But new ideas and concepts cannot break in and progressive elements are missing. That lack explains why Japan was late in joining the industrial revolution despite its many conducive sensibilities and attitudes.

After the war, Japan was luckily able to obtain a wealth of new ideas and concepts from abroad. And Japan, the eager pupil, used its traditional methods to excel at mastering them. Japan's mass-production society grew for forty-five years without recession, and many new goods, services, systems, and capabilities were created. But the ideas, whether for washing machines, televisions, tape recorders, or television programming, all came from abroad. Japan found models abroad for supermarkets, loan sharks, pro wrestling, and expressways. Even its export promotion and financial knowledge came from abroad.

Naturally, Japan has some great successes that were not imported. Pachinko, instant ramen, karaoke, and stores that sell moving and packaging supplies all come to mind. What these things all have in common is that they were not dreamed up by the big organizations or the elite. In fact, the reverse is true: Japan's elite, those top-notch "rounded" students from the standardized educational system, have proven unable to produce new ideas. What they *have* done is to introduce ideas gleaned from overseas, to study technology, and to add incremental improvements in the area of standardization and mass production.

This is the same method Japan used in the past when it created its giant works of bronze and when it mass-produced flintlocks. Japanese, in the past and today, excel at taking an introduced concept, refining its particulars, and mass-producing it. The culture takes what it considers best and leaves the rest, remaining ever diligent and group oriented, and paying a lot of attention to detail.

THE LIMITS OF THE ULTIMATE INDUSTRIAL SOCIETY: THE COMING JAPANESE TRANSFORMATION

JAPAN'S THREE BIG PROBLEMS

Japan has today come face-to-face with three thick walls: international criticism, quality of life, and scandals.

International criticism was the first of these problems to rear its head. While Japan has been criticized in many areas— for killing whales and sea turtles, for its weak response to the Gulf War—trade friction is easily the most significant of these issues. Rancor over the large surplus in Japan's international balance of payments has become intense.

International friction happens to every country and in every age. It is present whenever the interests of nations collide and has been a concern for Japan since the country opened to the world in the Meiji period. Since the end of World War II, Japan has never been completely free of it. But what we have experienced recently has been of an undeniably different order—not small, individual conflicts, but an over-arching critique of Japan's system of government and its economic and social structures.

The second problem Japan faces is consumer dissatisfaction with their quality of life. In the late eighties, the appreciation of the yen and the boom in domestic land and stock prices made the country very rich, to all appearances the richest on earth. And yet many people never felt any benefit of the nation's wealth in their personal lives. Instead, growing numbers felt forever locked out of buying a house, and it became much more expensive and difficult to improve public facilities. Unease about the future mounted, and people complained of a desperation that they would never share in Japan's prosperity no matter how hard they worked or how much the economy developed.

The third problem was the seemingly endless stream of scandals that began with the Recruit scandal of 1989. Major irregularities on the part of the major banks were revealed one after the other in the summer of 1991, from the Itoman affair to dummy deposit scandals. Securities firms were revealed to have *yakuza* connections, to whom they made loans of nearly $300 million with worthless securities as collateral. Prominent lawyers were arrested for malfeasance and flagrant criminals were let go by the police at the request of *yakuza* gangs.

What shocked the public most, however, was that securities companies were covering losses for their biggest customers. At least $1.4 billion in losses are known to have been covered up in fiscal 1989 and millions more in fiscal 1990. Almost seven hundred companies were beneficiaries of these deals. Most frightening of all was that the complicity of the Ministry of Finance made it all possible, since the money used to cover these losses was taken from the high commission rates approved by the ministry.

Every country experiences corruption. It happened in Japan before the war; it happened after the war. It happens in Europe and it happens in North America. Communist and ex-Communist countries have entrenched black markets, and the practice of politicians taking bribes and distributing them to family members and powerful supporters is widely accepted and even honored in many developing countries. What makes the current series of scandals different in character from even the flat-out bribery of the Lockheed Scandal is not just the massive amounts of money involved but their widespread, systemic nature and the lack of remorse shown by the perpetrators. Government agencies often formulated policy specifically to protect these people, so the problem can realistically be considered to be a structural corruption that is a pervasive, integral part of Japanese society.

The three major problems—international criticism, quality of life, and scandals—at first seem to be separate, but they arise from a common social structure. That structure is, of course, the industrially optimized society that was created by the same bureaucratically guided group behavior that turned Japan into an economic giant.

ADMINISTRATIVE GUIDANCE FAVORS PRODUCERS

The common foundation of these three problems is first and foremost the producer bias of the system. The biggest problem causing friction between Japan and other countries is the trade surplus. This surplus is due in large part to the many years of government assistance that encouraged the export of large quantities of mass-produced industrial products while keeping foreign products and foreign corporations out of the weak Japanese agricultural and distribution markets. The complete exclusion of rice imports is but a symbol of the many barriers erected in other areas.

Pharmaceuticals, for example, are restricted by a system of approvals. The homogeneity of educational materials keeps foreign products out of that system. Penetration of the distribution market was made almost impossible by the Large-Scale Retail Store Restriction Law. Finance and medicine are controlled by a system of permits and approvals. Even the Japanese automobile industry, which is extremely competitive, profits from restrictive laws like an idiosyncratic Road Transport Law and very strict emissions laws that require dozens of changes before foreign cars can be sold in Japan.

Behind all these controls are assumptions that have driven government agencies to protect and nourish producers since the Meiji period, as well as organizational principles the agencies adopted to accomplish this. The system of administrative guidance is of particular importance because it necessitates an even greater level of producer protection to eliminate the surplus production that inevitably results from the standardization and mass production adopted throughout industry. Administrative guidance promotes production-enhancing standardization even as it enforces industry-wide cooperation to hold down surplus production. Exports of industrial products become the outlet used to disgorge that surplus production. Protection of rice and small retailers are a vestige of the surplus production system.

Producer protection extends even to whalers and the tortoiseshell industry, which employs only eighteen hundred workers. Japanese think of themselves as a people that loves and honors nature, but when it comes to a choice between nature and producers, it is nature that loses out.

The lack of participation ordinary Japanese feel in their country's prosperity is also strongly linked to this attitude. Japan is a past master of mass production, and yet consumers have little freedom of choice and cannot satisfy their own desires. The compulsory education system eliminates choice from schooling; the standardized health system means hospitals do not offer patients choice of care. Since the import of rice is so strictly regulated, Japanese are also not free to choose imported rice. And the retail store law drastically limits shopping choices.

Even parks and public libraries are structured around the convenience of the people who run them, who fill the producer role, making the facilities a chore to use. Regulations that make life easier for administrators and police are adopted for roads, resulting in tremendous congestion during special events. The Japanese police never stop to consider how they can make life easier and more convenient for the people who use the roads.

SCANDALS ROOTED IN PROTECTION AND COLLUSION

The scandals that have been surfacing with such discouraging regularity trace their origins to exactly the same roots. Given the extremes of producer protection that exist, any business that can expand is guaranteed enormous profits. But to prevent an oversupply of goods, expansion is restricted by policies of administrative guidance. It is only natural that industrialists are thus constantly searching for holes in the administrative system and secretly scheming to expand their domain. The result is an expensive, time-consuming effort to build connections to bureaucrats and politicians with a plethora of kickbacks and compensation. The covering of losses by securities firms is but the tip of the iceberg.

The illicit and unsound loans made by the big banks are yet another product of this system. With their government protection, banks firmly believe that all they need to do to make a profit is increase the scale of their deposits and loans. This conviction is especially pronounced regarding the financing of land, since its supply is limited. For the construction of golf courses, this is even more so, as golf courses are not only limited but also constructed precisely for the building connections. The Japanese financial community is so reliant on government protection and supply restrictions, it even lacks the ability to evaluate collateral or check personal credit records.

This is not limited to the economic world. The habit of conforming to the direction of organizational superiors is felt far and wide. Farmers apply fertilizer at the times the agricultural directors indicate, even when such dictates run counter to weather changes or the state of the land. The amounts applied are thus excessive, but since the government price for rice includes compensation to cover the waste, no one bothers to complain.

Small retailers merely line up their products as instructed by the manufacturers and wholesalers. Any sense of entrepreneurial creativity or risk taking is totally absent; protection and restricted competition make them unnecessary. Doctors use expensive diagnostic machines and medicines and have lost their oral examination skills, again because of the narrowness of medical competition.

The case of education is the most extreme of all. Ever since compulsory public education was introduced, teachers have lost any inclination to make school life interesting for the pupils, since pupils have to attend in any case. The only responsibility teachers feel is to go through the textbooks as directed by the Ministry of Education and make the students comply with the oppressive school rules. For their part, the students surrender themselves to education, memorize their textbooks, and learn how to take exams. In Japan, this is an intelligent strategy.

This is Japan, the ultimate industrial society: a society in which no one possesses any individuality, no one exercises his or her creativity, and bureaucrats are satisfied with following regulations and standards developed through the precedent of history or the examples of other countries.

A FRUGAL AND GROUP-ORIENTED PEOPLE

The system of administrative guidance that protects producers is the common factor behind international criticism, dissatisfaction with the quality of life, and the pervasive scandals. Administrative guidance, however, is also what has transformed Japan into an economic giant. For that reason alone it is difficult for Japanese simply to discard it. The benefits it has provided are not easily foregone and it is the foundation of many social organizations. Many people have vested interests in its maintenance. And most crucial of all, Japan's educated elite, who have been the product of this system for almost half a century, are incapable of producing the ideas needed to change it. In a society that so values those who survive the grueling Japanese testing system, it is extremely difficult to reach out beyond this elite.

If that were the only stumbling block, however, the problem would be merely one of reforming the system. But it goes much deeper: the foundations of this system are Japan's long traditions of frugality, diligence, and group behavior.

The major problem facing Japan today, its trade surplus, is caused by the Japanese propensity to produce more than they consume. The ideals of frugality and diligence emphasized by the Ishida school of philosophy are still alive in Japan. The autarkic propositions of Ishida Baigan to maintain a macroeconomic balance by lowering productivity were acceptable during the Tokugawa period when the country was closed to the world and valued stability over efficiency. Today, Japan values efficiency, and new technologies and resources have been brought in from abroad. Far from lowering productivity, the ideals of Ishida Baigan have now made Japanese industrial productivity the highest in the world.

A powerful current is nevertheless still at work in the country, keeping productivity down in agriculture, distribution, planning surveys, and the knowledge-value creation industries. It can be seen in small shops that stay open late for marginal sales, polling companies that indiscriminately survey masses of people to create thick reports, filmmakers who pursue obsessions that film audiences cannot understand, and securities salesmen who approach total strangers whose names they glean from the tax rolls. The ideals of Ishida Baigan are still alive in these fields, protected as they are by the difficulty of learning the Japanese language, which keeps out foreign ideas and foreign workers with different work ethics; by the herd behavior of the corporate cadre; and by the protectionism of the government itself. The big difference now is that the reverence for efficiency leads the people in these fields to seek high levels of income and the government to enforce systems that restrict competition to keep prices high.

In a world that does not use as much as it produces, the higher productivity goes, the greater the surplus of goods that the country is forced to export. And if the capital thus obtained is not used, the resulting capital surplus must be invested abroad or chase the limited opportunities for investment within Japan, either encouraging criticism from Europe and North America or causing an explosion domestically in the prices of land, stock, golf memberships, and art objects (or both).

The Ishida school is a unique Japanese philosophy developed 250 years ago in response to a period of calamity. Although its roots are deep, in the greater Japanese context its history is not really so long. It is possible to change it in a Japan now grown prosperous. What keeps that change at bay are the ancient Japanese traditions and customs that predate even Ishida. The group orientation of Japanese dates back to the early days of rice cultivation and is characterized by a strong sense of belonging to the economic unit. Since that sense of belonging became focused solely on the place of employment in the early postwar years, no one has been able to escape. Surely the state of affairs where being disliked by one's work unit is a fate worse than death is desirable only to the producer.

To escape from their excessive diligence, Japanese must develop a sense of belonging that is focused on something outside the workplace. To escape from excessive frugality, a sensibility that holds consumption in some esteem is indispensable. Today, the only place such a sensibility is seen is in "producer consumption," the lavishness of business entertaining.

THREE SOURCES OF PRESSURES FOR JAPANESE REFORM

This can all make the future of Japan seem bleak. But Japanese are realists. Although most often this realism discourages change and directs dissatisfaction inward, in a few cases it has become the power for quite profound change indeed. Thinking can be changed to achieve real advantage, and once the object of that sense of belonging changes, pragmatic Japanese will be able to accept a new system of values.

Japanese history includes many major reforms that took place without widespread bloodshed and destruction. The Meiji Restoration and the post–World War II years are but two examples. Further back in history we find the destruction of the ancien régime at the birth of the Heian period society of nobility. The end of aristocratic court rule in favor of the Kamakura period warrior society is another example.

The inescapable flip side is that outdated systems may endure in Japan a very long time, despite many internal contradictions and much popular dissatisfaction. The Heian period lasted 398 years, enduring as a hollow shell a hundred years after the real power of the aristocratic classes was gone. The Tokugawa period lasted 260 years, but for its latter half the military-aristocratic *bakuhan* government was an empty structure divorced from real power. In both cases, the economy stagnated, the population was suppressed, and the culture decayed, but no revolution or violence occurred.

There is no knowing what path Japan will take in the future. The only certainty is that the direction will be set in this decade as powerful pressures for change build on Japan domestically and internationally.

The first of these pressures is the international environment. Japan today is not the semi-isolated island of the Heian or Tokugawa period. Trade on a massive scale is indispensable for the huge population to maintain its developed industry and comfortable living standards. And despite the protestations of Ministry of Agriculture and Forestry officials and protectionist politicians who attempt to shelter rice growers by prohibiting imports of rice, there is no way isolationist measures can provide Japan with food security. In the years immediately following the war, potatoes were grown in every available plot of land, from mountain tops to school exercise yards, in an effort to increase food production, and yet there was not enough to feed the population, which was then only seventy million. Today Japan is dependent on imported oil for tractors, fertilizer, and agricultural chemicals. Without trade, food production would be but a fraction of what it was after the war. If Japanese did not eat so much imported bread and noodles, the country wouldn't even be able to satisfy current domestic demand for rice. For Japan, self-sufficiency and war are no longer options.

No country needs world peace and free trade more than industrial monoculture societies like Japan. If Japanese are calm and wise, though the country's social character may change, the commitment to maintaining world peace and free trade will not. Peace and freedom create the international regime that is best for Japan. They are in Japan's national interest.

The second element of pressure is the effect of consumers seeking the fruits of prosperity. Japanese culture has been informed through most of its history by a shortage of things and a surplus of people. This psychological legacy endures today in a preference for making things, for favoring producers, for putting work first. But society has changed. Now things are in surplus and able hands in short supply. It is now more natural, if this situation is properly understood, that living standards be given more importance than the making of things and that quality of life come first. As the generation that has not experienced material deprivation grows in numbers, it is likely that this attitude will spread throughout society. Japan is not without the experience of sumptuousness and unfettered self-expression of the Nara and Warring States periods.

Resistance will be fierce. Within corporations, upper management will attempt to clamp down. The bureaucracies will step up the pressure on society as a whole. The backlash will draw much strength from the ethic of honoring frugality and labor, which is so basic to Japan. Those who value a consumer-oriented society and high quality of life and those who pursue their own happiness will be scorned and denounced. But if Japanese have the wisdom to comprehend their situation and the courage to be true to themselves, a new ethic suited to a society of material abundance will emerge, because that is the way to create a world in which that abundance can be felt.

AGING AND THE SPENDING OF ASSETS

The final element forcing the Japanese reformation is the changing demographic structure of society. Virtually throughout human history, the ratio of old (sixty-five years or older) to young (fifteen or younger) has been constant at about one to four. Societies were based on this premise. The numbers of persons who expected abundance to come from future growth vastly outnumbered those who were enjoying that abundance in the present. Japanese society today is based on these long traditions and habits.

In contemporary Japan, however, the numbers of children and elderly have drawn quite close, and by 1998 the elderly will predominate. This will result in changes far more significant than simply new structures of demand and styles of living. The number of consumers living off the fruits of their past labor will increase as the numbers expecting future growth shrink, causing a shift from a net producing economy to a net consuming economy.

Blessed with a warm, humid climate and fertile soil, Japan has always had a productive economy. As Japan changes to a society whose savings are greater than its production, major changes can be expected in the social environment and psychology. The expanding numbers of elderly who are pure consumers, no longer belonging to production organizations, will create a quiet revolution.

Opposition can be expected. Corporations, which are producer organizations, will probably wish to ignore the desires of these pure consumers. Bureaucratic structures, which are organized to protect producers, will probably try to contain the elderly with pensions and nursing homes. There will probably also be many among the elderly who will want to follow older aesthetic models that value deferring their own current desires to consume—out of love for their children. It has always been traditional in Japan to adopt ways that provide a better life for children.

But if Japanese love their elders and have the wisdom to understand the changing demographic structure, attitudes will change to match the new situation.

In the next ten years, Japan will experience significant pain as it grapples with the international environment, the society of abundance, and the changing demographic structure. As these are not problems that the outside world will solve for Japan, it is likely to experience deep pain similar to that of the turbulent seventh century, when Buddhism was encountered, or the harsh depression of the Kyoho era. The important task facing the Japanese is to develop, as they did then, a Japanese philosophy to solve the problems that confront them.

EPILOGUE TO THE ENGLISH LANGUAGE EDITION:

GETTING ALONG WITH JAPAN, OR, A WAY INTO THE JAPANESE MARKET

FINDING THE JAPANESE

In 1960, when I entered the Ministry of International Trade and Industry, Japan was in every way a small Oriental island nation. In that year Japan exported a mere $4.06 billion in goods and had an import tab of $4.49 billion. Its industrial exports were only 40 percent of British exports and 30 percent of American. And most of these were textiles and light industrial goods like toys. Exports to America were already growing rapidly, though, and Japanese were becoming steadily more familiar with the American market.

Postwar Japan's biggest problem was how to increase exports to big, rich America. With little land and a paucity of resources, Japan had to earn enough foreign currency to pay for its imports of food and fuels. This seemed an impossible task. America was rich in resources and had an overwhelming productive advantage in virtually every industry. Its technology was the most advanced in the world. What could poor Japan possibly have to sell to such a country? Raw silk had been Japan's primary export to America before the war, but the postwar popularity of nylon sent prices falling even as demand stagnated.

Japanese believed that Americans would buy expensive luxury goods only, so they first tried to sell expensive crafts and toys in the American market, without much success. Small and medium-size Japanese corporations watched the American troops in Japan during the occupation, and before long they noticed that Americans bought large quantities of cheap goods that were then used and discarded. This has since come to be called "the disposable culture." Japanese embarked on mass-producing simple export goods—the so-called dollar blouses, dollar radios, and dollar ballpoint pens (a dozen for a dollar)—which Japan then sold to America.

Information about the American market is actually quite easy to come by. Americans live in countries around the globe; people from around the globe live in America. Most countries learn much about America from emigrant compatriots and their descendants. Large numbers of foreigners also live in America to study or do business.

Non-Japanese have far fewer occasions to learn about Japan. Japanese soldiers have rarely been stationed in large numbers abroad. In recent years, more Japanese have begun living abroad on business, but because of the closed nature of the Japanese employment system they do not mix much with non-Japanese society. And of those who do, many are attracted to Western culture to an extent that so sets them apart from ordinary Japanese that they cannot provide non-Japanese with a realistic opportunity to know Japanese society. Non-Japanese also rarely immigrate to Japan. Substantial differences between what Japanese say and what they think also make intimate knowledge of Japanese daily life and the Japanese way of thinking hard to come by.

Today's Japanese business community is proud of the efforts they have made to penetrate the bountiful American market. They find it easy to criticize complaining Americans for not working hard enough to break into Japan. Japanese businesses *have* struggled hard to secure a place in the mind of the American consumer, and the Japanese government has spared no effort in supporting them. Japanese have tailored their products to American tastes and exhaustively studied American business practices. From the age of twelve, English is a Japanese student's most important subject.

In contrast, Americans have an undeniable lack of interest in Japan or the Japanese market. Japan's good fortune to observe the hundreds of thousands of Americans who were in Japan as occupation troops is an experience Americans have never had.

Let us take a look at three barriers that make the Japanese market more difficult to understand.

THREE BARRIERS TO JAPAN

For most non-Japanese, Japan remains an enigma, a black box belching forth industrial products. Businessmen trying to bring products into the Japanese arena perceive challenging, complex obstacles in their path. Island Japan is surrounded by a forbidding legal system, market peculiarities, and distinctive patterns of human interaction. These isolate Japan better than any body of water can.

The legal system has become considerably less of a barrier over the last twenty years. Tariff barriers and regulatory trade restrictions have been eased and are now, on paper, no more stringent than those of North America and Europe. As of 1992, Japan restricts imports of only twenty-two categories of goods, all of which are agricultural. Japan's total ban on imports of rice, its largest crop, was a major source of contention at the Uruguay Round of GATT talks, but the other restricted products are relatively minor. Tariffs are low, and with the exception of an extremely small number of products, problems with industrial goods are nil.

The Japanese market, however, is far from open. Japan has many domestic features that prevent foreign, and in some cases domestic, companies from joining existing markets.

Many school supplies and sporting goods, for example, are subject to fastidious standards set by the Ministry of Education or local education committees. Automobiles are saddled with strict exhaust restrictions that require imported cars to undergo expensive refitting. As an industrially optimized society, Japan is enveloped in rigorous regulations and standards.

These legal obstacles are not insurmountable. To overcome them, a foreign company must study Japanese law in detail and be prepared to outlast the arbitrary administrative guidance of bureaucrats. It is accepted practice for Japanese bureaucrats to apply regulations beyond their legal limits. They believe it is their moral duty to preserve the stability of the economy and the safety of the population.

The second barrier is the idiosyncrasy of the market. Japanese consumers and businessmen have their own peculiar value systems. Market competition is normally a matter of price and quality. In Japan (and particularly in the mass consumer marketplace), quality is more important than price. The standards Japanese use to judge quality are not those used by Americans and Europeans. From these different aesthetics arises what could be called a "design problem."

Where Europeans and Americans might look at overall performance and appearance, Japanese place intense scrutiny on fine detailing and packaging. As I have described earlier, Japanese believe diligent work builds character. The proof of the craftsman's character lies in the careful attention paid to hidden surfaces and obscure areas that the amateur would never notice. The ability to create a superior product is the mark of a superior character. The opposite is also true: if fine details and hidden surfaces are not well finished, the item is deemed the work of a morally inferior craftsman. This ethic extends to large corporations. A product that is not perfectly finished reflects poorly on the quality of the company's management and employees. All other products of that company are then considered likely also to have some kind of hidden defect. A flawed finish is a red flag that warns Japanese of the possibility of those minor breakdowns they most loathe.

To sell in the Japanese market requires an expert finish down to the last, hidden detail, even if this comes at greater expense. Packaging and wrapping must be excessive to the point of redundancy. Labels and markings must be sharp, correctly positioned, and neatly applied. These seemingly wasteful efforts are the bait that catches the Japanese consumer.

The third barrier is social interaction. The Japanese propensity toward groups became established long ago, as the islands' narrow valleys forced the people to engage in rice cultivation that was highly productive but required close cooperation. Small village communities were tightly knit and mobility was low, so personal relationships could be expected to last for a lifetime. People felt very strongly tied to their villages. Modern industrial Japan preserves this strong sense of belonging, but the focus has shifted to work communities. Close interpersonal relationships are still prized, and information is still gained through gradual observation. Continuity over decades is also valued in corporate relationships, as businesses come to know and trust one another on a personal level.

In Japanese organizations, authority is dispersed down to the lowest echelons, and the opinions of those in direct contact with customers are given more weight than the views of the president. To forge a relationship with a Japanese company, it is more important to build a good sympathetic relationship of patronage with the purchasing agent than to play golf with the president. One must have dinner together often and talk about family life, the children's education, and the like. Japanese spend six times more on business entertaining as a percent of GNP than Europeans and Americans precisely to build these bonds. Japanese businessmen golf, drink, and play mah-jongg with their colleagues and business partners. These activities provide occasions for those long-term observations of others—of the way one golfs, the way one drinks—

that are the basis for forming judgments. In a society where much direct expression is superficial, intensive after-hours socializing provides a way to reveal the underlying intentions. And no consideration of Japanese political life would be complete without noting the importance of the constant giving and receiving of favors that sustains the cultivation of personal connections that is so deeply a part of Japanese society.

For most non-Japanese, spending so much "free" time with work colleagues would be burdensome and maybe even a source of shame. The idea of repeatedly socializing with the same work colleagues and contacts for dozens of nights might seem unappealing. But all Japanese do it. And contrary to expectation, it is not the sort of thing Japanese are particularly unwilling to do with non-Japanese, either. Most Japanese find this kind of interaction with foreigners to be stimulating, and the human bonds are formed all the faster.

Within Japan: The Impenetrable East, the Accessible West

The Japanese instinct for group behavior is strongest in eastern Japan, and particularly so in the greater Tokyo region, which is its heart. Japanese soil is warm and wet, and in premodern times roads were poor and cartwheels tended to become stuck. Wheeled vehicles were used only in urban areas, and ships were favored for most long-distance transport.

Eastern Japan has few ocean and river inlets that can be exploited by boats, so movement of goods was difficult. To get rice from Akita to Edo, a distance of 300 miles, grain was shipped by boat around the western tip of the island of Honshu to Osaka, where it was off-loaded and carried 1,200 miles to Edo.

One result was that prices varied considerably within eastern Japan and commercial rights were vested. During the Edo period of feudal-military government, certain merchant houses were granted exclusive rights, and business transactions came to depend on political connections that required extensive cultivation of interpersonal relationships. In modern Japan, it is still difficult for new players to enter the Tokyo milieu.

River and ocean routes were far more accessible and developed in western Japan, which is centered on Osaka. Transport of goods over the Inland Sea was far easier. Prices were more nearly uniform throughout the region, and risk-taking businesses could grow. Today, the vast majority of new Japanese businesses still spring up in western Japan and Osaka. Vested interests and commercial rights in Tokyo usually prevent new products or services from developing, and consumers in eastern Japan have developed a resistance to innovation. In western Japan, consumers are far more receptive.

For a non-Japanese company trying to break into the Japanese marketplace, especially one dealing in consumer goods, the Osaka area is a more congenial place to begin than Tokyo. In fact, most foreign companies successfully selling foodstuffs and household products in Japan have their headquarters in Osaka and neighboring Kobe.

Japan is a homogeneous society, but there are important regional differences, though the bureaucry and national mass media in Tokyo are reluctant to acknowledge them. Ever since the system of administrative guidance was devised in 1941, abolishing regional disparities has been an important goal of Japanese government policy. Some differences nevertheless endure that affect product sales, especially in the initial stages.

Because of Tokyo's prominence as Japan's information center, foreign companies must rely on the Tokyo mass media for advertising and publicity, even when targeting Osaka or Kyushu. Nevertheless, the inconvenience of a location outside of Tokyo should not be overstated, since major advertising agencies have branch offices around the country for that very reason.

This interplay between regional identity and national uniformity is yet another factor that makes the Japanese market a little more inaccessible. The need to rely on mass media on a national scale has the added effect of raising the initial publicity costs for new entrants into a market.

The Japanese market today remains a difficult one for foreign businessmen, requiring of both Japanese and non-Japanese patient effort and persistent information gathering on products and business partners that may deter the fainthearted. But it is no longer a closed market, and the prospective foreign business considering Japan now should bear in mind that success is entirely possible.

Major Events in Japanese History

Period	Year	Event
	400 b.c.	Paleolithic Jomon culture. Neolithic Yayoi culture.
	200 b.c.	Rice cultivation begins.
	a.d. 57	Japanese ambassador receives stamp from China.
	circa 200	Small states coalesce.
	circa 300	Spread of iron tools.
	circa 350	Trade with Korean peninsula.
	369	Mimana colony started in Korea.
	390	Japanese troops fight in Korea.
	413	Japan sends ambassador to southern Chinese dynasty.
	456	Yamato court unifies most of Japan. Immigration from Korea grows. Japanese learn Confucianism from Korea.
	538	Yamato court permits Buddhist worship.
Asuka begins about this time	552	Buddhism may also have entered the country.
	562	Mimana colony lost.

PERIOD	YEAR	EVENT
	587	Religious wars over Buddhism.
		Buddhists triumph.
	593	Prince Shotoku becomes regent.
		National Buddhist temple established.
	596	Ambassador sent to China. Sent regularly thereafter.
	609	Prince Shotoku begins Shinto worship.
		Proclaims both Shinto and Buddhism can be worshiped.
	645	Fujiwara family overthrows the Soga family.
NARA	710	Large capital built at Nara.
	742	Construction of Great Buddha begins.
	749	Great Buddha completed.
HEIAN	794	Capital moved to Kyoto.
	circa 830	Yamato court weakens, power of Fujiwara aristocracy grows. Resources shrinking.
	873	The crown prince confers new name on the Minamoto family.
	889	The crown prince confers new name on the Taira family.

PERIOD	YEAR	EVENT
	894	Dispatch of ambassadors to China formally ceases.
	circa 1000	Aristocratic society at its zenith.
	circa 1100	Regions rebel, bandits thrive, warriors become powerful.
WAR BETWEEN MINAMOTOS AND TAIRAS	circa 1150	War between the Minamotos and Tairas spreads.
	1185	Minamoto Yoritomo defeats the Tairas.
KAMAKURA	1192	Minamoto Yoritomo becomes *seii taishogun,* establishing the Kamakura *bakufu.*
	1219	Minamoto descendants wiped out. Hojo family rules as regents.
	1274	First Mongol invasion destroyed by typhoon.
	1281	Second Mongol invasion destroyed by typhoon.
NORTH AND SOUTH COURTS	1331	Emperor stages failed coup d'etat.
	1333	Kamakura *bakufu* falls. Imperial house divides into north and south lines, starting a civil war.

PERIOD	YEAR	EVENT
	1338	Ashikaga Takauji appointed *seii taishogun* by the north, begins Muromachi *bakufu*.
	1392	Imperial houses unified.
MUROMACHI	1397	Ashikaga Yoshimitsu sends ambassadors to Ming China. Chinese technology begins to enter Japan again.
	1404	Formal trade with China.
	1426	Common people rebel often.
	1467–77	Onin war. Widespread fighting shakes Ashikaga rule.
	1520	Daimyo lords appear throughout the country, increasing the scale of war.
	1543	Portuguese appear, bringing guns.
	1549	Francisco Xavier comes to Japan, bringing Western technology.
WARRING COUNTRIES	1560	Oda Nobunaga appears.
	1568	Oda Nobunaga takes Kyoto.
	1573	Ashikaga government completely destroyed.
	1582	Oda assassinated.

PERIOD	YEAR	EVENT
	1583	Toyotomi Hideyoshi builds Osaka castle and unifies Japan.
	1592–98	Toyotomi Hideyoshi sends troops to Korea.
	1598	Toyotomi Hideyoshi dies.
	1600	The Battle of Sekigahara ends with victory for Tokugawa Ieyasu.
TOKUGAWA	1603	Tokugawa Ieyasu starts Tokugawa *bakufu*, with its capital at Edo (Tokyo).
	1639	Japan becomes closed country. Land, waterways, and commerce develop greatly.
	1702	Events of Chushingura occur.
	1716	Economic decline bottoms in the Kyoho era.
	1729	Ishida Baigan begins lecturing in his home.
	1731	Price of rice crashes, major shortages occur. Famine in western Japan.
	1793	Ishida Baigan dies.
	1803	American ships are denied commercial rights. Britain and Russia also press Japan to open the country.

PERIOD	YEAR	EVENT
		1831	Decade of famines begins.
	1841	Material shortages reach their peak.
	1853	Black ships of Admiral Perry and Russian ambassador Putyatin come to Japan.
MODERN	1867–68	Meiji Restoration opens Japan.
	1882	Modern cotton spinning begins.
	1890	Diet inaugurated.
	1894–95	Sino-Japanese War.
	1902	British-Japanese alliance.
	1904–05	Russo-Japanese War.
	1907	Stock market crash.
	1910	Treaty merging Japan and Korea.
	1914–18	World War I. Japan booms.
	1920	Postwar panic.
	1923	Great Kanto earthquake destroys Tokyo.
	1929	Great worldwide depression begins.
	1931	Japan invades Manchuria.
	1937	Japan invades China proper.
	1941	Pacific War begins.
	1945	World War II ends in defeat for Japan.

Facts About Modern Japan

Area: Approximately 222,000 square miles (California is 254,400 square miles. Figure for Japan is approximate because of territorial disputes with Russia.)

Habitable area: About 60,000 square miles

Population: 123 million (49.5 percent of U.S. population)

Population density: 332 per square km (11.9 times U.S. density)

Per-capita GNP: $19,035 (109.5 percent of U.S.)

Average yearly economic growth in 1980s: 4.2 percent

Yearly trade (1991 figures): $551.2 billion (exports $314.5 billion, imports $236.7 billion)

International balance of trade: $77.8 billion surplus (surplus over last five years: $3.324 trillion)

Educational levels

Primary attendance: almost 100 percent

Percent who go on to high school: 95.9 percent

Percent who go on to higher education: 38.9 percent

Divorce rate: 0.27 (United States, 0.47)

Income distribution (top fifth/bottom fifth): 2.9 (United States, 9.1)

GLOSSARY

Administrative guidance: The practice by the Japanese bureaucracy of using its powers and authority to gain the compliance of Japanese industry with its policies.

Amidha: The great savior deity worshipped by members of the Pure Land denomination of Japanese Buddhism.

Ashikaga Yoshiaki: Shogun at the end of the Muromachi period. (1537–1597)

Asuka period: A.D. 552–710, when the capital of Japan was at Asuka, in the south of the Nara valley.

Azuchi and Momoyama periods: 1573–1598, the reigns of Oda and Toyotomi.

Bakufu: Literally "tent government," *bakufu* refers to a regime that combined a military government structure with support from feudal lords around Japan. There were three *bakufus*, the Kamakura *bakufu*, founded by Minamoto Yoritomo in 1192; the Muromachi *bakufu*, founded by Ashikaga Takauji in 1338; and the Tokugawa *bakufu*, founded by Tokugawa Ieyasu in 1603.

Battle of Sekigahara: A battle in 1600 in which the forces allied to Tokugawa Ieyasu bested their rivals amid great bloodshed.

Emperor Bidatsu: Reigned 573–585.

Black ships: The American fleet led by Admiral Matthew Perry that won concessions from the Tokugawa government in 1853.

***Bon* festival:** The festival of lanterns. Japanese families gather together and make offerings to their ancestors.

Chushingura: A play based on the events of 1701–1703, when forty-seven *ronin* fought their way into the compound of a shogun official to avenge the death of their lord.

Civilization and enlightenment *(Bunmei kaika)*: Slogan of the Restoration patriots.

Daimyo: A hereditary ruler of a Japanese fief.

Edo: Premodern Tokyo.

Era names: Reigns of Japanese emperors are given names. In recent times emperors have had but a single era each, but emperors have in the past had multiple eras. Era names are commonly used to refer to events in Japanese history.

Extralegal official *(ryogenokan)*: The officials of the shadow governments of the Tokugawa, Kamakura, and Muromachi periods whose power was nowhere provided for in law.

Famicon: Short for "family computer," a small portable popular in Japan used for games and simple programs.

Genroku era: 1688–1703, the cultural and economic height of the Tokugawa period, when Japanese culture flowered.

Han dynasty: The dynasty of China's classical flowering, 206 B.C. to A.D. 220. Divided into Early Han and Later Han, also called Eastern Han and Western Han.

Heian period: 794–1191, when the capital of Japan was at Heian-kyo (Kyoto).

Heiankyo: Ancient name of Kyoto.

Heisei era: The name of the era of Japan's current emperor, Akihito.

Hideyoshi: See **Toyotomi Hideyoshi.**

Hikaru Genji: The hero of the novel *The Tale of Genji*, by Lady Murasaki. (circa 1163–1244)

The History of the Three Kingdoms: A medieval Chinese romance novel written by Chen Shou describing the exploits of three blood brothers and the dastardly Cao Cao of Wei.

Hojo Tokimasa: The first regent of the Kamakura government from the Hojo family. The Hojo family regents became the true ruling powers of the Kamakura *bakufu.* (1138–1215)

Honno-ji incident: Akechi Mitsuharu assassinated Oda Nobunaga at Honno-ji temple.

Honor the emperor, Expel the Barbarians *(Sonno joi)*: Slogan of the final days of the Tokugawa *bakufu* opposing Tokugawa concessions to foreign powers.

Ieyasu: See **Tokugawa Ieyasu.**

Ishida Baigan: Japanese philosopher who believed in an inborn sense of duty. (1685–1744)

Japan National Railways: A public corporation that ran Japan's railways and was characterized by overemployment, politicized labor-management conflicts, and yearly rising deficits. It was privatized and broken up into regional passenger railways, a freight railway, and other related companies in the late 1980s.

Japan–U.S. Structural Impediments Initiative (SII): Talks between Japan and the United States concerning barriers to trade within the Japanese economy other than tariffs and trade regulations.

Japanese-style management: A business organizational system characterized by lifetime employment, wages by seniority, company unions, dispersed decision making, consensus, low dividends, and high business entertainment spending.

JIS: Japan Industrial Standards. The letters *JIS* are placed on products to indicate that they conform to the standards.

Kaei era: 1848–1853. One of the last eras of Tokugawa rule.

Kamakura period: 1192–1330, when Japan was governed by the Kamakura *bakufu,* founded by Minamoto Yoritomo.

Kanban system: The word *kanban* means sign and refers to the labels indicating where parts and supplies are to be shipped. Also known as just-in-time inventory control.

Kan'ei era: 1624–1629. One of the early eras of Tokugawa rule.

Emperor Kinmei: Reigned 539–571.

Knowledge creation industries: Any industry that is based primarily on a knowledge or information component, such as advertising, design, software, publishing, and fashion.

Kojiki: *Records of Ancient Matters,* Japan's oldest text, which describes the exploits of Japan's gods in a linear chronology.

Kokinshu: *Ancient and Modern Collection,* an early anthology of Japanese *waka* and haiku poetry compiled in 905.

Koku: A Japanese unit that measures volume, equal to approximately five bushels.

Kyoho era: An era (1744–1747) in which a period of economic decline peaked in great deprivation and devastation under the Tokugawa shogun Yoshimune.

Large-Scale Retail Store Restriction Law: A law that keeps large retail stores from opening except under specific circumstances. It is used to keep discount stores from pushing smaller stores out of business.

Later Han History: A history of the Later Han dynasty that contains a passage describing the country of Yamatai.

Look East: A Malaysian government program developed in the 1980s to adopt Japanese rather than British practices in order to improve the economy.

Lü-ling: A Tang dynasty Chinese system of civil and criminal law.

Manyoshu: The *Ten Thousand Leaves Collection,* an early anthology of Japanese poetry in various styles, compiled in the eighth century.

Meiji period: The reign of the Meiji Emperor (1868–1912). See also **Meiji Restoration.**

Meiji Restoration: A series of events leading to the overthrow of the Tokugawa military-feudal government and restoration of real authority to the imperial government.

Mimana domain: An area of the Korean peninsula that was under Japanese rule from the fifth century to A.D. 562.

Minamoto Yoritomo: Established the Kamakura *bakufu,* Japan's first military government, by defeating Taira Kiyomori of the rival Taira clan. (1147–1199)

Ming dynasty: The last "Chinese" dynasty, 1368–1644. Overthrown by the Manchus, who founded the Qing dynasty.

Mono no Be: The leader of Shinto opposition to Buddhism becoming Japan's state religion.

Muromachi period: 1397–1559, when Japan was governed by the Muromachi *bakufu* founded by Ashikaga Takauji, who became *seii taishogun* of the northern dynasty. Japan's medieval period.

Myogakin: A compulsory "contribution" charged by the Tokugawa government on merchants.

Nara period: 710–793, when the capital of Japan was at Nara.

National Schools Ordinance: An ordinance that stipulates the form of education in Japan.

Nihon Hoso Kyokai (NHK): Japan's public television agency.

No: A stylized Japanese dramatic form.

Nobunaga: See **Oda Nobunaga.**

North and South dynasties period: 1331–1396, when a failed coup by the imperial family against the Kamakura *bakufu* led to the fall of the *bakufu*, two parallel dynasties, and civil war.

Northern and Southern dynasties period: A period of Chinese history, 420–581.

Oda Nobunaga: One of the warring feudal lords of the Warring Countries period. Considered a military genius, he was the first lord to capture Kyoto, the center of Japanese power, in 1573, ending the Muromachi *bakufu* and beginning the process of unifying Japan later completed by his general Toyotomi Hideyoshi. He was assassinated in the Honno-ji incident. (1534–1582)

Okawa Shumei: Nationalist Japanese economist in the 1930s who propounded a theory of "universal brotherhood" advocating brotherhood among Asians and that Japan militarily replace European colonial powers within East Asia. (1886–1957)

Onin era: 1467–1468. An era of widespread destruction in which rival generals sacked Kyoto. The period of *Rashomon.*

Owari fief: Oda Nobunaga's home region.

Paekche: The southernmost of three medieval Korean kingdoms that competed to rule the Korean peninsula. Taken over by the Korean kingdom of Silla in the year 660.

Frajna Paramita Sutra: The "Heart Sutra," a brief distillation of the "Perfection of Wisdom" writings, much reproduced and recited throughout Asia.

Emperor Qin: China's first emperor. Overthrown by Liu Bang, who founded the Han dynasty.

Qing dynasty: The Manchu dynasty that was China's last dynasty. 1644–1912. The last empress dowager, Cu-xi, was noted for her misrule.

Recruit scandal: A 1989 scandal in which it was revealed a Japanese company named Recruit had paid numerous politicians large amounts of money for favors.

Restoration patriots: The men who led the proimperial forces against the Tokugawa, ending the Tokugawa *bakufu* and beginning a program of modernization that transformed Japan into an industrial nation. Also called the "elder statesmen of the Meiji."

Ritsu-ryo: The Japanese adaptation of Chinese lü-ling law.

Ronin: Samurai who have lost their lord through the lord's death.

Ryo: An old Japanese monetary unit.

Sanya and Kamagasaki incidents: Riots in 1961 in Tokyo and Osaka slum areas over poor living conditions.

Security Treaty riots: Huge demonstrations in Tokyo in which students opposed renewal of the Japan–U.S. Treaty of Mutual Cooperation and Security.

Seppuku: Ritual suicide by disembowelment.

Shinto: A polytheistic Japanese religion that incorporates worship of ethnic deities. The emperor is believed to be descended from the chief of these, Amaterasu.

Shitenno-ji: Temple of the Four Heavenly Kings, Japan's first national Buddhist temple, located in Settsu Province. Founded by Prince Shotoku.

Shogi: Japanese chess.

Prince Shotoku: Literally the "virtuous prince," Prince Shotoku served as regent for Empress Suiko until he was murdered in 622. He overcame the Soga family and fused Shintoism with Buddhism and Confucianism to preserve the authority of the imperial family. (574–622)

Shrine: A Shinto house of worship. Compare **temple.**

Shumei Okawa: See **Okawa Shumei**

Soga: A family of Buddhists who rivaled the imperial family in the sixth and seventh centuries.

Soga no Iname: The first member of the Soga family to become a Buddhist. (?–570)

Soga no Umako: A powerful member of the Soga family who caused Buddhism to become a state religion of Japan. (?–626)

Soka Gakkai: "Value Creation Society," a religious group associated with the Nichiren denomination of Buddhism.

Song dynasty: China's "little modernization," characterized by a flurry of technological advances. (960–1279)

Spring and Autumn period: A period of Chinese history, 722–484 B.C.

Sugawara Michizane: An outstanding scholar of Chinese who was appointed minister of the right in the ninth century. (1537–1597)

Sui dynasty: A short turbulent dynasty, 581–618.

Empress Suiko: Reigned 592–628 with Prince Shotoku as her regent. Asia's first female sovereign.

Sukhavati Sutra: The fundamental scripture of Pure Land Buddhism.

Emperor Sushun: Reigned 587–592. Originally pro-Buddhist emperor who later opposed the Soga family and was murdered.

Tang dynasty: A period of cultural flowering. 618–907.

Taoism: Belief in the Taoist immortals, from the thought of Laozi and Zhuangzi.

Temple: A Buddhist house of worship. Compare **shrine.**

Teritiary functions: All industries that depend on primary industries (materials) and secondary industries (manufacturing). These include knowledge creation industries, government, and medicine.

Tokonoma: An alcove in the receiving room of Japanese homes in which a scroll is often hung with an arrangement of flowers.

Tokugawa: A family that ruled Japan as shoguns, or generals, for over 250 years, from 1603 till their overthrow in the Meiji Restoration of 1868.

Tokugawa Hidetada: The second Tokugawa shogun, son of Ieyasu. (1579–1632)

Tokugawa Ieyasu: The first Tokugawa shogun, who established the Tokugawa military government around 1600. (1542–1616)

Tokugawa period: 1603–1867, when Japan was governed by the Tokugawa *bakufu*, founded by Tokugawa Ieyasu.

Tokugawa Tsunayoshi: Flamboyant fifth Tokugawa shogun who ruled during the sumptuous Genroku era, Tokugawa Japan's cultural and economic peak, but is despised as a tyrant. (1646–1709)

Tokugawa Yoshimune: Ascetic eighth Tokugawa shogun who presided over a period of drastic economic decline but is nonetheless revered. (1684–1751)

Toyotomi Hideyoshi: The shogun who succeeded Oda Nobunaga and completed the unification of Japan and invaded Korea in 1592 and 1597. (1536–1598)

Tsubo: A Japanese unit that measures area. One tsubo is about four square yards.

Tsunayoshi: See **Tokugawa Tsunayoshi**

Tungus: A nomadic people of north central Asia.

Ukiyo-e: A style of Japanese painting from the 1700s depicting scenes from everyday life.

Ultimate industrial society: A society in which everything is designed to facilitate mass production.

Umayado no Toyotomimi no Ooji: See **Prince Shotoku.**

Warring Countries period: A period in Japanese history (1560–1600) after the collapse of the Muromachi military government during which feudal lords fought to dominate Japan.

Warring States period: A period in Chinese history (475–221 B.C.) in the late Zhou dynasty during which regional states contested.

Wei dynasty: A period in Chinese history, 220–265.

Wei Zhi: An early Chinese work of history (third century A.D.)

Wu Xu reform: An ill-fated attempt at reform in 1894 that was overturned after a mere one hundred days by Empress Dowager Cu-xi.

Yakuza: The Japanese mafia.

Yamato court: Japan's imperial family, who have ruled Japan as titular rulers since at least the sixth century, and their court officials.

Yasukuni shrine: A Tokyo shrine where war dead are worshiped. It has recently become a focus of controversy because the prime ministers worship there each year.

Yin dynasty: One of China's ancient dynasties, overthrown by King Wen of Zhou, who founded the Zhou dynasty.

Emperor Yomei: Reigned 585–587. First emperor to engage in Buddhist worship.

Yoritomo: See **Minamoto Yoritomo.**

Yoshimune: See **Tokugawa Yoshimune**

Yuan dynasty: The dynasty founded by Genghiz and Kublai Khan when they overthrew the Jin dynasty. (1271–1368)

Zaibatsu: A grouping of Japanese companies bound together by ties of family ownership.

Zhou dynasty: Dynasty founded by King Wen (1126–255 B.C.).

INDEX

303

ABOUT THE TRANSLATOR

Steven Karpa is a San Francisco writer and translator of Japanese and Chinese.

About the Author

Taichi Sakaiya was born in 1935 in Osaka, Japan. After receiving an Economics Degree from Tokyo University he joined Japan's Ministry of International Trade and Industry (MITI), where he was responsible for planning and presenting the 1970 Osaka Expo and the 1975 Okinawa Marine Expo. Since leaving MITI, he has become a best-selling author in Japan, publishing novels and nonfiction books that are widely read and very influential. Mr. Sakaiya is the author of more than thirty books. *The Knowledge-Value Revolution* (Kodansha International, 1991) was his first book to be translated into English.